CIB ASSOCIATESHIP SERIES

THE MONETARY AND FINANCIAL SYSTEM

Third Edition

B. Julian Beecham, FCIB

PITMAN PUBLISHING

To my students

Pitman Publishing
128 Long Acre, London WC2E 9AN

A Division of Longman Group UK Limited

First published as *Monetary Economics* in 1986
Second impression with amendments 1986
Second edition 1988
Third edition retitled *The Monetary and Financial System* 1990
Second retitled edition 1993
Third retitled edition 1994

© Longman Group UK Ltd 1986, 1988, 1990, 1993, 1994

British Library Cataloguing in Publication Data
A CIP catalogue record for this book is available from the British Library.

ISBN 0 273 60554 2

Typeset by Avocet Typesetters, Bicester, Oxon
Printed in England by Clays Ltd, St Ives plc

Contents

Preface

This book is one of the Pitman Publishing series of textbooks which are written to cover the *merged* syllabi of the Associateship exams of the Chartered Institute of Bankers (CIB) and the Chartered Building Societies Institute (CBSI).

The book has been designed as the most direct route to meeting the requirements of the Monetary and Financial System (MFS) examination paper of the CIB. The MFS exam paper will consist of eight questions, covering eight of the ten subject areas of the syllabus, from which you will be expected to select and answer four questions in the essay or detailed note form. The new syllabus is distinctly divided into eleven sections to focus attention on the individual subject areas. However, you should not regard each section as being totally self-contained; it is in the nature of the subject that a full understanding of one area of the syllabus demands knowledge of other areas, and the questions set in the examinations will inevitably reflect this.

Chapter 1 provides pointers on how best to use your private study time in preparing for the examination. It also gives suggestions on examination technique, i.e. on how you actually conduct yourself during the examination itself. Adherence to both should help you to achieve success in the examinations you take. Chapters 2 to 12 are arranged in sequence with the layout of the MFS syllabus. Each chapter begins by stating the requirements of the syllabus for the topic covered in that chapter. This is followed by a section which briefly defines the technical terms involved and which gives an overview of the topic area in question, to help you get started. Then follow two sections dealing with the essential theories and principles connected with the topic; one dealing with their explanation and the other with their application to the UK MFS. These sections are backed up by approximately six examination questions recently set in that topic area, together with outline answers. There then follows a full specimen answer to a carefully chosen recent examination question: this is to help you improve your technique in how best to answer the question, the whole question and nothing but the question. Finally, each chapter ends with advice on how to take a step further in keeping yourself fully abreast of movements in the subject matter of each topic. The text in each chapter is divided into sections and sub-sections, giving you an opportunity to think upon and digest what you have been reading before proceeding further.

The general thrust of the examination will be direct, seeking precise and up-to-date information and understanding — and that could make the questions difficult for those candidates who have learned out-of-date material, instead of concentrating on acquiring a finely-focused perspective of the *evolving* practices of the monetary and financial system of a developed economy. I believe that this book, and the series as a whole, will help you to a well-grounded understanding of the required knowledge and exam techniques which will help you to do your best in the exams you take. Good luck!

B. Julian Beecham, FCIB
Cardiff

Acknowledgements

My grateful thanks to:

The Chartered Institute of Bankers and the Chartered Building Societies Institute for permission to use the Monetary and Financial System and Economics *Examiners' Reports*, Monetary and Financial System *Syllabus, Updating Notes* and Waterlow Publishers Ltd for permission to use Signpost articles from *Banking World*.

The Bank of England for permission to refer to articles in their *Quarterly Bulletins* and published papers, the Barclays Bank's Regional Corporate Division in Cardiff for providing and permitting the use of their material in the writing of Chapter 11, and the *Financial Times* for allowing the use of their London Money Market Rates table.

And to Enid, my wife, for her invaluable assistance.

B. Julian Beecham, FCIB
Cardiff
1993

CHAPTER 1
Study Techniques

If you *know* where you're going, you're halfway there.

A careful use of your private study time in preparation for the examination, and a well-practised examination technique, are perhaps the two most important requirements for examination 'success'.

▮ Preparation

(a) Make sure that you fully know, and have in your possession, the latest CIB syllabus for the Monetary and Financial System, or the syllabus for the examination you plan to sit.

(b) Create study time within your weekly activities. Discipline yourself to stick to the study time. Within the study time allocate time to *all* subjects within the course you are studying. Set study targets so that you cover the whole syllabus and endeavour to achieve them: few things are worse than leaving things *half* done. This last point is even more important where students are taking examinations by correspondence course and by private study.

(c) Read as much as you can about each topic from the quality daily and weekly newspapers, banking magazines and other learned journals and bulletins. Watch and listen to appropriate programmes on the television and radio. These activities will help you to update your knowledge and to understand technical terms more fully. They will also help you appreciate the context in which to place your essays, home assignments and answers to examination questions.

(d) When you come to write essays or home assignments, you should first collect all the relevant data and information from the references suggested by your tutors. Make good use of the college and public libraries. Your opening paragraph should clearly state the scope of the essay/assignment and how you intend to meet it. It is extremely helpful to make an answer plan, in which you identify the main points to be covered. Arrange these points in a cohesive form *before* you begin to write the essay/assignment: this will give your essay a clear structure. Write one paragraph on each point, using headings if you feel this makes the answer clearer. Keep a dictionary handy to avoid spelling mistakes. Also avoid bad grammar, emotive language and unnecessary repetition. Wherever appropriate bring the points you have made together in a conclusion. Remember to answer the question, the whole question and nothing but the question!

(e) Read the chief examiner's reports and *Signpost* articles carefully to find out which topics usually cause most problems and why!

(f) Read any article that the chief examiner might write or refer to about the subject.

(g) Design your overall study programme in such a way that you leave time for *revision* before the examination: *this is vitally important.*

▌ Examination technique

(a) Keep calm in the examination room and read the question paper through and spend five to ten minutes deciding which questions you will answer. Use time too to make sure you understand *exactly* what the examiner is asking. Spot and underline the key words/phrases on each question you have chosen to answer, so that you may write precise answers to the specific points in the questions.

(b) Allocate your time to the required number of questions.

(c) Tackle first the question which you can answer best − build up confidence.

(d) Prepare an answer plan for each question you answer by setting down the main points and arranging them in their logical order *before* beginning to write in detail. Do not waste time in copying the question on the answer book, simply state the number of the question you intend to answer.

(e) Always start the answer to a question on a new page; this will give you room to write something relevant, which may have slipped your mind, later on when you revise what you have written.

(f) Be brief and relevant − you will get no marks for irrelevant material, however well it is expressed. Draw the attention of the examiner to key words and phrases in your answers by underlining them.

(g) If there is more than one part to a question, make sure you answer all parts.

(h) Answer the right number of questions. If you are required to answer four, then the examiner will mark the first four you have done and will ignore anything else.

(i) Finally, read what you have written, correct as necessary, and cut out anything which does not make sense.

(j) Write answers to questions, where appropriate, in point form.

▌ Overall

Remember, this is not a subject you can memorise or swot; it is one that requires *understanding*, which can be acquired only by application throughout the course. Last-minute cramming alone almost certainly spells disaster.

CHAPTER 2
Money and Inflation

Syllabus requirements
- The nature and functions of money and liquidity.
- The meaning and measurement of the value of money including a simple understanding of the use of indices in measuring changes in money's value.
- The causes and the problems of inflation.
- The composition of the 'narrow' and 'broad' money in the UK.
- Alternative measures of money in a modern economy (and in the UK in particular).

▌ Getting started

Money is anything that is generally and instantly accepted in payment for purchases and in settling debts. It is generally accepted because it is the legal tender (notes and coins) or a representative of notes and coins (demand deposits with financial institutions). Since money is accepted in exchange for all things, it measures the values of all things, by comparing their prices: values measured in terms of money are called prices. Thus money, by performing its essential functions, enables money-based economies to function smoothly. It makes specialisation possible by making exchange possible and by streamlining the activities of banking and financial institutions. It therefore makes possible a higher standard of living in advanced money economies.

Since money measures the value of all other things, it follows, therefore, that other things measure the value of money. If money purchases less of other things than, say, it did last year, then its value, its instant purchasing power, has fallen. Conversely, if it purchases more than it did in the past, its value has risen. Thus the value of money is *inversely* related to the prices of other things, i.e. the general price level, as measured by, say, a retail prices index: when the retail prices index rises (inflation), the purchasing power of money falls, and vice versa. The main cause of inflation is too much money chasing too few goods. Inflation erodes the value of money and, by doing so, strikes at the heart of money economies. Therefore the authorities of money economies try to control the supply of money in the economy mainly by controlling the spending ability of the general public. If and when they succeed, the cancerous growth of inflation is rooted out of the monetary and financial system, and money, once again, begins to perform its functions satisfactorily.

In sophisticated economies, where the banking and financial system is well-developed, the monetary authorities make a distinction between 'narrow' and 'broad' money aggregates. The narrow money aggregate is the sum total of instant purchasing power in the economy, i.e. the total of cash, sight deposits, unused limits on overdrafts and credit cards, and the broad money aggregate is the sum total of the total instant purchasing power *plus* the total of *potential* purchasing power in the economy, i.e. narrow money *plus* easily, but not instantly, encashable financial assets. The potential purchasing power is instant purchasing power, but one stage removed. The distinction between narrow and broad money measures assists the authorities in devising appropriate policies to control whichever type of the money supply is getting out of hand. It is not the money, but the uncontrolled supply of money which is the root of all evil in money economies.

■ Essential principles

Functions of money

The commodity which possesses instant and general acceptability can perform at once all the four *functions* of money, viz.:

1. *Medium of exchange.* It splits exchange, first, into a process of sale of one's goods and services for money, and second, into a process of purchase of the goods and services wanted in exchange. It facilitates buying and selling by overcoming the problems of barter. It acts as wealth with liquid purchasing power, giving its possessor the freedom of choice in the satisfaction of wants, and enabling him to save and lend easily. From this function arises the definition of the 'narrow' money: the sum total of instantly spendable money balances.
2. *Store of value.* It enables wealth to be stored up indefinitely without deterioration in value, except in times of rapidly rising inflation. It can then be exchanged for other goods, now and in the future, without loss in purchasing power. From this and the previous function of money arise the definition of 'broad' money: the sum total of instantly spendable money balances (narrow money) *plus* stored money balances which can be spent almost instantly with no or little financial loss.
3. *Unit of account or standard of value.* It measures the values of all other things because they are exchanged for it. 'Price' is the value of a good in terms of money; by comparing the prices of various goods their values can be compared. As the unit of account, it enables accounts to be kept, costs to be assessed precisely and choices to be made between competing projects by comparing the costs and returns from each project. This function helps explain the economic concept of 'opportunity cost'; the true cost of a good is the alternative good which was not bought.
4. *Standard for deferred payments.* It enables contracts to be fulfilled in the future to be assessed now, thereby equating present and future values. The equation of present and future values is crucial to lenders making loans to borrowers who contract to repay an agreed sum regularly over several months or even years.

Importance of money to advanced economies

By performing all its functions, money makes possible division of labour and specialisation; division of labour presupposes exchange: money helps in the payment of rent, wages, profit and interest; as a store of value and a standard of deferred payments, money enables investment of capital in plant, machinery, etc. It streamlines the activities of banking and financial institutions as financial intermediaries, safely linking lenders to borrowers. It makes possible a higher standard of living in advanced money economies, via its four functions. It has a dynamic role as well; governments control its supply to achieve economic aims.

Sight deposits with financial institutions

In countries where the banking and financial system is not developed, coins and paper money (bank notes) form the major proportion of their total money supply. In countries with highly developed monetary and financial systems, deposits with banks and other financial institutions (e.g. building societies in the UK) are also an important component of the money supply. The *sight* bank deposits are deposits which can be withdrawn on demand, either in part or in full. Sight or demand deposits are clearly money since they possess the major *characteristics* of money, being generally acceptable, divisible and transferable by cheque and other means; they also perform all the functions of money.

Types of money

There are three main types of money:

1. *Primary money*. It comprises money which is the liability of monetary authorities, e.g. notes and coins, and the operational deposits of commercial banks with the central bank. Primary money is the ultimate means of payment, therefore it is also known as 'high powered' money. Only an injection of high powered money into the bank and building society deposits in the UK − as you will see later on − sparks off the credit creation process by these financial institutions.
2. *Secondary money*. It consists of the primary money claims which the UK public can make against its deposits with banks and building societies. It comprises the deposit liabilities of banks and building societies. The credit creation process generates an increase in the secondary, or 'low powered' money; low powered money does not of itself trigger the credit-creation process.
3. *Near money*. It comprises financial assets of the public which can be cashed quickly with little or no financial loss, e.g. building society shares and deposits, Treasury bills (issued by the authorities for short-term borrowing), certificates of deposit (issued by financial institutions) which are held as investments and not as means of payment.

You should now be able to see the relationship between money and near money and the narrow and broad definitions of money supply: the narrow definition of money comprises solely spending money, and the broad money definition comprises the transaction-based spending money *plus* the savings-orientated near money. The near money assets have two functions:

1. To earn interest and to act as a store of wealth. Thus they are attractive to those who are able to save. In most cases, money yields no interest and therefore, unlike near money, provides no hedge against inflation.
2. To be fairly quickly convertible into cash, without significant risk of loss, either of interest or of capital. It may therefore be attractive to plan to make larger payments out of near money assets rather than out of money.

The technical definition of 'liquidity' separates money from near money: money *is* liquid purchasing power and can be directly exchanged for goods and services, whereas near money is *not* liquid purchasing power. If near money is to be used directly to purchase goods and services, it must first be converted into money, i.e. cash or sight deposits; this requirement of conversion into cash or sight deposits, with the consequent risk of monetary loss and time loss, differentiates near money assets from money. Near money is money, one stage removed.

■ Liquidity spectrum

It is absolutely essential to understand that the concept of money is very closely linked with the concept of liquidity. A liquid asset is one that can instantly be turned into cash without risk of loss. On the one extreme of the liquidity spectrum we have money with instant liquid purchasing power, notes and coins and sight deposits with financial institutions. In the middle we have near money assets which have a definite money value but which do not directly function as a medium of exchange, e.g. Treasury bills and savings deposits. On the other extreme, we have 'non-money', i.e. non-financial assets which are least liquid in their ability to act as a medium of exchange, e.g. houses, business premises and lands. The conversion of such assets into money will involve marketing costs, inconvenience and often waiting. The liquidity spectrum is a scale on which financial and other assets are placed in order of their liquidity, measured by the liquidity standard of money, because money, by definition, is *liquidity*.

In the liquidity spectrum, it would be wrong to draw absolute dividing lines between various types of money and other financial assets because there *is* substitutability, especially at the margins, between various types of money and financial assets. The more complex, sophisticated and stable the financial institutions a country has, the greater the variety of financial assets available to the public and the greater the degree of substitutability there is likely to be among these financial assets.

As financial innovation becomes more sophisticated, many near money assets become available, e.g. higher interest deposits with banks and building societies, which are generally available, like sight deposits, on demand and without financial penalty.

■ The value of money

The value of money is its purchasing power, i.e. the goods and services it obtains through exchange. Therefore a fall in the value of money is the same thing as a general rise in prices and vice versa. Thus the value of money changes *inversely* with changes in the general price level. A major cause of a fall in the value of money is inflation, as you'll see below.

Index numbers and the value of money

In most countries the changes in the value of money are measured by a number of statistical devices, known as *index numbers*. These indices attempt to measure changes in the purchasing power of money over given periods.

Retail price index (RPI)

The RPI, published by the Department of Employment, is commonly used in the UK to measure changes in the value of money, and therefore real incomes, over a given period. It is based on the 'weighted' prices of a 'basket' of goods and services, which are seen as reflecting average expenditure patterns in UK households. The 'weighting' given to each item in the 'basket' is related to the share of the household's expenditure in purchasing it. If the purchase price of the basket in a given month is, say, 10 per cent higher than on the base date, then it is assumed by the public, trade unions, employers and the government that the value of money in the UK has fallen by 10 per cent; the same sum of money buys 10 per cent less now than it did on the base date. Such a general assumption can be misleading. Large groups of the population will have different expenditure patterns and may not be similarly affected by changes in the prices of the goods in the basket. For example, a rise in mortgage rates or 'motor tax' will not affect those with no mortgage debt or motor cars. Consumption patterns change at different levels of income or with individual tastes.

The RPI has two other major drawbacks in this respect: first, it is difficult to assess changes in the quality of goods purchased now and in the base year. For example, it is difficult to compare the current prices of, say, television sets with those of 10 or 15 years ago, because this product, like many others, has been considerably improved over the years. This improvement is partly reflected in the current higher prices which may not, therefore, reflect a 'true' fall in the real value of money incomes. Second, it is not easy to assess the effects of changes in tastes or demand. Higher prices may, in part, reflect an increased preference by society for certain goods and services, resulting in increased demand, rather than a fall in the real value of money incomes.

The changes in RPI and therefore in the value of money (its purchasing power), can be calculated by usng the following formula:

$$\text{RPI at a selected index date} = \frac{\text{Price of the basket of goods at selected date}}{\text{Price of the same basket of goods at base date}} \times 100$$

Wholesale Price Index (WPI)

The WPI measures changes in the wholesale prices of a number of representative commodities, ranging from raw materials to finished goods. The WPI 'weights' products, compares their prices as a percentage of prices in the base year in order to show changes in the value of money. It measures costs of inputs for manufacturers or prices of manufactured output. The drawback with the WPI is that the prices are list prices quoted by manufacturers (i.e. wholesale prices) rather than current prices at which the goods are actually traded (i.e. retail prices).

Tax Price Index (TPI)

The TPI attempts to show how an increase in indirect taxes (e.g. VAT) and a decrease in direct taxes (e.g. income tax) may leave people's purchasing capacities unchanged. In other words, they pay more for goods and services but have more money to pay for them. Some economists consider that the TPI is more reliable in determining the purchasing power of individuals than the RPI. The major drawback of the TPI is that it ignores the effects of change in the indirect and direct taxation rates upon those whose incomes are *below* the income tax threshold. These people pay more for goods and services *without* being compensated by cuts in income tax rates.

One important point to note in connection with index numbers is that all price indices suffer from statistical errors, imprecision and misrepresentation. Due to these drawbacks, changes in the value of money cannot be measured *precisely*. It is useful to be fully aware of this fact.

▌ Fisher's equation and the value of money

There are several theories of the value of money; however, Fisher's equation has become the more important because of the preoccupation of most governments in recent years with controlling the money supply in order to maintain the real value of money. This equation attempts to show the link between the quantity of money in the economy and the level of prices. It maintains that the level of prices is directly proportional to the quantity of money in circulation and that if the growth in the money supply is not controlled prices will rise (causing the value of money to fall).

According to this equation, $MV = PT$, where

M = quantity of money (cash and chequeable accounts) in circulation
V = velocity of circulation (the rate of turnover of M), i.e. the speed with which money is circulating through the economy in a given period; an increase in V implies an increase in M, because both increase spending
P = general price level (or a price index, say, RPI)
T = total number of transactions during a given time period.

The equation further claims that in the short term V and T are constant; therefore any increase in M is reflected in a proportional increase in P.

Drawbacks of Fisher's equation

1. There is no one generally acceptable definition of M.
2. The equation is a truism: total spending (MV) must equal total sales (PT).
3. Increase in P may also be caused by the excess of demand over supply, even though M is stationary.
4. V and T are not constant: changes in the demand for money are reflected in changes in V, to which this supply-based equation pays insufficient attention. During the upswing of the economic activity, when prices are rising, an expansion of credit may increase the money supply, thus the increase in the money supply is the *result*, not the cause, of rising prices, as the equation maintains.

▌ Inflation, deflation and the value of money

The phenomena of *inflation* and *deflation* cause changes in the value of money.

The outward sign of *inflation* in an economy is a sustained increase in the general price level. The reason for a rise in prices is increased total spending relative to the supply of goods and services on sale: too much money chasing too few goods and services. Thus inflation is caused by either an excess of the money supply, or an excess of demand in the economy. The group of economists called the 'monetarists' maintain that it is the excess of money supply which causes rising prices: 'inflation is always and everywhere a monetary phenomenon' (Milton Friedman). Another group of economists, the 'Keynesians' (after the famous English economist, J. M. Keynes), maintain that when the total money demand in the economy exceeds the available or potentially producible output, an inflationary gap develops, and that generates rising prices. The net result of inflation on the value of money is to decrease its purchasing power.

There are four major causes of inflation.

1. High demand for loans from financial institutions, mainly banks and building societies in the UK, which, when granted and spent, increases the money supply (see Ch. 5). The resulting increase in demand pulls up the prices of consumer and capital goods. This in turn increases the demand for more bank loans, which pulls up prices still more.

The cause of this type of inflation is *demand pull*. Demand pull can also be triggered by a sharp and significant rise in the demand for exports, with the result that too much money is chasing too few goods in the domestic economy.

2. Heavy government spending to reflate the economy, in order to bring it out of deep recession, can also create inflation: prices will rise if the increased output does not match increased aggregate demand.

3. A successful and continuous demand for higher wages will cause businessmen to raise prices continuously in order to recoup their higher labour costs. The rise in prices then triggers off demand for still higher wages. This cause of inflation is called *cost push*: prices are pushed up, at least initially, by higher labour costs.

4. An inflationary psychology which motivates people to spend savings quickly in order to avoid a further decline in the purchasing power of their money. This will increase the general price level, owing to increased total spending relative to the goods and services available in the market.

Since the purchasing power of money is *inversely* related to the level of general prices, inflation, by eroding the value of money, causes a loss of confidence in money's ability to perform its functions satisfactorily. Money's ability to perform its functions is affected to different degrees at various levels of inflation; therefore the *rate* of inflation is crucial.

(a) With the inflation rate up to about 2 per cent p.a. (creeping inflation), money fulfils all its functions.

(b) As the rate of inflation increases, the 'store of value' is the first function to suffer: no one wants to hold on to savings in wasting assets. Non-financial assets (antiques, old master paintings) begin to be preferred over financial assets. Savers demand a rate of interest at least equal to the rate of inflation.

(c) The 'unit of account function' is next to suffer: adjustments to business accounts (inflation accounting) are needed to enable meaningful comparisons over time.

(d) With further increases in the inflation rate, the next function to suffer is the 'standard of deferred payments': upward adjustment clauses are built into future calculations of debt contracts (e.g. rent agreements) to avoid debtors gaining at the expense of creditors. The rate of interest demanded forward by lenders would become so enormous as to make the justification of taking a loan very difficult.

(e) Finally, and rarely, if the inflation rate reaches astronomical levels (hyper-inflation), the 'medium of exchange' function suffers: people begin to revert to barter, and the authorities revalue (up value) the unit of money to make buying and selling more manageable (e.g. 1 unit of new money = say, 1000 units of the old money).

Despite the UK authorities' attempts in recent years to focus attention on the *underlying* rate of inflation (which excludes mortgage interest payments) and away from the *headline* rate of inflation (which includes mortgage interest payments), the headline rate remains of particular relevance in influencing wage bargaining.

Deflation, on the other hand, is a phenomenon which causes a *decrease* in the general price level, due to a decrease in total spending. Deflation increases the purchasing power of money, and deflationary psychology causes companies and households to defer purchases to buy them later at lower prices. It benefits, in the short term, those on fixed incomes and creditors. Deflation can cause businesses to decline, unemployment to rise and incomes to fall. However, when prices fall producers reduce production and retailers carry less stock and the demand for labour and therefore money incomes falls. The consequent reduction in spending leads through unsold stocks to a further lowering of output and a further increase in unemployment. Thus unchecked deflation through a chain reaction gives momentum to a downswing in economic activity. Deflation has not really occurred in Britain since the 1930s. Economic **recession** (technically a fall in economic growth for two consecutive quarters) is a less severe form of deflation. Britain has experienced economic recession twice during the past decade.

∎ Disinflation and reflation

Under inflation, the general price level rises and therefore the value of money falls. The authorities may take *disinflationary* or *deflationary* measures, namely increase in interest rates and taxes, decrease in government spending and imposition of credit restraints, to keep the rise in prices and incomes in check. Without such disinflationary measures the rate of inflation could reach astronomical levels, i.e. become hyper-inflation.

Under deflation, the general level of prices falls and therefore the value of money rises. Unhindered deflation would, in theory, reduce prices and profits to zero! The authorities may take *reflationary* measures, i.e. measures which are the *reverse* of deflationary measures, to counteract the damaging effects of deflation on the economy. Reflationary measures aim directly to increase aggregate expenditure in the economy.

The relationship between (a) inflation and disinflation and (b) deflation and reflation is shown in Fig. 2.1.

∎ Legal tender

While money is something which people will generally accept in settlement of debts, legal tender is what the law says they must accept if it is offered. Legal tender may be *limited* legal tender, i.e. people must accept it if it is offered, but only up to specified limits of payment; on the other hand it may be *unlimited* tender, i.e. it must be accepted in settlement of debts of any amount. Legal tender is high-powered money

∎ Useful applied material

Bank and building society deposits

The chequeable sight deposits in Britain, as in other countries with highly developed banking systems, are an important feature of the money in the economy. The medium of exchange in Britain consists of notes and coins and chequeable current accounts. The leading building societies also provide full chequeing accounts payable on demand which therefore must be regarded as, and is, money (see Ch. 3).

The *near money* assets in Britain include postal orders, money orders, bills of exchange, bank and building society short notice deposits, national savings securities except National Savings Certificates and Save As You Earn contracts — these are too illiquid. Also included are Treasury bills, short-dated gilts, local authority deposits, certificates of tax deposit (for the corporation tax paid in advance by business companies), certificates of deposit (sold by banks and building societies to large depositors), and National Savings Bank accounts.

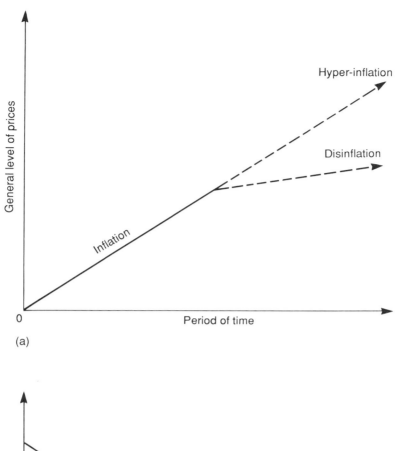

(a)

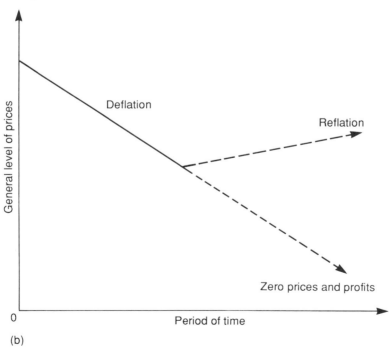

(b)

Fig. 2.1

Official monetary aggregates in Britain

The meaning, measurement and control of money are interrelated concepts. If the monetary authorities (the Treasury and the Bank of England) do not know precisely what money is, and what forms it can take, then they will not be able to measure it or control its supply.

In the UK, as in most other countries, a distinction is made between 'narrow' and 'broad' measures of money. The *narrow* money measures include those assets which represent immediate purchasing power, i.e. those assets which perform the medium of exchange function of money. Narrow money comprising *immediately* available purchasing power might well understate the *potential* purchasing power in the economy, given the existence of liquid assets which could quickly, and without the risk of significant financial loss, be converted into cash; hence the need for *broad* money measures.

In order to understand why there is more than one official definition of money, you must first and foremost understand the concept of the liquidity spectrum (see p. 6). The various aggregates differ in their composition and in their response to changes in interest rates, incomes and inflation.

There are at present in Britain three main measures of sterling-dominated money, namely M0, M2 and M4. The components of each aggregate and the relationship between them are as follows:

1. *M0* = notes and coins in circulation outside the Bank of England *plus* bankers' operational deposits with the Bank of England.

   M0 is also called the 'wide monetary base', which can be misleading, because over 99.5 per cent of its total is made up of notes and coins: M0 is mainly cash. However, it is the only monetary aggregate which the authorities target: 0−4 per cent for 1993−4.

   M0, as the narrow monetary aggregate, emphasises the distinction between transaction balances, which respond *inversely* to the changes in short-term interest rates, and the broad money, which has particular relevance for government decisions relating to the tax revenue, public spending and borrowing, i.e. the official fiscal policy decisions.

2. *M2* = notes and coins in circulation with 'M4 private sector' (i.e. non-bank and non-building society UK public) *plus* M4 private sector's interest-bearing and non-interest-bearing *retail deposits* with banks and building societies and building society shares and deposits.

   Sterling retail deposits include the following:
   (a) All sterling deposits (regardless of size and maturity) on which standing orders, direct debit mandates, or other payments to third parties may be made.
   (b) Other deposits of less than £100,000 having a maturity of less than one month: deposits of £100,000 and over, or with maturities over one month are held mainly as investment, and not transaction, balances.

   M2 provides a monetary aggregate that comprises retail (transaction) balances of the M4 private sector in modern times, an aggregate which is neither so narrow as to be confined to notes and coins and sight deposits, nor so broad as to include large investment balances.

3. *M4* = M2 *plus* bank and building society *wholesale* deposits (including certificates of deposits) of the M4 private sector.

   M4 consists of both retail and wholesale deposits, i.e. transaction and investment balances of the M4 private sector.

M0 is mainly cash and as such performs only the medium of exchange function of money. M2 comprises cash and near money assets, and performs the medium of exchange and, to some extent, the store of value functions of money. M4, of which M2 is a *subset*, also performs the medium of exchange and store of value functions of money, although the emphasis is on investment balances.

The authorities emphasise the distinction between retail and wholesale deposits or funds of the banks, building societies and M4 private sector, because a sizeable increase in the retail balances can trigger inflation, but an increase in the level of short-term interest rates may divert a proportion of the retail funds to wholesale funds and thereby reduce the possibility of inflation rearing its head. On the other hand, in times when the economy is going through an economic recession, a sizeable proportion of the wholesale funds may be encouraged to move into retail funds by the lowering of the short-term interest rates, and thereby encouraging spending and discouraging saving. And, as you will see later, the Bank of England has the power to influence short-term interest rates in the UK. For all practical purposes, there are, at present, only two monetary aggrgates: M0 and M4.

Liquidity outside M4

M4 is made up of sterling cash and deposits with banks and building societies in the UK held by the M4 private sector. Certain *liquid* assets have developed *outside* M4, and the Bank of England publishes figures for these assets. In assessing the liquidity of these assets, it should be remembered that M4 itself contains some comparatively illiquid elements (e.g. deposits of any maturity with banks and building societies and certain paper and other capital market instruments of not more than five years' original maturity – though in practice the great majority of M4 is of under three months to maturity).

The main components of the liquid assets outside M4 are as follows:

M4 private sector's deposits etc.

(a) *Sterling bank bills.*. These are sterling commercial bank bills which have been accepted by a bank in the UK. They are very similar in status and liquidity to sterling certificates of deposit issued by UK banks (which are inlcuded in M4 if owned by the M4 private sector).

(b) *Sterling deposits with UK offshore institutions.* At present about one-third of the banking institutions in the Channel Islands and Isle of Man comply with the Bank's monetary control arrangements and are treated as UK banks for statistical purposes; M4 private sector's deposits with these institutions are included within M4. The remainder of the banking institutions are treated as 'other financial institutions' (OFIs), and the deposits with them are not included in M4. However, the deposits of the OFIs with the UK banks and building societies are included in M4. Therefore, to the extent that the OFIs take funds and redeposit them in the UK, there is no leakage from M4.

(c) *Sterling deposits at banks in the BIS area.* Banks in twenty-four countries are included in the territorial statistics published by the Bank for International Settlements (BIS). Deposits from the UK offshore institutions that are part of the M4 private sector may be included in the BIS statistics as deposits from banks rather than M4 private sector; hence the identification of the UK M4 private sector in the BIS statistics may not be precise.

(d) *Foreign currency deposits with UK banks and building societies.* These deposits held by the M4 private sector at banks and building societies in the UK, or at UK offshore institutions – or even held at banks abroad – may be destined for spending in the UK or may represent a store of wealth relevant to UK economic activity. Any significant conversion of these deposits into sterling for spending in the UK would impact upon the money supply and interest rates and would tend to raise the exchange rate (within the constraints imposed by membership of the Exchange Rate Mechanism (ERM)).

Overseas sector's sterling deposits

These deposits held at banks in the UK may be for spending in the UK, or may be held as a store of wealth, but their conversion into foreign currency might affect UK economic activity via an effect on the exchange rate. (See Ch. 9.)

M4 private sector's public sector debt

(a) *Sterling Treasury bills.* These bills with an original maturity of six months or less are marketable and are considered as liquid by their holders.

(b) *Local authority temporary debt.* This covers a variety of instruments, all with an original maturity of one year; in general, the holders of these instruments will view them as fairly liquid.

(c) *Certificates of tax deposits.* These are not marketable. The return on them is greater when used to pay tax; their holders may not consider them liquid for other purposes.

(d) *Gilts.* All gilts are marketable, and may be considered liquid by their holders, especially nearer to their maturity. However their longer original terms make them less liquid.

(e) *National Savings and National Savings Certificates.* These are, both in the fixed interest and index-linked forms, the largest single item within the national savings total. During their five-year term, withdrawals are subject to a penalty. On maturity they normally go automatically on variable interest rate extension terms, and repayment on demand. In principal, this makes mature NSCs liquid. *Yearly plan* is a fixed-interest, tax-free scheme involving monthly payments for one year, after which a certificate guaranteeing the rate of interest for the next four years is provided. It is non-marketable. Matured yearly plans, like the NSCs, are liquid. The *Save As You Earn* schemes are illiquid until maturity.

(f) *Deposits with the National Savings Bank:*
   (i) *Ordinary accounts.* Since withdrawals can be made on demand at any post office, these deposits are liquid.
   (ii) *Investment accounts.* Repayments require one month's notice, therefore they are fairly liquid.
   (iii) *Premium Savings Bonds.* These can be cashed in immediately, and in lieu of an interest return they provide opportunities of winning tax-free cash prizes.
   (iv) *Income Bonds.* The life of the bond is ten years. Repayments are at three months' notice. Interest is taxable and paid gross each month after one year of purchase.
   (v) *Capital Bonds.* Their life is five years. Interest is taxable and is paid gross.
   All the National Savings products are non-marketable.

Other assets etc.

(a) *Sterling commercial paper (SCP).* This is marketable paper issued with maturity of up to and including one year. The paper issued, and owned, by banks and building societies is excluded from calculation.

(b) *Sterling medium-term notes.* These are marketable securities issued with original maturities of over one year and up to five years. They include both fixed- and floating-rate notes; the floating-rate notes are more capital-certain and therefore more liquid than fixed-rate notes. Notes issued by banks and building societies are excluded from this heading.

(c) *Other sterling paper maturing within one year.* Included under this heading are all holdings of sterling (including eurosterling) bonds of original maturity of five years issued by the UK private sector and the overseas sector that are due to mature within one year. Their liquidity varies with the size of the issue and with the status of the issuer. The majority are floating issues and may be considered more liquid (being more capital-certain) than fixed-rate issues.

(d) *Residual maturites of gilts.* Their maturity breakdown cannot be allocated into sectors and hence gilts maturing within one year and gilts maturing in one to five years are included.

(e) *Sterling unused credit facilities.* It is sometimes argued that unused credit facilities may be seen by potential borrowers as a form of liquidity. Some banks report no unutilised facilites (although requests by borrowers to increase the credit limits are often met). Coverage is incomplete – notably, the unused portion of credit card holders' limits is not included. On the other hand, borrowers may have facilities with several institutions without ever intending to draw on them all simultaneously. Therefore, all sterling unused credit facilities reported by UK banks are included in the figures of liquidity outside M4 under this heading.

▌ Recent examination questions

The following six questions taken from past papers give an indication of the type of questions you may encounter on 'Money and Inflation'. You could usefully spend ten minutes or so on each question, trying to identify the main points you would use in your answers, before turning to the section on 'outline answers' which follows.

Question 1

(a) What is meant by index-linking of financial assets? Include some examples of index-linked assets in your answer.
(b) To what extent is index-linking likely to succeed in curbing inflation? How else might governments attempt to deal with the problem.

Question 2

Since 1984 the UK monetary authorities have set a target for the growth of the monetary aggregate M0, also known as the 'wide monetary base'.

(a) Define M0 and explain the reasons for its introduction.
(b) Is the behaviour of M0 alone sufficient to provide a clear picture of monetary conditions in the UK?

Question 3

(a) What attributes must an asset possess in order to be considered liquid?
(b) To what extent do the following possess the attributes referred to in (a) necessary for them to be considered liquid?

  (i) Treasury bills.
  (ii) Gilt-edged stock.
  (iii) Bank notes.
  (iv) Building society term shares.
  (v) Certificates of deposit issued by a commercial bank.
(c) Classify the assets set out in (b) above according to whether they are included in the measures of the money stock in the UK.

Question 4

Compare and contrast the principal liabilities of commercial banks and building societies with particular reference to the following:

(a) Money as a medium of exchange.
(b) Money as a store of value.
(c) The control of money supply.

Question 5

(a) How do the authorities of a country measure the rate of inflation?
(b) Describe the relationship between the money supply and the rate of inflation.
(c) What problems are created by inflation?

Question 6

Some of the functions of money are performed by other liquid assets. What are these assets? Why are they held in preference to bank notes and bank deposits in the performance of these functions?

▍Outline answers

Answer 1

(a) (i) Inflation erodes the capital value of financial assets.
    (ii) Index-linking gives full protection against the effects of inflation by linking the capital value in line with increases in prices as (usually) measured by the retail price index.
    (iii) Index-linking of the rate of return on securities etc. brings the rate of interest into line with the rate of inflation.
    (iv) Examples of index-linked assets in the UK:
        − Certain gilt-edged stock.
        − Certain National Savings Certificates.
        − (Also) the pensions of civil servants.
(b) (i) Index-linking, by encouraging the public to save safely, curbs inflation.
    (ii) Index-linking, however, only attacks the symptoms and not the roots of inflation.
    (iii) Experience world-wide shows that index-linking becomes institutionalised, making it more difficult for the economy to return to a low rate of inflation.
    (iv) Government may take the following measures to deal with the roots of the inflation problem:

- Control money supply growth – raise interest rates.
- Discourage spending by the public and private sectors via fiscal measures (e.g. higher taxes, lower spending limits for the local and central governments).
- Introduce, in the short term, a prices and incomes policy to keep wages, profits and prices in check.
- Keep the exchange rate of the currency, via central bank intervention, at a level high enough to curb the price rises of imported goods, yet not so high as to discourage exports by overpricing them (see Ch. 8).

Answer 2

(a) (i) M0 comprises notes and coins in circulation, banks' till money and their operational deposits with the Bank of England.
   (ii) M0 is a very narrow measure of the money supply and so it is confusing to term it the 'wide monetary base'.
  (iii) M0 was introduced because:
      - M1 (abolished), the traditional measure of narrow money, became unreliable owing to the inclusion of a large and volatile element of interest-bearing deposits.
      - M0, as an alternative, seemed to offer a less distorted and less misleading indicator of changes in narrow money, and a guide to inflation.
(b) (i) Although M0's credibility has been questioned since its introduction in 1984 it grows much more slowly and remains mostly within its target range.
   (ii) No *single* monetary aggregate can fully encapsulate monetary conditions and provide a correct basis for controlling the complex relationships between monetary growth and prices and incomes, because there is substitutability between the components of various monetary aggregates.
  (iii) M0 is too narrow as a money supply aggregate and its behaviour cannot provide a comprehensive view of the purchasing power in the economy.

Answer 3

(a) Attributes of liquidity:
   (i) Quickly convertible into means of payments; such conversion is without risk of financial loss.
(b) (i) *Treasury bills.* Quickly convertible into means of payments (i.e. through secondary markets), but suffer from risk of loss: their value during their 91-day life fluctuates in line with short-term interest rate movements. Considered liquid.
   (ii) *Gilt-edged stock.* Maturities vary, from five to fifteen years to undated, but all marketable. Significant risk of loss in value because of their long maturities and high responsiveness to interest rate movements. Those close to maturity are liquid.
  (iii) *Bank notes.* Most liquid: instant purchasing power without any risk of financial loss. Inflationary loss irrelevant to this concept of liquidity because it relates to an asset maintaining its value in money, not 'real', terms.
   (iv) *Building society term shares.* Illiquid (except those nearing maturity): cash tied up for the term, or available on demand with significant penalty.
    (v) *Certificates of deposit.* Generally regarded as liquid: issued for short maturities (maturities may range from three months to one year); easily marketable in secondary money markets; risk of loss due to interest rate changes is similar to that of Treasury bills. Those close to maturity are liquid.

(c) (i) Treasury bills included in liquid assets outside M4.
    (ii) Gilt-edged stock are included in liquid assets outside M4.
    (iii) Bank notes included in all measures of money – M0, M2, M4.
    (iv) Building society term shares are included in M4 measure of money.
    (v) Certificates of deposits included in M4. Those held by overseas residents are excluded from any measure of money.

Answer 4

(a) (i) Both bank and building society current accounts (not cheques) may be classed as medium of exchange: available as a *direct* means of payment.
    (ii) The cheques received by depositors from a building society may be used as a direct means of payment but these cheques are drawn upon a *bank current* account of the building society. Recent changes in money transmission services may blur the distinction between bank current accounts and building society ordinary accounts.
    (iii) All other bank and building society accounts do not act as medium of exchange: they have to be converted into cash or chequeable current accounts before performing the medium of exchange role – it is the *cash* which is withdrawn on demand that constitutes the medium of exchange, not the bank deposit from which it is withdrawn.
(b) (i) Bank current accounts are not a store of value: they earn little or no interest. This is changing fast.
    (ii) All other banks and building society accounts are a store of value: they all earn, albeit differing, rates of return; the term deposits generally earn the highest rate of return; they provide a 'real' rate of pre-tax returns.
    (iii) Inflation rates higher than rates of returns tend to undermine their role as a store of value.
    (iv) Money in bank current accounts, earning little or no interest, suffers from erosion in purchasing power during inflationary times.
(c) (i) Define M4 measure of the money supply.
    (ii) Traditionally the authorities have sought to control only bank deposits (together with notes and coins) in controlling the money supply.
    (iii) There is close substitutability between bank and building society deposits, hence the introduction of the wider monetary aggregate, M4.

Answer 5

(a) To measure inflation, a 'basket' of goods is created and the amount of money required to purchase that basket is identified at different points in time. A price index is thus created, such as the Retail Price Index (RPI) in the UK.

It is not only the RPI which is used to measure inflation. In 1990, the RPI (headline rate) showed a faster rise than the underlying rate (which excludes mortgage interest payments). Wholesale price inflation, measuring cost of inputs for manufacturers or prices of manufactured output, is calculated via a wholesale price index.

(b) There is a close connection between growth in the money supply and the rate of inflation, as expressed by Fisher's equation: $MV = PT$. V (velocity of circulation of money) and T (total number of transactions) in a given period are assumed to remain constant; therefore an increase in M (money supply) will cause a proportionate increase in P (price level), i.e. an *increase* in the rate of inflation.

(c) Problems caused by inflation:
   (i) Exports become uncompetitive and, if the demand for export of goods and services is *elastic*, may result in balance of payments problems.
   (ii) An arbitrary redistribution of income takes place: e.g. those on fixed income or in a weak wage bargaining position lose.
   (iii) At higher and rising rates of inflation, the functions of money are adversely affected. Money ceases to be a store of value, and its effectiveness as a unit of account and as a standard for deferred payments is eroded, making sensible financial decisions more difficult.
   (iv) With hyper-inflation there is great economic uncertainty and a breakdown of the price mechanism, causing money to cease functioning as the medium of exchange.

Answer 6

Briefly explain the concept of the liquidity spectrum, emphasising the substitutability at the margins between real and near money assets.

(a) Near money assets perform the store of value function of money and, once removed, the means of exchange function.

(b) Near money assets held by the UK non-bank and bank sectors: postal orders, money orders, bills of exchange, building society deposits, National Savings securities and accounts, Treasury bills, local authority deposits, certificates of tax deposits, certificates of deposits, gilt-edged securities, money at call and short notice, and interest-bearing deposits with banks.

(c) Reasons for holding near money assets in preference to bank notes and current accounts with banks:
   (i) Bank notes and current accounts with banks generally earn no or little interest. Therefore inflation erodes their actual purchasing power and makes them unattractive as a store of value.
   (ii) Near money assets provide a hedge against inflation, and sometimes a 'real' increase in the rate of return, which makes them more attractive as a store of value.
   (iii) Most near money assets can be converted into cash or chequeable accounts fairly quickly and without significant loss of interest or capital, therefore larger payments can be planned easily and without financial loss in terms of near money assets.

▌ A tutor's answer

The following question is highly relevant in view of there being several measures of money at present. The answer highlights the fact that in a sophisticated modern economy there are many financial assets which perform some, if not all, the functions of money. Also, that there is such substitutability among these assets in the public's mind as to make it impossible to give one unambiguous definition of money in modern economies. The specimen answer should help you to assess the scope of the question, to make a relevant answer plan and to write within the scope of the question.

Question

(a) Explain briefly why a country's monetary authorities consider the behaviour of the money supply to be important.

(b) Discuss the problems which arise in modern economies in defining the money supply.

Answer plan

(a) To control inflation:
  (i) Fisher's analysis,
  (ii) expectation of future inflation rate,
  (iii) exchange rate,
  (iv) economic growth rate.
(b) Some assets:
  (i) perform some of the functions of money,
  (ii) have varying degrees of liquidity,
  (iii) have substitutability.

Specimen answer

(a) If the money supply grows faster than the growth in output then, other things being equal, there will be too much money in the economy chasing too few goods. This will lead to an increase in the general price level (e.g. RPI in the UK). Rising prices are a symptom that the economy is suffering from inflation.

The monetarists use Fisher's equation to explain the above analysis: $MV = PT$, where M = quantity of money; V = velocity of circulation of M; P = general price level; T = total number of transactions. Since V and T are assumed to be stationary, an increase in M will be reflected by an increase in P.

The effects of inflation badly damage the national economy. Rising prices cause employees to ask for higher wages, lenders to ask for higher interest returns and landlords to ask for higher rents. In such circumstances, the profit margins of business firms are depressed, which causes a reduction in investment, and that leads to an increase in unemployment.

High-priced domestic goods are difficult to sell abroad, whereas comparatively lower priced imports increase. This leads to deficit on the balance of trade, which, in time, leads to a fall in the foreign exchange value of the national currency. Thus a country with a rate of inflation higher than the inflation rates of its trading partners will find that its currency buys less both domestically and internationally.

Inflationary psychology motivates the inclusion of anticipated inflationary increase clauses into contracts for wages, loans and rents: inflationary psychology materialises inflationary *expectations*.

In extreme cases, unchecked growth in inflation leads to hyper-inflation (e.g. in Weimar Republic Germany during 1922/3). Hyper-inflation means that the citizens refuse to accept the national legal tender in settlement of debts.

It is for the above reasons that the control of the money supply has been an important aspect of economic policy in major countries for many years.

(b) In modern economies there exists a diversity of assets which can be called money. Each of them performs *some* of the functions of money because they each have *varying degrees of liquidity* (e.g. *near money* assets perform the store of value, but not the medium of exchange function of money). It is therefore difficult to establish precisely where the line should be drawn in defining money.

Nevertheless, a distinction is usually made in developed economies between narrow and broad definitions of money. *Narrow* money (e.g. M0 in the UK) stresses money's means of exchange function; *broad* money definitions extend beyond cash and bank deposits and include liabilities of several other financial institutions (e.g. M4 in the UK includes all the sterling balances with the banks and building societies). The issue, however, is to what extent should financial instruments not included (e.g. unused credit card facilities) in even the broadest definition of money (e.g. M4, in the UK) also be included in money aggregates monitored by the authorities, because there exists considerable *substitutability* between various assets.

There are two main reasons why it is difficult to provide an unambiguous definition of money supply in a modern economy. First, in the developed economies the banking and financial institutions are sufficiently sophisticated to be able to create a growing variety of financial assets capable of performing some, if not all, of the traditional functions of money. Second, in the eyes of the public, there is substitutability among these financial assets, especially at the margins.

∎ A step further

If you wish to obtain up-to-date information on changes of definition of the various monetary aggregates, then the *Quarterly Bulletin of the Bank of England* (*BEQB*) and the *Financial Times* are invaluable sources. Read carefully 'Measures of Broad Money' in the *BEQB* in the June 1989 and February 1991 issues and 'Liquid assets outside M4' in the May 1991 issue. There are useful articles, especially the *Signpost* articles, on money which can be found in The Chartered Institute of Bankers' *Banking World*, and in the past editions of the *Financial Times*. These articles can be located by using the *Financial Times Monthly Index* in your college or public libraries. Fairly frequently you will find articles interpreting the definitional changes of monetary aggregates in the daily quality newspapers. Sometimes there are excellent programmes on the television dealing with various aspects of money. The Chartered Institute of Bankers publishes excellent *Updating Notes*, especially on definitional changes, and these keep candidates abreast of monetary matters.

Note: In the August 1992 issue of *BEQB*, the Bank of England outlined a new monetary aggregate: M3H. *M3H* = M4 *plus* foreign currency deposits of UK residents with banks and building societies in the UK *plus* sterling and foreign currency deposits of UK public corporations with banks and building societies in the UK. In effect, M3H is about 8% larger than M4. It has been introduced throughout the EC to enable comparisons to be made among member states on the movements in broad money aggregates. In most EC states M3 title is preferred for the major broad money aggregates. H probably stands for 'Harmonised'.

CHAPTER 3
UK Financial Institutions

▋ Getting started

To gain a clear insight into the mechanics of the UK financial system, you need to understand the role and functions of the financial institutions operating in the UK, the operations of the various specialised UK financial markets and the types of financial instrument bought and sold on the financial markets (see Fig. 3.1).

In this chapter, we shall look at the roles and functions of the principal banking and non-banking financial institutions in the UK, and in the next chapter, we shall study the operation of the financial markets in the UK and the financial instruments traded in these markets.

The UK *financial institutions* are an integral part of the UK financial intermediation mechanism through which the savings of households, firms, public corporations and even overseas residents are made available to borrowers at home and abroad. Financial intermediation channels the funds from the potential surplus units to potential deficit units quickly, cheaply, safely and conveniently.

The principal financial institutions in the UK financial system may be classified into *bank* and *non-bank* financial intermediaries (BFIs and NBFIs). The BFIs include the Banking Department of the Bank of England, commercial banks (including overseas banks), discount houses, Girobank plc, National Savings Bank and finance houses. The NBFIs include building societies, insurance companies and unit and investment trusts. By and large, the BFIs constitute the UK *monetary sector*.

Most countries in the world have a *central bank* as their principal banking institution to exercise monetary control, supervision of financial institutions and financial assistance to commerce, trade and industry. In the UK, the *Bank of England* stands at the heart of the UK banking system. It supervises, monitors, guides and advises the bank financial institutions, so that the government's monetary policy objectives are fulfilled in the interest of the nation.

In the balance sheets of the financial institutions, savings received from depositors/lenders constitute the *liabilities* of these institutions, and loans and advances made to borrowers

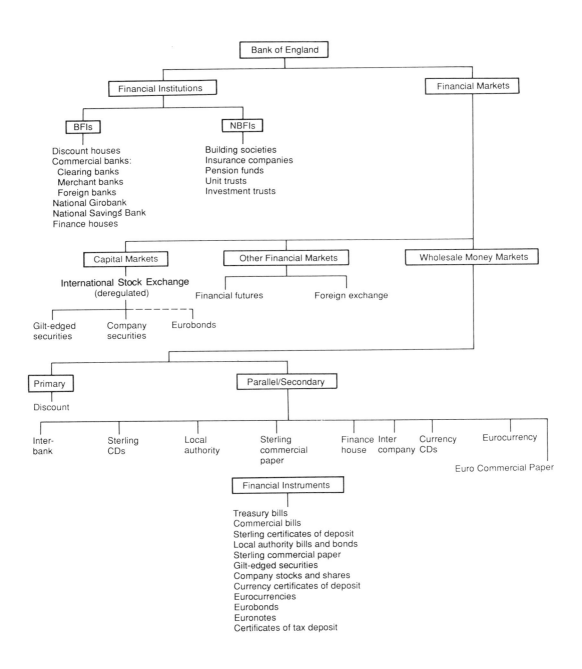

Fig. 3.1 The UK financial system

represent the *assets* of these institutions. Their liabilities, in the main, provide them with resources with which to create their assets.

Those among the BFIs and NBFIs which are *commercial, joint stock companies* have responsibility, like other commercial companies, not only for the safety of their depositors'/investors' money, but also for the profitability of their shareholders. This dual responsibility often creates a counter-pull, i.e. safety versus profitability, and the successful institutions have to resolve this dilemma satisfactorily.

▎Essential principles

The central bank

Most countries have a central banking institution, and as such it is under some degree of state control. On the one hand it functions in close contact with the government department responsible for finance, and on the other with the country's financial institutions, with the aim of meeting the needs of commerce, trade and industry.

The role of the central bank in the national economy relates to monetary control, supervision and last resort financial assistance. Generally speaking, its main functions are as follows:

(a) To act as the banker to the government by undertaking the following tasks:
  (i) Maintaining the accounts of the government departments.
  (ii) Handling the government's short-term borrowing needs via the sale of Treasury bills.
  (iii) Managing the issue, payment of interest, repayment or renewal at maturity of government stocks; i.e. managing the National Debt.
(b) To act as banker to commercial banks by holding their transaction balances (e.g. for clearing in the UK), and assisting their settlement of mutual indebtedness and their payments to and from the public authorities.
(c) To act as lender of last resort to the financial system, by lending to banks either directly or indirectly through open market operations.
(d) To apply prudential control to ensure that financial institutions and markets are run soundly and honestly.
(e) To stabilise the domestic currency exchange rate in foreign exchange markets, by intervening directly or through exchange controls.
(f) To implement the official monetary policy: basically this means varying the cost and availability of credit in the economy, thereby controlling money supply growth. It attempts to achieve this by the following methods:
  (i) By varying the terms of last resort assistance and other financial support, to relieve liquidity problems in the market.
  (ii) By buying and selling government and other first-class bills in the money market.
  (iii) By imposing direct controls on lending and interest rates, and imposing restrictions on asset and liability management by the banks so as to control the 'credit multiplier' (see Ch. 5). The directives issued by the central bank to the financial institutions under its control are binding upon them.
(g) To regulate the issue of the legal tender in order to meet the demand of the public for cash.

Is it essential for a country to have a central bank?

Not all the central banks perform all the above functions. In many cases some of the functions are undertaken by a government department (e.g. the Treasury in the UK or the Finance Ministries elsewhere) and bank regulatory and supervisory commissions. The central banks themselves may share some of their functions with private sector institutions.

Governments need not channel their financial business, including the production and issue of the legal tender, through a central institution; instead they may seek competitive private tenders for the work involved. When a central bank intervenes in the foreign exchange markets to influence the exchange rate (see Ch. 9), it does so as the agent of the government, and uses commercial banks as its agents. There is no real reason preventing the monetary authorities from using private sector banks directly in exchange rate management, which is essentially what happens in Hong Kong.

In many countries the central bank acts as a consultant to the authorities over monetary policy but the authorities make the final decision and the central bank acts as the agent of the authorities in implementing the policy, as is the case in the UK (but not in Germany, where the Bundesbank has constitutional independence in the setting of monetary policy). Here again, there's no real reason why the implementation of the policy may not be done via private sector financial institutions.

The private sector banks may set up their own central clearing agency, empowering it to hold their settlement accounts, oversee the money transmission service, and even to act as lender of last resort, provided regulations are in place preventing banks from taking unwarranted risks and protecting the agency's resources against excessive claims.

It may, however, prove more efficient if a central bank, free from commercial pressures, performs such functions as lender of last resort with supervisory and regulatory powers; this will enhance the confidence of the public at home and abroad in the national financial system. Some central banks, however, such as the Swiss National Bank, seem to be trying to divest themselves of supervisory responsibilities in order to concentrate more on monetary policy and exchange rate-related activities. The Federal Reserve of the United States of America has a very complex regulatory system, involving many agencies.

Secondly, if confidentiality were essential in the government's financial business and could not be guaranteed if the private sector institutions were involved, then a non-commercial bank might be considered a necessity.

Thirdly, a non-commercial central bank will be able to provide the government with an *independent* link with the commercial financial sector.

Central banks are *not* responsible for implementing the fiscal policy of the government (i.e. management of the economy by varying the size and composition of taxation and public expenditure). They are *not* members of the International Monetary Fund; representation at the IMF is by member governments, although the central banks can act as its directors. They *are* members of the Bank for International Settlements.

▌ Financial intermediation

Whilst the inflow and outflow of funds provide the financial institutions with the major source of their profits, the process of channelling most of the savings in the economy to borrowers is also of great benefit to both the savers and borrowers and to the national economy. This process of matching for a fee the needs of the ultimate lenders, i.e. the possessors of surplus loanable funds in the personal, corporate and public sectors, with those of the ultimate borrowers, i.e. those units or sectors in the economy which are in need of liquid funds, is called *financial intermediation*, and the institutions performing the financial intermediation are known as the 'financial intermediaries' (FIs).

A financial intermediary may be a deposit-taking institution, such as a bank or building society, or a non-deposit-taking institution, such as an insurance company or a pension fund. Financial intermediaries are reservoirs through which the funds of surplus units flow to the deficit units in society. Financial intermediation makes lending and borrowing indirect and in doing so has a number of important advantages over direct borrowing and lending; arguably these more than justify the cost of FIs, and also make the FIs indispensable to financially developed economies.

▌ Advantages of financial intermediation

Minimising lending risks

Default

Under direct lending, if the borrower fails to repay, then the lender may lose all or most of his capital. The risk of default is either removed or minimised if lending and borrowing take place via an FI. By interposing itself between the ultimate lender and ultimate borrower, the FI takes over from the lender the risk of loss through default by the borrower. The FI can do this for two main reasons.

1. A financial intermediary *transforms the lending risks* by spreading its risks. The FI can reduce its risk, and therefore the risks of the ultimate lenders, through making a large number of loans of varying degrees of risks, returns and maturities. Diversification spreads the lending risks, and thereby minimises them. Besides, the FI can adjust its interest charges or fees to borrowers so that in the long run the loss through bad debts is covered.
2. FIs are traditionally financially sound institutions; their capital and reserves are sufficiently large and their deposit base is sufficiently stable to meet possible loan losses, whilst still protecting the funds of their depositors.

Loss of liquidity

Other things being equal, lenders prefer to lend short-term to avoid the loss of liquidity for long periods, especially if they suspect a possible need for liquidity arising, or an increase in interest rates occurring, before the borrower repays. On the other hand, borrowers prefer to borrow long-term to take full advantage of the productivity of the capital borrowed before it is to be repaid. The FIs are, by and large, able to resolve the problem of such opposing time-preferences by *maturity transformation*, i.e. borrowing short and lending long. Three main reasons enable the FIs to do this.

1. Unlike individual lenders or borrowers, FIs, due to their large-scale operations, are able to benefit from the statistical 'laws' of large numbers; e.g. the probability of an event occurring comes closer to the probability of its not occurring as the scale of operations gets larger. For example, the larger the number of accounts a bank holds, the greater the statistical probability that withdrawals will match, rather than exceed, deposits.
2. Their long experience enables FIs to anticipate seasonal changes in the outflow of their

funds. They can therefore arrange to hold such interest bearing assets as will mature in time to meet the seasonal pressure of outflow of funds.

3. By paying competitive deposit rates and by maintaining the confidence of depositors, FIs are able to maintain the overall level of their deposits while still providing their depositors with the benefit of liquidity: depositors are able to convert deposits into cash quickly and without loss of capital value.

Minimising borrowing risks

Funds may not be available when required

Borrowers may be unable to obtain funds when needed, due in part to a shortage of funds from regular sources, and in part to a lack of knowledge of other sources from which funds may be available. The FIs are able to minimise this borrowing risk for two main reasons.

1. They are able to supply funds in quantities, at the required times and for appropriate maturities to the borrowers by *aggregating* the small savings of a large number of depositors and direct borrowing from the money markets.
2. Unlike individual lenders and borrowers, FIs specialise in taking deposits from, and making loans to, many sources; hence they possess up-to-date information on the sources and terms under which funds are supplied and demanded.

Lenders may terminate lending at a time most inconvenient to borrowers

The FIs are able to minimise this borrowing risk via the fact that the economic basis of their financial intermediation lies in specialised large-scale operations. This enables them to do the following:

(a) To spread default and other risks.
(b) To hold a more balanced mix of asset portfolios, with regard to types and maturities, thereby reducing the risk of losses. FIs are therefore able to lend, on a contractual basis, such period loans as are most suitable to the needs of borrowers.

Borrowers wish to borrow at the lowest cost

First, due to their large-scale operations, FIs benefit from specialisation and economies of large scale; hence they are able to keep their transaction costs down. Second, because the FIs are able to reduce lending risks, lenders are prepared to accept a lower rate of return from FIs. FIs are therefore able to lend at lower interest rates to borrowers.

The nature and practice of financial intermediation shows that FIs are not parasitic middlemen. Despite carrying liabilities (claims against them) which are more liquid than their assets (claims against borrowers), FIs are able to provide a unique financial service at reasonable cost that assists both ultimate lenders and borrowers *and*, via encouraging additional savings and investment, promotes economic growth for the nation as a whole. (See also 'A tutor's answer' on pp. 48–9 below.)

Reasons for the decline in financial intermediation

Despite the advantage of financial intermediation to lenders and borrowers, the practice of financial intermediation has declined in recent years. This is due to the deregulation of financial services, which is making lenders and borrowers realise that the traditional advantages of financial intermediation are being overcome by the advantages of direct borrowing and lending, called *disintermediation*. To some investors, large companies are no more risky than a financial intermediary, hence the direct issue of short-term securities, such as the sterling commercial paper (see Ch. 4), to investors by the companies. The decline in financial intermediation has increasingly caused the financial intermediaries (especially the commercial banks) merely to act as guarantors and brokers of corporate debt; this has increased their income from commissions but has decreased their traditional source of income: interest receipts. Since guaranteeing and broking are off-balance sheet transactions, they incur reduced capital/liquidity costs to financial intermediaries, which strengthens their balance sheets.

■ BFIs and NBFIs as financial intermediaries

The distinction between a bank and a building society has almost disappeared since the passing of the Building Societies Act 1986. BFIs (including building societies) and NBFIs (excluding building societies), have some common fundamental characteristics: both rely on large-scale operations in order to benefit from statistical probabilities and from the economies which result from specialisation in:

(a) matching anticipated changes in their liabilities and assets;
(b) remaining solvent despite their liabilities being more liquid than their assets.

However, there are some economists who argue that BFIs and NBFIs are different kinds of FIs. Briefly they put their point of view as follows: when a BFI makes a loan, it creates a deposit of equal value (see Ch. 5). Therefore the liabilities (deposits) of BFIs may be used actually to increase the volume of spending in the economy, because BFI sight deposits are generally accepted in settlement of debts. In contrast, NBFIs merely *transmit* funds created elsewhere, i.e. notes and coins by the monetary authorities and bank deposits by the banking system. Hence BFIs, because they can create credit and thereby actually increase money supply, are different in kind from NBFIs who cannot do either of these two things.

■ The UK monetary sector

Since 1982, the monetary authorities have established a much wider UK monetary sector. The Bank of England recognises the following institutions as the participants of the widened monetary sector: the UK offices of authorised banks, Girobank plc, the Banking Department of the Bank of England and some banks in the Channel Islands and Isle of Man which are under the UK monetary control arrangements. By the end of February 1989, there were 295 UK incorporated banks, and 256 were incorporated outside the UK, giving a total of 551 authorised institutions under the 1987 Banking Act (see Ch. 10).

It is noteworthy that not all major UK financial institutions are included even in the widened monetary sector. The notable exceptions are building societies, the National Savings Bank, insurance companies and pension funds.

■ The UK commercial banks

As commercial enterprises, these aim to make profit for their shareholders, to whom they are accountable. The main UK commercial banks are the London Clearing Banks (Barclays, Lloyds, Midland, National Westminster, TSB and Coutts), the Scottish Clearing Banks (Bank of Scotland, Royal Bank of Scotland, Clydesdale Bank), the Northern Irish Banks (Northern Bank, Ulster Bank, Allied Irish Banks, Bank of Ireland) and some other joint stock banks, who are not, like the London clearing banks, members of the Bankers' Clearing House, and whose cheques and credits are cleared via members of the Clearing House (Isle of Man Bank, C. Hoare and Co., Standard Chartered, Yorkshire Bank).

Sometimes the clearing banks, especially the London clearers, are called *retail* banks on account of their direct participation in the UK clearing system and their vast branch network serving the banking needs of hundreds of thousands of personal and corporate customers. However, the distinction between 'retail' and *wholesale* banks − e.g. the merchant banks, who provide for the specialised financial needs of large corporate customers and therefore do not require the expensive branch network − has blurred in recent years.

The wholesale banks include accepting houses (they accept bills of exchange for customers), the overseas banks and consortium banks (these are owned by other banks). The other main differences between wholesale and retail banking are that the wholesale deposits, as compared to retail deposits, might offer a higher rate to depositors, and wholesale loans, as compared to retail loans, might be at a lower rate, because wholesale lending and borrowing rates are related to London Inter-Bank Offered Rate (LIBOR) and London Inter-Bank Bid Rate (LIBID) rather than, as in the case of retail borrowing and lending, to banks' base rates. Both retail and wholesale banks raise wholesale (large) funds through the inter-bank and certificate of deposit (CDs) markets.

Most clearers are now 'banking groups', providing through their subsidiaries retail *and* wholesale banking and non-banking services 'under one roof'. They have acquired controlling interests in merchant banks and finance houses, opened leasing and factoring companies and set up unit trusts. They have established offices overseas for foreign operations and have a substantial share in the eurocurrency market, both directly and in conjunction with the London-based consortium banks. Their main role, however, is to act as financial intermediaries for the sterling and currency funds.

The clearing banks may be distinguished from other banks by the extent to which they provide current account facilities and money transmission services; because of this distinction, the volume of their demand deposits forms a major component of the total purchasing power in the UK economy. It is also for this reason that they are sometimes called *primary* banks, as distinct from *secondary* banks, which (with the exception of some American and Japanese banks) take term deposits and not sight deposits. Therefore secondary banks, unlike primary banks, cannot provide money transmission services. The *secondary* banks include accepting houses, merchant banks, foreign banks, consortium banks and unit and investment trusts.

■ The balance sheet approach

The best way to determine the structure, functions and operations of retail banks, say clearing banks, is by analysing the items on the liabilities and assets sides of their balance sheets.

The liabilities side

Share capital and reserves

These liabilities represent amounts owed to the bank's equity (and preference) shareholders. The bank must show profit in its operations in order to pay adequate dividends to its shareholders. Profitability is therefore very important to a commercial bank.

Loan capital

These are the aggregate fixed interest commitments of the bank; loan interest must be paid before any dividend distribution to shareholders.

Customers' sterling deposits

The volume of these deposits forms the largest liability of a retail bank, but it is also the main source of its profitable operations; banks pivot the credit multiplier on the deposits they take, which generally comprise the following:

(a) *Current account balances*. These are safe repositories of immediate liquidity; banks operate their money transmission services through these accounts. Either no or modest interest is paid to current account holders; but the holders of large overnight balances, usually big corporate customers, receive interest on call accounts, which are similar to current accounts.
(b) *Seven-day and high interest rate deposits*. These are an example of 'near' money assets, yielding a rate of return yet convertible into cash or current account on demand, with only a seven-day interest loss in lieu of notice, and no interest loss with high-rate deposits. *Savings opportunities* at competitive rates are also provided.
(c) *Term deposits*. These cannot be withdrawn by depositors before the end of the term; long-term deposits are 'wholesale' deposits and tend to be larger in amount than 'retail' deposits which are generally small sight and other easily withdrawable deposits.

For their depositors, other than term depositors, retail banks provide the main payments mechanism through the Bankers' Automated Clearing System (BACS) and the Clearing House Automated Payments System (CHAPS).

Customers' currency deposits

There are no exchange controls in the UK and therefore UK residents, personal and corporate, can hold deposits in foreign currencies of their choice. These currency resources assist banks to participate in the eurocurrency markets. Banks pivot the *currency* credit multiplier on currency deposits as they do the ordinary credit multiplier on their sterling deposits (see Ch. 5). Note that if a bank fails, then its sterling and currency depositors are treated as a special class of creditor with increased rights and are paid before its loan stockholders or any class of shareholder. This shows that the safety of depositors' funds is of paramount concern to the banks.

Certificates of deposit

These are really large receipted term deposits with one major difference, that the receipts are bearer documents which are easily marketable and negotiable items in the CDs market.

Since they are liquid-cum-safe investments, banks selling them offer a lower interest rate than on term deposits. Inter-bank and CDs markets borrowings provide banks' main wholesale funding sources.

Other liabilities

These include amounts owing at the balance sheet date, such as the proposed dividend to shareholders, amounts due to subsidiary companies in the 'group' and to the Inland Revenue towards corporation tax commitments.

The assets side

The assets of a bank result from the deployment of its loans and share capital and its deposits. The following are the main assets of a commercial bank.

Liquid assets

These are immediately available:

(a) to meet cash withdrawals from demand deposits, e.g. notes and coins in the till;
(b) to effect clearing settlements and to meet unforeseen contingencies.

The most liquid assets of a bank, in addition to the *till money*, are the first four of the following assets.

Operational deposits held at the Bank of England

Retail banks hold non-interest bearing operational balances with the Bank of England, these balances are treated as cash. The banks are obliged to keep operational balances large enough to cover their daily *clearing* needs and are expected not to overdraw. If a bank becomes overdrawn at the Bank of England, then the Bank may charge it the highest overnight interest rate of the day.

Money at call and short notice

This includes funds lent to discount houses to help them balance their books (outflow of funds on bills discounted and on purchases of Treasury bills and other short-term financial assets *minus* the inflow of funds from the maturity of discounted bills and from the sale of other short-term financial assets); also funds lent to Gilt-Edged Market Makers (GEMMs); to money and bullion brokers, to corporate customers and to other banks (the latter can be very important). Money 'at call' means that it is repayable by the borrower on demand. Money 'at short notice' implies that a notice of repayment of up to fourteen days will be given by the lending bank. These monies are usually secured loans (always so in the case of discount houses) and earn interest; the rate depends upon the availability of such funds and the period of loan. After cash, these are the most liquid assets of a bank. These funds provide a suitable outlet for the surplus liquidity of the banks, and are therefore one of the principal means by which banks adjust their cash and liquidity requirements.

Eligible bills

The Bank of England is prepared to buy these first-class, easily marketable bills, mainly from discount houses. Items qualifying as eligible bills are Treasury bills, local authority bills and first-class trade bills which have been accepted by eligible banks. Banks do not usually tender for Treasury bills directly but buy them from discount houses later on, as part of their easily realisable short-term assets. Local authorities also issue bills to raise short-term funds. The holding of eligible bills forms a significant percentage of the total assets of a bank. They are held because they provide a safe rate of return and are easily discounted by the discount houses in the bill market in the course of open market operations of the Bank of England.

Certificates of deposit and other market loans

Although a bank's holdings of CDs issued by other banks represents its short-term investments, these can easily be cashed at current rates in the CDs market. The market loans are short-term loans made to non-bank borrowers via specialised markets, to other banks via the inter-bank market and to other large customers; these loans are, of course, linked to LIBOR.

Investment other than trade investments

These are safe short- and medium-term fixed interest rate investments, mainly in gilt-edged securities of the central government. Besides being quite safe, these instruments are held both for their yield and also for the possibility of capital gain, which occurs when interest rates fall. However, even though they are liquid, there is the danger of financial loss on realisation if the current market interest rates are higher than those operating when the financial asset was purchased.

Advances and loans to personal and corporate customers

These items form the largest proportion of a bank's assets and are traditionally seen as the most profitable. They include all types of bank lending, namely overdrafts, term loans, credit card finance, hire purchase finance (through subsidiaries), home mortgage and insurance. In theory, overdrafts, but not fixed term loans, are call money, but in practice, very rarely would a bank call for their immediate repayment. In fact, therefore, these balances represent a bank's illiquid assets, and, as such are prone to lending risks; this point is reflected in the higher interest rates banks charge on them. A bank widely diversifies its advances and loans in terms of maturity and sectors. Changes in these balances have a significant influence upon the size of the money supply. Short-term loans, e.g. an overnight loan to a company like ICI, are very liquid; whereas loans that have a definite repayment period have a liquidity that is determined by the time remaining to maturity.

Investment in subsidiary and associate companies

A subsidiary is a company in which the bank has controlling power; an associate company is one in which it owns at least 20 per cent of the share capital. Most commercial banks, especially the clearers, are now fully fledged banking groups providing banking and non-banking services 'under one roof'. Their investments in *subsidiary* companies assist them in providing services beyond the range of traditional banking services, such as factoring, leasing, insurance, estate agency. Their investments in *associated* companies often provide the commercial banks with the means through which to operate their banking services more efficiently, e.g. Bankers' Automated Clearing System (BACS).

Trade investments

Investments in a company in which the investor has less than a 20 per cent stake are called trade investments; these investments give a bank access to specialist services, as with the Agricultural Mortgage Corporation, Finance for Industry and the Bankers' Clearing House. Trade investments may also assist it in opening overseas offices, e.g. in conjunction with a consortium bank.

Non-operational deposits with the Bank of England

The Bank of England requires all institutions in the UK monetary sector with 'eligible liabilities' (broadly speaking, its sterling deposit liabilities) of £10 million or over to:

(a) Keep 0.35 per cent of its sterling deposit base in non-interest bearing and non-operational deposits with the Bank. These cash deposit ratios are designed to provide the Bank with a major source of its income to enable it to carry out its functions and to pay salaries to its staff. One of its main functions is its 'open market operations', which may take place in order to relieve a shortage of cash in the money markets, or to influence short-term interest rates.
(b) Be ready to receive 'calls' for special deposits from the Bank. As a part of the UK monetary control regulations, the Bank of England is empowered to call, from time to time, for non-operational but interest-bearing special deposits from the institutions in the 'monetary sector' (see Ch. 5). Such calls for special deposits are a means of withdrawing cash from the money market, thereby reducing the commercial banks' ability to create credit, by 'freezing' some of their funds in special deposits.

Premises and equipment

These are the bank's fixed assets, which are necessary for its operations. They include head office and branch bank premises, other buildings, computers, equipment and vehicles. The book value of a bank's premises and other buildings, which is much less than their market value, represents hidden reserves. An increase in investment in fixed assets reduces banks' ability to create credit.

The asset structure of a bank reflects a successful compromise between its two main objectives: safety of its depositors' funds and profitability for its shareholders. If the composition of a bank's liabilities changes, e.g. there are more current accounts and less savings deposits, then its asset structure will be adjusted accordingly, with more liquid assets and less long-term investments.

Other services

More recently retail banks, in addition to their well-established services (standing orders, direct debits, tax advice, ATMs and executor and trustee work) are also providing insurance broking, unit trusts, investment advice, merchant banking, factoring (buying from corporate customers their invoiced debts), mortgage finance and leasing (hiring to customers assets for the duration of their economic life).The retail commercial banks are now *financial conglomerates*, and not just takers of deposits and makers of loans.

▌ Foreign banks

There are about 550 banks in the UK; just under half of them are branches of foreign banks. Foreign banks are represented in London through branches, subsidiaries, representative offices and through minority holdings in 'consortium banks', i.e. institutions which specialise in international banking activity and which are owned jointly by a group of established banks.

Foreign banks are attracted to London for several reasons:

(a) To participate in the eurocurrency transactions, because London is a major eurocurrency market (see Ch. 4).
(c) To serve the financial needs of companies from their own countries which are operating in the UK.
(c) To participate in financing trade between the UK and their own countries, and indeed between the UK and other countries.
(d) To have stakes in consortium banks which specialise in international banking activity.
(e) To cater for specific ethnic communities now resident in the UK.
(f) To compete with the UK banks, since the 'Big Bang' in October 1986, in the investment business, mortgage finance and merchant banking, either directly or through acquired stockbroking and jobbing firms.

Therefore, the presence of foreign banks is not restricted to London; some banks are establishing networks of strategically placed offices in major UK cities, e.g. Birmingham, Bradford, Cardiff and Liverpool.

Like the UK retail and merchant banks, foreign banks are 'authorised' institutions under the 1987 Banking Act, and the regulatory changes of the past few years, i.e. capital adequacy ratios and liquidity criteria (see Ch. 10), have not in fact driven off any foreign banks. On the completion of the Single European Market by the end of 1992, overseas participation in the UK banking sector might be expected to increase, just as British banks are likely to increase their interests in Continental European markets. (Completion of the Single Market will change the supervisory regime for EC-incorporated banks.)

Among the foreign banks, the American and Japanese banks are the most prevalent. Therefore, for statistical purposes, the Bank of England classifies foreign banks as American Banks, Japanese Banks and Other Overseas Banks. In terms of balance sheet trading, the American banks account for around 45.0 per cent of foreign banks' business in London and around 12.5 per cent of all lending to British corporate customers. Their prowess in oil and energy finance has enabled them to take a sizeable slice of the North Sea oil business.

The American and Japanese banks, along with a few other foreign banks, are engaged in the UK domestic wholesale banking, and in particular in providing funds to large companies. They are also competing with the UK clearing banks in retail banking in sterling, particularly that denominated in foreign currencies.

The Japanese banks were among the most aggressive international lenders in Europe in the late 1980s, driving down margins and profitability for European banks. The margins of UK banks only recovered as the Japanese banks retrenched their operations during the current recession. The intense competition in financial services has contributed to excessive lending, fuelling inflation and keeping real interest rates high.

▌The Bank of England

The Bank of England has a history of private banking but has since become a public sector institution (1946), unlike the Bundesbank (West Germany) and Federal Reserve Board (USA), which were set up from scratch by legislation. It became the central bank because it had been adopted as the government's banker. Due to its implicit government backing and its favoured position, often being designated as sole bank note issuer, it naturally evolved as agent/adviser of the government.

It is the central bank of the UK and as such its relationship with the Treasury and its functions and operations in the UK financial system are of extreme importance.

Functions of the Bank of England

Adviser and agent to the government

One of the Bank of England's functions is to act as the adviser and agent to the UK government and assist in formulating and implementing the official monetary policy. It is uniquely placed, on account of its specialised knowledge, contacts and experience of the UK financial market acquired over many years, to give advice to the government on the technical aspects of monetary policy as it is being formulated. Its advisory role has widened in recent years: the Bank officials serve on a wide range of official committees concerned with economic and monetary matters, bringing to these committees the Bank's economic forecasts and views on financial matters. Thus the monetary policy, when finalised, is likely both to be in line with government objectives and to meet with a large measure of agreement from within the financial community.

Since the Bank is the agent of the government for implementing monetary policy measures, its 'advice' to banks and to other financial institutions has to be obeyed. In implementing monetary policy, the Bank seeks to influence both the cost and availability of credit; this can be done by varying the terms of 'last resort' assistance to the banking system, by making calls for special deposits, by introducing direct controls on bank lending and interest rates, and by reactivating the Minimum Lending Rate (MLR), i.e. its lending rate to the money markets.

Banker to the government

It is the banker to the government, and in that capacity its activities include:

(a) Keeping the government's main banking accounts, through which payment of taxes *to* the government and payments *by* the government for social security, defence and so on are ultimately made. Any surplus of funds is invested in the money markets or used to reduce the government's short-term debt.

(b) Arranging for the government's short-term borrowing needs by handling the weekly issue of Treasury bills.

(c) Acting as registrar to the gilt-edged stock holders, thereby providing for the long-term borrowing requirements of the public sector, paying interest, arranging renewal or redemption at maturity and issuing new gilt-edged stocks. In effect, the Bank acts as the manager of the National Debt. Since 1986, it operates the new Central Gilts Office which deals in all gilts deals done by GEMMS and the commercial banks.

(d) It holds and protects the UK gold reserves and manages the UK foreign currency reserves via the Exchange Equalisation Account (EEA). It often uses its management of the EEA to stabilise the foreign exchange value of the pound sterling directly against other currencies by buying and selling sterling in the foreign exchange markets.

(e) As the central note issuing authority in the UK, it is responsible for the printing, issue, withdrawal and destruction of bank notes; roughly in a working day an average of £35.5 million worth of notes are destroyed.

Banker to the banking system

(a) A traditional role of any central bank is as lender of last resort, whereby it makes funds available when the banking system as a whole is short of liquidity, caused mainly due to large *net* payments to the central bank on account of tax payments and sale of gilt-edged securities. The Bank of England, in performing this traditional function, uses a unique method: rather than deal directly with each individual bank, it uses the *discount houses* as an intermediary. Discount houses are highly specialised banks (dealers) who hold large stocks of commercial bills and with whom the major banks place their surplus cash on a call or short-notice basis. They have borrowing facilites at the Bank, who may provide cash either by purchasing securities from them, or by lending to them direct. The discount houses can then return the call and short-notice money to the banking system, thereby removing the banks' liquidity shortage; the discount houses can then continue to cover the weekly Treasury bill issue (see below). Sometimes (e.g. during the tax gathering season) it may lend directly to banks through repurchase agreements (REPOS), i.e. the Bank buys gilts at fixed rates and for fixed periods from the banks, which the banks agree to buy back at the end of the period.

(b) As the bankers' bank, it holds their operational balances, their current accounts, which the banks use for obtaining cash and for settling clearing and other transactions among themselves and with the public sector.

Supervision and prudential control of authorised banks

The Banking Act 1987 has not only made the supervision of the monetary sector a function of the Bank of England but has also given it *statutory* powers to supervise authorised banks to ensure that they are soundly run, so that any recurrence of the banking crisis can be avoided. More generally, the Bank has responsibility for overseeing the soundness of the UK financial system as a whole. It also applies prudential supervision and control in respect of capital and liquidity adequacy requirements (see Ch. 10).

∎ The discount houses

The following eight discount houses, all recognised as authorised banks, are members of the London Discount Market Association: Alexanders Discount plc; Cater Allen Ltd; Clive Discount Co. Ltd; Gerrard & National plc; King & Shaxson plc; Gerald Quin, Cope & Co. Ltd; Seccombe Marshall & Campion plc; The Union Discount Company of London plc.

Discount houses are a type of banking institution unique to the London money market.

They provide a remunerative outlet for banks' liquid funds by taking secured call deposits. They provide a mechanism whereby the commercial banks adjust their liquidity positions (the advent of the inter-bank and CDs market has reduced the importance of this mechanism). When the banks call in their loans, it suggests general liquidity shortage in the system and the need for the Bank of England's open market operations. These funds are then used for the purchase of Treasury bills, commercial bills and gilt-edged securities. They are the principal market-makers in short-term, first-class bills.

Their uniqueness stems from their special relationship with the Bank of England. They are the focus of the Bank's open-market operations, and act as a 'buffer' between the Bank and the rest of the banking system. They provide a mechanism whereby the Bank supplies the banking system with funds when any shortage occurs and through which it withdraws funds when there is a surplus. It is through these open market operations that the Bank influences short-term money market interest rates. The rates at which the Bank deals with the discount houses are quickly passed on through the financial system, influencing interest rates for the whole economy. When the Bank changes its dealing rate significantly the commercial banks promptly change their own base rates from which deposit and lending rates are calculated.

For the company sector, their primary function is the provision of borrowing facilities through discounting bills of exchange, whilst as a secondary function they offer various forms of short-term investments for the companies.

In the sphere of government finance, their major function is to cover in full the weekly Treasury bill tender, which is an essential part of the government's short-term borrowing requirements. They are active dealers in short-dated government stocks and local authority bills and bonds.

They are also active in the secondary market for bills, negotiable dollar and sterling CDs, and by providing marketability to them, they have directly contributed to the success of this form of investment. They will usually only buy bank-accepted bills.

In the balance sheet of a discount house, the largest item, by a long margin, is its sterling and currency *liabilities* relating to funds it has borrowed from the banking sector. And the largest item on its *asset* side, again by a long margin, is 'other bills', i.e. bills other than UK and Northern Ireland Treasury bills. These statistics reflect the complementary relationship between the discount houses and the commercial banks and the importance of commercial bills in the discount market.

In 1982, new rules for the prudential supervision of discount houses by the Bank of England were introduced. Under the new system, which is designed mainly to ensure that the houses can cover any losses they may sustain if the value of their assets drops, they are allowed to carry assets up to forty times their capital base, but the types of asset which they hold are now more tightly controlled by the Bank.

▌ Merchant banks

They provide finance to industry by accepting bills of exchange, making loans on a wholesale basis and underwriting capital issues. The Accepting Houses Committee represents the leading merchant banks. In addition to the finance of international trade, they are now very much involved in corporate finance, investment management, financial advisory services, interest rate and foreign exchange hedging instruments.

On the *deposit* side, whilst a number of them operate a current account service, only a small proportion of their sterling deposits are sight deposits. Most of their sterling deposits are term deposits. Their foreign currency deposits are much larger than their sterling deposits.

On the *lending* side, they are active suppliers of corporate finance, by accepting bills of exchange issued by companies concentrating on medium-term lending in sterling and eurocurrencies. Most of their sterling and foreign currency assets are in the form of market loans. Bills accepted by the accepting houses can be discounted at fine (low) rates.

They are very active in the money markets and have contributed greatly towards the success of negotiable CDs. They account for a large proportion of the total bank bills (bills accepted by banks and then sold to discount houses). They help their clients in raising capital in the domestic and international capital markets.

Like the clearers, several US and other overseas banks in the UK have established their own wholly owned subsidiaries undertaking merchant and wholesale banking; it is with these subsidiaries that the merchant banks are in keen competition.

Deregulation (see Ch. 4) within the City of London has accelerated, for the clearers, discount houses and merchant banks, the process of diversification of financial services. There are a number of alliances between merchant banks and the stock exchange member firms. Merchant banks are 'authorised' institutions. Many of their specialised functions are now being performed by the clearing banks, so that a clear distinction between the clearers and merchant banks is fading fast.

▌ Girobank plc

Alliance and Leicester Building Society bought it from the UK Post Office in 1990, with the main objective of acquiring its ready-made current account and credit card operations.

Girobank plc's money transmission service is operated through the postal system and its cash facilities are provided through post offices. Despite increasing use of its payment services by local authorities, nationalised industries and government departments, and despite the introduction of a personal loan scheme and the extension of its cash and money transmission services to the business sector, its growth has been slow. To increase the public's awareness of its banking facilities, it was renamed, in 1978, National Girobank (the previous name was National Giro). It was incorporated in 1985, when its name was changed again to *Girobank plc*. It is a full member of the London Bankers' Clearing House. It forms a part of the UK monetary sector and, like other constituents of the monetary sector, is subject to the monetary control measures.

▌ National Savings Bank (NSB)

NSB has 20 million active accounts and its banking business is handled by 20,000 post offices.

It offers two main types of account, ordinary and investment. From the *ordinary account* small withdrawals can be made on demand, but withdrawals from the *investment account* are subject to one month's notice, which is why it offers a higher rate of interest than the ordinary account. Since the NSB funds are invested in government securities and contribute towards the government's spending requirements, certain tax benefits are offered to savers with the NSB; the first £70 of interest income from an ordinary account deposit is tax free.

NSB is part of the Department of National Savings and not part of the UK monetary sector. However, its ordinary and investment account deposits are included in the liquid assets outside M4.

▌ Finance houses

These provide loans to finance leasing and hire purchase transactions. At present forty-five finance houses, who are members of the Finance Houses Association, control 80 per cent of the instalment credit business, which amounted to some £24 billion at the end of 1986. The majority of the finance houses are owned by the authorised banks and other financial institutions. As subsidiaries of authorised institutions, they form a part of the UK monetary sector.

Those finance houses owned by the major banks are listed below:

Finance house	Parent bank
Lombard North Central plc	NatWest
Mercantile Credit Co. Ltd	Barclays
Lloyds Bowmaker Ltd	Lloyds
Forward Trust Group Ltd	Midland
United Dominions Trust Ltd	TSB
North West Securities Ltd	Bank of Scotland
RoyScot Trust Ltd	Royal Bank of Scotland

On the *deposit* side, a large proportion of their deposits comes from banks, other financial institutions and also from industrial and commercial companies. Personal sector deposits are insignificant.

On the *lending* side, most of their funds are used to finance motor trade, equipment leasing, insurance, factoring and property bonds, and the remainder for giving loans for home improvement, house purchase, leisure and holiday activities.

Their finance flows mainly to and from companies rather than individuals. Therefore finance houses compete with banks in the company sector rather than the personal sector. However, the scale of their deposit taking and lending activities is too small to threaten the clearing banks.

▌ Investment trusts and unit trusts

These two financial intermediaries have several features in common, but as organisations they are not identical. Both spread investment risk on behalf of each individual investor, thus avoiding investors putting 'all eggs in one basket'. Both generally provide the investors with expert management at reasonable costs. Both mainly invest in the securities of UK and overseas companies. The types of claims that both hold (their assets) are of the same kind as the claims they create (their liabilities).

Investment trusts are public limited companies and, like any other public company, raise funds by the sale of shares and loan stock on the Stock Exchange. Nearly 90 per cent of their funds are invested in company securities and the rest in short-term assets such as sterling CDs, British government securities and local authority temporary debt. By buying shares in an investment trust, the investor is, in effect, buying a 'share' in a wide spread of assets owned by the investment trust company. Their shares can be traded on the Stock Exchange.

Unit trusts are really two companies which are independent of each other: one acts as the trustee (a bank or an insurance company) and the other manages the trust's funds obtained by selling units to investors. The Department of Trade and Industry (DTI) exercises close control over all unit trusts to protect unit holders. Units can be sold to the fund managers quite easily. When units are purchased, *new* units are *created*, and when units are sold units are *eliminated*; with investment trusts investors buy and sell *existing* shares. Hence, unlike investment trusts, there is no limit to the funds of unit trusts.

The value of the investment trust shares and the units of unit trusts depends upon the performance of the companies whose securities form their underlying assets.

In so far as most clearers have established their own unit trust schemes, the unit and investment trusts compete with the clearers for the investing public's funds.

▌Building societies (see also Chs. 10 and 12)

Traditionally, Britain's savers save with banks, building societies and national savings, although unit trusts, particularly those with life assurance links, and investment trusts are increasingly challenging the dominance of the 'big three'. Building societies were popularly regarded merely as savings and mortgage institutions. In fact they are major financial institutions: their total sterling assets were £248 billion at the end of January 1992, as compared to £298 billion for the banks. They are also major deposit taking institutions. They totally dominated the mortgage market until the banks entered the market in a significant way in 1981. Building societies are major holders and traders in short-term gilt-edged securities, substantial investors in the money markets and lately significant borrowers in wholesale markets. The similarity between bank and building society deposits has led to the inclusion of building society deposits in the official definitions of money supply, M2 and M4.

As building societies are not a component of the UK monetary sector they are not subject to the Banking Act 1987. Their supervision, at present, is the responsibility of the Building Societies Commission, a government department, under the Building Societies Act 1986. Building societies are non-profit-making *mutual* organisations. Mutuality means that a society cannot be purchased against the wishes of its depositors. Under the Building Societies Act 1986, which became effective on 1 January 1987, the societies are not only empowered to compete fully in the financial industry market but can also opt to become banks. The 1986 Act provides for conversion of mutual societies into corporate bodies, with effective control of the societies going 'public', and for the protection of the members' rights. The Act sets out criteria for prudent management which includes capital adequacy and liquidity requirements (see pp. 45, 46–47).

Abbey National Building Society became a public limited company in July 1989, and became an 'authorised' bank under the 1987 Banking Act.

Between 75 and 80 per cent of their assets are held as mortgage advances, over periods normally up to twenty-five years. Although these are long-term loans, they are secured against property, which is usually an appreciating asset, and the risk of loss is low. Their remaining assets are held in liquid form to provide working capital, and to cover any short-term excess of withdrawals and lendings over deposits. Their liquid assets must equal at least 7.5 per cent of their total assets.

The type and maturity distribution of the liquid assets is regulated by the Building Societies Commission. In practice, the societies have been cautious, usually maintaining a liquidity ratio of between 15 and 20 per cent.

▌Competition between banks and building societies

A major feature of financial intermediation since 1980 has been the intensity of competition between banks and building societies. The distinction between the banks and the larger building societies has become progressively blurred, and will become more so as the societies exploit the freedoms given to them in the 1986 Building Societies Act. In particular, building society deposits, which are traditionally dominated by savings balances, have increasingly been used for transaction purposes in recent years; larger societies provide money transmission services. The provision by some societies of accounts with cheque book facilities, and the spread of cash dispensers has facilitated this change in usage, which may well proceed further with the introduction of cheque guarantee cards. At the moment, societies can make unsecured personal loans up to a limit of £15,000 per customer. Under the Building Societies Act there have been strict limits on services which societies can offer to companies. However, in February 1989 the Treasury allowed the societies to offer companies 'temporary or occasional overdrafts'. Until this loosening of restraints, societies were forced to give up clients who wanted to borrow more than £15,000 or who decided to take on company status for their financial affairs. Another relaxation allows societies to acquire mortgage portfolios from *other* institutions.

The initial focus of competition (from 1980) between banks and building societies was *mortgage lending*. One result of the banks' successful inroads into the mortgage market was the break-up of the societies' cartel arrangements for setting interest rates. Rationing of mortgage lending had helped to sustain the societies' interest rate cartel, but this became untenable after the banks' entry into the mortgage market. In consequence, building society interest rates have become more flexible and market-related.

The reason why the banks have become aggressively involved in mortgage business is that they found mortgage lending to be very profitable, especially as lending on the security of a house is safer than lending on the security of a business, and mortgage loans can be used as a lead-in for the sale of their other financial services, such as insurance, tax planning and house improvement loans. In the circumstances, it was unlikely that increased competition between the banks and building societies would be confined to mortgage lending.

Until recently, the societies were able to attack the banks where they are most vulnerable, i.e. in the personal savings sector. The societies were able to achieve this because they could offer better terms to depositors. Building societies have been able to operate on a narrower margin than banks between their rates to the depositors and borrowers (an average interest margin for a representative clearing bank is 6.2 per cent compared with a little over 1.0 per cent for a typical large building society) because of (a) their low management cost (due to their less complicated specialised business); (b) no requirements to pay dividends; (c) low capital requirements due to the low-risk nature of their assets; and (d) because the banks have tended to subsidise their money transmission service by their deposit accounts, which lessens their ability to compete in the savings market.

However, the personal retail deposits of the building societies have declined during the past few years due to the government's highly successful privatisation schemes, the flotation of very popular private sector new issues, the increased importance given to national savings in the financing of the Public Sector Borrowing Requirements (PSBR) and the introduction by banks of their higher interest rate sight deposits. The profitability of the societies' main business – mortgage lending – has been hit by the high cost in attracting retail funds. Until the societies were allowed access to wholesale funds, their rates have been as much as 2 per cent above the wholesale money market rates. Therefore the banks were able to increase returns to their new depositors towards the societies' rates in order to attract customers for mortgage loans to whom they could cross-sell their other financial services.

In order to attract more inflows of deposits, the building societies' ordinary share accounts were progressively replaced in importance first by term shares, and then by various high interest accounts. Although the new kinds of accounts were introduced in the mid-1970s, their scope was broadened during the 1980s. Whereas initially the conditions associated with these new accounts meant that they were less liquid than existing share accounts or bank deposits, these conditions were progressively relaxed through the 1980s by, for example, the introduction of term shares with withdrawal facilities and by the reductions in interest penalties for early withdrawal from term accounts.

The larger societies are able to raise wholesale funds in the form of Sterling Commercial Papers, CDs and through floating rate notes. The societies have eagerly taken the opportunity to raise money in the wholesale markets − which has frequently proved to be a cheaper source of wholesale funds − and have used these funds to even out any shortfall in the inflow of retail funds to meet the mortgage demand. (*Wholesale funds* are large deposits placed by companies and financial institutions, bearing an interest rate in line with the market rate rather than base rates.) In 1983 the societies were allowed to pay interest gross on certificates of deposit and on time deposits, and by 1986 some 40 per cent of their new funds were raised from this source. Also in 1983 they first had access to the eurobond market. (The *eurobond market* is the international market which raises long-term funds in various capital markets and in different currencies against the issue of bonds.) This has allowed the societies to borrow longer maturities more in line with the average life of mortgages. From April 1986 they have been permitted to pay interest gross on eurobonds. This enabled them to launch issues on the eurobond market. This gives the societies access to an even cheaper source of funds. The new legislation is expected to allow them to raise funds in foreign currency which they would then be able to swap into sterling at very fine terms. Inevitably all these developments have led to a change in the relationship of building society interest rates to other market interest rates.

By the end of 1984, the banks' share of deposit inflows had fallen sharply. This loss of share encouraged intensification of competition, and the extension of the composite rate arrangements (now abolished) provided the trigger for the introduction by the banks of high-interest retail accounts, some with chequeing facilities. These accounts substantially narrowed the gap between the interest rate offered by the building societies and those previously offered by the banks.

It seems clear that, though still constrained somewhat by the 40 per cent ceiling on wholesale borrowing, under the 1986 Act, the larger societies, at least, have shifted away from *asset management* during the period of their interest rate cartel, towards a *liability management*. A similar shift in behaviour occurred among banks after *Competition and Credit Control* in 1971, when they abandoned their collective agreement on interest rates.

Larger building societies, to increase capital, can issue Permanent Interest-Bearing shares (PIBs). PIBs are fixed-interest, irredeemable investments and can be bought and sold on the Stock Exchange. PIB holders are not covered by the Investor Compensation Scheme (see p. 180) if the society issuing them goes bankrupt (highly unlikely). PIBs are very sensitive to long-term interest rates and, like all fixed-interest investments, their market value is inversely related to interest rate movements.

▊ Banks and building societies compared and contrasted

The following is a summary of the major similarities and dissimilarities between banks and building societies.

(a) *Major similarities:*
- (i) Both are allowed to undertake unsecured personal lending, issue cheque books, offer money transmission services, give advice on investment, insurance and conveyancing, administer pension schemes, and provide foreign exchange to individuals.
- (ii) Both can give overdrafts to corporate customers.
- (iii) Both offer home mortgage loans and a wide variety of savings accounts.
- (iv) Societies can, if they choose, like the banks, become public limited companies and be 'authorised' as banks.
- (v) Both can raise wholesale funds.
- (vi) Both pay interest to depositors gross.
- (vii) Deposits of both are included in broad money aggregates.
- (viii) Both are empowered to offer Tax Exempt Special Savings Accounts (TESSA).

(a) *Major dissimilarities:*
- (i) Unlike banks, societies have a 40 per cent ceiling on raising wholesale funds.
- (ii) Societies can offer only temporary or occasional overdrafts to corporate customers. They have not yet become significant lenders to industry.
- (iii) Unlike banks, the unsecured lending ceiling for the societies is £15,000.
- (iv) Banks are profit-orientated institutions, societies are mutual bodies.
- (v) Banks are a part of the UK monetary sector, building societies are not.
- (vi) Banks are supervised by the Bank of England under the provisions of the 1987 Banking Act; societies are supervised by the Building Societies Commission under the 1986 Building Societies Act, with different rules on capital adequacy, liquidity and deposit protection.
- (vii) Banks still offer a far wider range of services than the societies, particularly if their group's in-house services are taken into account.

Although the distinction between banks and larger building societies has been considerably blurred, and continues to be blurred further with the passage of time, it is still valid and useful to distinguish between the two sets of institutions.

▊ Insurance companies (see also Chs. 10 and 12)

They provide general insurance to policy holders against particular risks, such as theft, fire and accident, and provide life assurance to those seeking life cover.

Their income comes from the deposits of premiums by policy holders and from the returns on the assets in which they invest the premium income. The claims against insurance companies (their liabilities) arising out of their general insurance business tend to be short term, and those arising out of their life business are long term. Therefore, insurance companies have to exercise financial prudence by adjusting their asset maturity structures to cope with the short-term and long-term nature of their liabilities and, at the same time, so to adjust their asset portfolios as to obtain maximum benefit from asset diversification. The long-term investment of insurance companies is mainly in government securities, company shares, mortgage and other loans and property and their short-term investment (liquid assets) is in general funds.

Although the insurance companies receive their funds from specific sources and for particular purposes, nevertheless their life-linked unit trusts and insurance business compete with the unit trust and insurance business of the banks.

▌ Pension funds

Their 'deposits' come from the contributions paid by employers and employees and in return they undertake to provide pensions on employees' retirement. Their other source of income is the returns from the investment of accumulated and accumulating contributions. By and large, it is from the investment income that pensions are paid. Hence the paramount need in their investment policy is to maximise current and future profits from investments.

Until recently a major proportion of their funds was used in purchasing mainly the ordinary shares of domestic and overseas companies, because that was one of the ways of ensuring that the return from and the value of investment kept pace with inflationary growth of incomes. With falling inflation and interest rates there has been a heavy switch to government securities. Even so, their funds are heavily committed to the purchase of existing and new issues of the company sector. Their other investments include loans, mortgage finance and property.

The trustees of pension funds usually hand over the investment management responsibility of a significant proportion of their funds to life assurance companies, because the operation of a pension fund involves the same sort of considerations as those involved in organising life assurance business. Therefore the investment strategy is similar for both these organisations: long-term assets which continue to increase in value in order to discharge long-term liabilities which also tend to continue increasing in money terms.

Pension funds and insurance companies dominate the purchase of existing and new issues of ordinary shares as well as 'making a market' in existing securities of the Stock Exchange. By channelling funds into the equity market they increase the depth and liquidity of the market, thus improving its effectiveness as a source of company finance.

▌ Recent examination questions

The following five recent questions reflect the type and depth of knowledge required to answer questions placed in the UK Financial Institutions section of the syllabus. First try to locate, from the contents of this chapter, the main points you consider essential in answering each of these questions. Then spend ten minutes or so planning your answer to each question before turning to the section on 'Outline answers' which follows.

Question 1

Why and how does a bank raise funds in the following markets?

(a) The retail market.
(b) The wholesale market.
(c) The capital market.

Question 2

Outline the ways in which the Bank of England carries out its role as:

(a) banker to the government;
(b) banker to the banks;
(c) lender of last resort to the banking system.

Question 3

What are the advantages and disadvantages to building societies of converting to plc status?

Question 4

For what reasons does a commercial bank need liquidity and how may it be provided? How has Bank of England supervision in this area evolved since 1981?

Question 5

With particular reference to the Bank of England's day-to-day operations in the money markets, discuss the Bank's present role as 'lender of last resort'. How has this role changed since 1981?

■ Outline answers

Answer 1

(a)   (i) Reasons for raising funds in the retail market:
      – To finance lending.
      – To market other products to borrowing customers.
  (ii) How the retail funds are raised:
      – Through extensive branch network.
      – Through successful advertising.
      – Into accounts offering money transmission and savings services, mainly to the personal and small business sector.

(b)   (i) Reasons for raising funds in the wholesale market:
      – To supplement funds raised from retail activities for additional lending (retail bank).
      – To match and improve the maturity structure of deposits (retail bank).
      – To tap the only source of finance for its activities (wholesale bank).
      – To manage their foreign currency positions (retail and wholesale bank) via inter-bank eurocurrency borrowing.
  (ii) How the wholesale funds are raised:
      – By issuing sterling and currency CDs on the CDs market.
      – By sterling and currency borrowing on the inter-bank market.

(c)   (i) Reasons for raising funds on the capital market:
      – To maintain capital adequacy.
      – To absorb bad debts and bad investments.
      – To inspire confidence.

(ii) How the capital market funds are raised:
- By rights issues.
- By issuing new shares.
- By issuing loan capital.

Answer 2

(a) As the *banker* to the government, it:
  (i) holds the government's main accounts: the National Loan Fund, the Consolidated Fund, the Paymaster-General, including the Exchange Equalisation Account;
  (ii) ensures that short-term (the Treasury bills) and longer term (sale of government gilt-edged securities) finance is always available to the government;
  (iii) pays interest to government stockholders and reduces the total cost of government borrowing by purchasing securities with surplus government funds;
  (iv) issues bank notes;
  (v) implements the official monetary policy.
(b) As the *banker* to the banks, it:
  (i) holds banks' operational deposits and facilitates the settlement of clearing transactions between banks;
  (ii) sells bank notes to banks;
  (iii) holds the mandatory 0.35 per cent non-operational and non-interest bearing cash ratio deposits of the banks, *not* as an element of monetary control, but as a source of income for itself (a tax on banks!);
  (iv) holds the accounts of overseas central banks.
(c) As *lender of last resort* to the banking system, it:
  (i) ensures that the banking system as a whole is not short of cash on a daily basis;
  (ii) makes good any shortages, primarily by the purchase of eligible bills from discount houses;
  (iii) mounts a lifeboat operation to save a bank in difficulties;
  (iv) ensures prudential supervision over banks.

Answer 3

Advantages

(a) The societies' unsecured loans (Class 3 Assets) are limited to 15 per cent of their commercial assets; no such restriction on the banks.
(b) At least 75 per cent of the societies' commercial assets must be loans secured by first mortgage of an owner-occupied residential property (Class 1 Assets); this is a serious restriction on their ability to lend to corporate customers.
(c) Although the societies are allowed by the Building Societies Act to increase their Tier 1 capital by issuing Permanent Interest Bearing Shares (PIBS), banks, as plcs, can raise capital by issuing shares and bonds and therefore can expand more quickly.
(d) Although the societies can merge with other societies to expand geographically, they cannot, unlike banks, engage in takeovers of or mergers with other financial institutions in order to expand substantially and rapidly their breadth of operations.
(e) Although not an onerous constraint, the societies are restricted to raising wholesale funding to 40 per cent of their liabilities.

Disadvantages

(a) As plcs, they will be supervised by the Bank of England, and not by the Building Societies Commission, and may find it difficult and time consuming to comply with the different technical requirements.

(b) As plcs, they will be under pressure to pay high dividends to shareholders; this will reduce retained earnings.

(c) They will be susceptible to takeover bids.

(d) Shareholding may become concentrated with institutional investors who may seek to exercise some degree of influence on the society's activities.

(e) Change of status may have adverse effects on their image with customers and may undermine their ability to compete directly with traditional building societies which remain mutuals.

(f) As they expand the range of their activities they will require more broadly skilled staff and this could drive up their operating costs.

Answer 4

(a) A bank needs liquidity:
   (i) to meet cash withdrawals from deposits;
   (ii) to effect clearing settlements via operational balances with the Bank of England;
   (iii) to meet unforeseeable problems in financing known future commitments (e.g. unused overdrafts);
   (iv) to maintain the confidence of the public.

(b) It provides for liquidity:
   (i) by maintaining a certain percentage of its assets in liquid assets (e.g. cash in tills, Treasury bills, call money with discount houses, short-dated gilt-edged securities);
   (ii) by the extent of maturity diversification in its deposit base;
   (iii) by its ability to raise loans when needed from the inter-bank and the CD markets;
   (iv) by the cash flow generated from maturing assets, and the matching with maturing liabilities.

(c) Liquidity criteria applicable to all banks: the Bank of England ensures that individual banks are adopting prudential policies in the light of their individual circumstances, taking into account all the factors relevant to liquidity (see Ch. 10).

Answer 5

(a) Bank of England's traditional role as lender of last resort: it makes available funds when the banking system as a whole is short of liquid resources.

(b) In its day-to-day operations in the money markets, the Bank carries out this role involving eligible bill purchases only from the discount houses.

(c) The Bank announces a daily estimated shortage (or surplus) of 'cash'; it is prepared to buy eligible bills from discount houses which are offered at *their* own prices, but which the Bank may not accept. The Bank will, however, make good any shortage at a price acceptable to it. With the sale proceeds, discount houses discount more bills and return banks' call money.

(d) Sale and repurchase (REPOS) of gilts and other securities with banks at fixed rates and for fixed periods:
   (i) to relieve cash shortage during the tax gathering season (January and February);
   (ii) to influence short rates and stabilisation.

(e) Main changes since 1981: little direct lending to discount houses; abandoning the weekly announcement of the MLR, to which direct lending was generally linked; bill purchasing within four bands, depending upon maturity of the bill, is now the pivot of the 'lender of last resort' role; main change in carrying out this role is in the method of operation; discount houses remain the buffer between the Bank and the commercial banks (see Ch. 4).

■ A tutor's answer

The following question touches on various important aspects of the UK financial intermediation. The tutor's answer in *point* form is intended to help you establish the scope of the question and then to write cohesive relevant information in answering the whole question.

Question

(a) What are the main problems which would arise in the absence of financial intermediation? How does financial intermediation overcome these problems?
(b) What do you understand by the term 'disintermediation'?
(c) Outline the basic characteristics of each of the following and state whether it is an example of financial intermediation or disintermediation:
  (i) eurocurrency deposits;
  (ii) sterling commercial paper.

Answer plan

(a) State the problems and benefits of FIs to borrowers and lenders.
(b) State that disintermediation is direct borrowing and lending, by-passing financial intermediaries.
(c) Define eurocurrency deposits and sterling commercial paper and link them to intermediation/disintermediation.

Specimen answer

(a) The problems that financial intermediation overcomes are as follows:
  (i) *Size of loan.* A corporate borrower would find it difficult to find enough people to lend him the sum required.
  (ii) *Term of loan.* It is unlikely that the time-scale of ultimate lenders and borrowers would coincide. In general, depositors will require liquidity and borrowers long-term use of funds.
  (iii) *Risk.* Individual lenders would bear the whole risk of default, and individual borrowers bear the whole risk of locating suitable lenders lending at acceptable rates.

Financial intermediation *overcomes* the above problems in the following ways:
  (i) *Aggregation.* By pooling the deposits of many individuals it is possible to provide large loans.
  (ii) *Maturity transformation.* By providing depositors/investors and borrowers such financial instruments and loan maturities as would suit their respective needs.

(iii) *Risk diversification.* By being sound, the financial intermediary gives confidence to depositors that their funds are safe, and at the same time, by diversifying its lending portfolio, the financial intermediary minimises its own risk.

(b) *Disintermediation.* This refers to the by-passing of financial intermediaries, with ultimate lenders and borrowers dealing with each other directly. Disintermediation may arise when official restrictions limit lending by established intermediaries, or when companies with high credit rating can raise funds in their own name.

(c) (i) *Eurocurrency deposits.* These represent examples of intermediation; these are time deposits of currencies placed with banks outside the currency's country of origin. The banks taking the eurocurrency deposits on-lend them to borrowers needing eurocurrency loans.

(ii) *Sterling Commercial Paper (SCP).* SCP is an example of disintermediation. SCPs are seven-day to one-year notes issued by medium and large companies (with assets of at least £25 million) of good standing (with their shares listed on the Stock Market) as an alternative source of funds to traditional bank loans or bills. In contrast to commercial bills, SCP does not have to be issued as a counterpart to a specific transaction.

▌ A step further

This section of the Monetary and Financial System syllabus requires a lot of study. What you learn in this chapter impinges on other parts of the syllabus. However, changes in the UK financial institutions do not occur too frequently. Therefore, once the characteristics and practices of the existing institutions are clearly and fully grasped, and your knowledge is kept updated, you should be able to answer questions asked on this topic in the exam question paper, which invariably seek precise information.

A comprehensive knowledge of the UK financial system, of which the financial institutions form a part, is essential to your understanding of other topic areas within the Monetary and Financial System.

To keep abreast with changes as they occur, you need to update your knowledge by reading *Banking World*, *BEQB*, the Chartered Institute of Bankers' *Updating Notes* and *Examiners' Reports* and the financial press.

The Banking Information Service have published a very useful book, *A Guide to the British Financial System*, which covers the fundamentals of the UK financial system. Another useful publication is *The British Banking System*, published by National Westminster Bank. There is a very useful section on competition between banks and building societies in 'Measures of Broad Money' which appeared in *BEQB*, May 1987. See *Bank of England Report and Accounts 1987* for good reference to the Banking Act 1987. Very useful information is provided in the *Bank of England Banking Act Annual Reports*.

CHAPTER 4

Financial Markets in the UK

Syllabus requirements
- The nature and function of the discount market.
- The role of parallel markets.
- Financial instruments traded in the financial markets.
- The role of the capital markets in the UK economy.
- The impact of 'deregulation' on the capital market.
- The role of banks in the deregulated securities market.
- The role of the Bank of England in the money markets.
- The role of the eurocurrency market in the provision of international finance.

▌ Getting started

To complete the study of the UK financial system, we shall in this chapter look at the operation of the organised specialised financial markets and the characteristics of the financial instruments traded on them.

The UK financial markets may be divided into money markets and capital markets. The *money markets* match borrowers and lenders of large short-term (less than five years) sterling and currency funds, the discount market being of this type but having a special relationship with the Bank of England. The *capital markets* match borrowers and lenders/investors of medium- (five to fifteen years) and long-term (over fifteen years) sterling and currency funds. The distinction between short- and long-term capital is, however, less clear cut now than it used to be.

The financial instruments are used by depositors/investors as a means of holding surplus wealth and they can be traded in the financial markets. *Treasury bills* are short-term promissory notes of HM Treasury and carry capital gains in lieu of fixed interest returns; *commercial bills* are short-term fixed yield securities; *sterling commercial paper* represents short-term fixed interest negotiable borrowing by companies; *certificates of deposit* are bearer, short-term fixed yield securities expressed in sterling and US dollars; *gilt-edged securities* are British government short-, medium- and long-term fixed interest stocks; *stocks and bonds* are longer-term fixed interest instruments; *equities* are ordinary shares of private sector companies with no fixed rate of return; *deposits* in sterling and currency with financial institutions reflect the amounts of demand and time deposits, although interest rates vary.

There is a wide and growing variety of financial instruments on offer in the financial markets to satisfy the various objectives of numerous depositors and investors, each instrument with its own peculiar features.

In October 1986, a process of *deregulation* of the financial institutions began, starting with the reshaping of the Stock Exchange rules and continuing with the freeing of financial markets and the removal and modification of barriers between different classes of financial services institutions. Domestically this has led to increased competition among existing institutions and to the emergence of new sources of competition.

The *Bank of England*, as the pivot of the UK financial system, is an active participant in the financial markets (mainly through the discount market), raising short- and long-term funds for government spending, and implementing the official monetary policy as regards money supply and interest rates.

A eurocurrency deposit is in a currency other than the local currency, and hence outside the control of the central bank which issued it. The *eurocurrency markets* have arisen and developed quickly, partly due to the inadequate availability of international liquidity from traditional sources, and partly due to eurocurrency markets being not fully regulated. The margin between their borrowing and lending is narrow. The activity in the eurocurrency markets is different from the activity in the foreign exchange market; in the former foreign currencies are lent and borrowed, and in the latter they are bought and sold.

▌ Essential principles

Wholesale money markets

The discount market and the Bank's role as lender of last resort

The main participants of the discount market are the eight discount houses which are members of the London Discount Market Association (LDMA). Discount houses are specialised institutions; they borrow mainly from the banking system and invest by discounting commercial bills and purchasing short-term assets, chiefly Treasury bills and gilt-edged securities. The discount houses constitute a buffer between the Bank of England and the rest of the banking system and it is through them that the Bank, as lender of last resort, regulates the availability of its funds to the commercial banks, thereby relieving shortages of liquid funds within the banking system. The discount market is used by the Bank to smooth out cash fluctuations between government and banks and to influence short-term interest rates via the cost of its *last resort* assistance.

It is very important that the mechanics of *how* the Bank of England performs its traditional role of lender of last resort are clearly understood. The present arrangement of relieving cash shortages of the banking system involves the Bank purchasing eligible bills exclusively from the discount houses; the latter maintain a portfolio of eligible bills, purchased with the funds deposited with them.

The clearing banks inform the Bank of England daily of the target level of daily balances they are aiming at. On the basis of this, and the Bank's own estimate of flows between the banks and the public sector, the Bank assesses the size of the likely shortage (or surplus) of liquidity each day. The shortage (or surplus) is announced to the money markets every morning. The Bank then informs the discount houses that it is prepared to buy bills from them (to relieve shortage), or to sell bills to them (to mop up surplus). The discount houses then offer bills to the Bank at prices of their own choosing. The Bank may or may not accept the prices offered, but will always relieve the shortage, or surplus, at a price acceptable to itself.

Until 1981, the Bank of England could have lent to the discount houses directly at the *Minimum Lending Rate* (MLR). In 1981, MLR was suspended (but not abolished) and direct lending by the Bank to the discount houses is now used only rarely. Instead, bill purchases, primarily eligible commercial bills within the following four bands of various maturities, have become the pivot of the system by which the Bank provides its lender of last resort assistance to the banking system.

The Bank has defined a number of 'maturity bands' which refer to the periods remaining before the bills mature. Band 1 has bills from one to 14 days to maturity; Band 2, 15–33 days; Band 3, 34–63 days; and Band 4, 64–91 days. While the Bank concentrates mainly on dealing in bills within Bands 1 and 2, dealings in Bands 3 and 4 are not uncommon. As well as outright purchases of bills, the Bank sometimes engages in sale and repurchase agreements with the banks, i.e. the Bank provides funds to the banks by buying bills from them with an arrangement that the banks will buy the bills back on an agreed day.

The discount market is one means by which commercial banks adjust their liquidity positions, because the discount houses mainly borrow surplus funds from the banks on a call/overnight basis. Thus the discount market provides a highly suitable and profitable place where the banks can place their surplus-to-need liquidity on a call basis. This gives the banks a means of holding near-liquid assets that can be drawn on when their operational deposits at the Bank of England get too low, due to withdrawals from operational deposits, notes and coins for more till money or settlement of debts with other banks or the government. This liquidity function is now increasingly shared with the inter-bank and the certificate of deposit markets (see below).

The discount market is an important provider of short-term finance to business companies; it does this by discounting commercial bills of exchange. In fact, the discount market is market-maker in Treasury bills, local authority or commercial bank bills, and to promote the bill market the Bank of England increased the number of eligible banks. The discount houses compete in underwriting the weekly Treasury bill tender. They maintain a secondary market in CDs and are prominent in the short-dated gilt-edged securities market. The discount market helps finance the government's short-term debt by agreeing to purchase all the Treasury bills issued by the Bank of England.

The discount market is the oldest money market for short-term funds and is often referred to as the 'traditional' money market. The newer money markets which have emerged since the 1960s, and in particular the inter-bank and certificates of deposit markets, are known as 'parallel' or 'secondary' money markets.

■ Secondary parallel money markets

The certificates of deposit (CDs) market

Banks have issued CDs since 1968, and building societies since 1983. CDs are receipts issued by banks certifying that a deposit has been made of a certain sum, for a given period, and at a fixed (and also variable) rate of interest. The depositor or the holder will be paid in due course by the issuing bank at maturity of the CD. Sterling CDs are issued by London banks in multiples of £10,000, with a minimum of £50,000 and a maximum of £500,000, for periods ranging between three months and five years. On CDs issued for a period of less than one year, interest is paid at maturity, along with the capital sum invested. For CDs issued for periods longer than one year, interest is payable annually. CDs are flexible instruments which offer advantages to both the depositor and the borrower. The depositor obtains for his minimum £50,000 investment maximum security, a good fixed rate of interest and easy marketability in the secondary CDs market, making them liquid and therefore attractive to holders. Discount houses are very active in the secondary CDs market. For the original borrowing bank, a CD is a fixed period loan, and therefore not withdrawable until the expiry of that period. The CDs market is an extension of, or alternative to the inter-bank market (see below). Banks hold CDs issued by other banks both as investments and as liquid assets. Societies find the wholesale funds in this market very reliable for their mortgage lendings.

The main attraction of CDs is that they can be sold before maturity in the secondary market. The certificates show the deposits as repayable to 'bearer' and thus anyone legally acquiring them is entitled to repayment. The value of CDs traded in the secondary market is calculated from a uniform agreed formula, which takes into account the interest rate at the date of issue and the original issue period, together with ruling interest rates and the period remaining to maturity.

The CDs may be purchased by banks, in preference to making inter-bank loans for fixed terms; by discount houses as traders in CDs; and by industrial and commercial companies as safe and near-liquid investment.

The inter-bank market

This is a short-term wholesale market where banks, money brokers and other financial institutions lend to each other for periods from overnight to five years. The minimum amount of loans in sterling and currency is £250,000, normally unsecured. The rates of interest in this market for overnight money are higher than those offered in the discount market for call money. The inter-bank lending rate, i.e. LIBOR, is an important determinant of banks' base rates. Many loans, especially wholesale loans, are linked to LIBOR. The fundamental significance of the inter-bank market to the UK banking system is not only that it, together with the CDs market, is the largest sterling parallel market, but also that it, like the discount market, allows individual banks to adjust their day-to-day liquidity positions quickly. Banks with surpluses can lend on the inter-bank market to banks with shortages, thus reducing the need for individual banks to keep large holdings of liquid assets; this increases their profitable lending operations.

The main participants in the inter-bank market are merchant banks, overseas and foreign banks in London, the clearing banks and large building societies. In addition, pension funds, insurance companies, commercial and industrial companies and finance companies also participate in the inter-bank market. A small number of money brokers synchronise the needs of the participants in the market.

The development of the market for CDs and the inter-bank market in the early 1970s has had an important effect on how the UK banking system works. Before these markets existed, whilst a bank could increase its retail deposits by offering higher interest rates, it could not be sure of doing this by a given amount quickly and with certainty. Thus, prior to the existence of these markets, a bank's lending activity, and therefore profitability, was to some extent limited by the amount of its customers' *retail* deposits. Nowadays, however, banks have much more flexibility. In the inter-bank market, banks with surpluses can lend wholesale funds to other banks with shortages, while banks with shortages can also borrow large sums by issuing CDs. Often the clearing banks have to raise large deposits from the inter-bank market. This reflects the success the building societies have had in garnering retail deposits through, and then the inter-bank market recirculating them back to the banking system at higher rates.

The local authority market

In 1955, the central government prevented local authorities from gaining access to central government funds. The local authorities therefore had to raise their own funds: this led to the development of the *local authority market*.

Local authority borrowing is of three kinds:

1. *Temporary deposit receipts.* The terms of these receipts range from two days to about one year; most have a maturity of seven days or less, hence these receipts are fairly liquid instruments.
2. *Local authority bills.* These are similar to the central government Treasury bills and first-class short-term commercial bills. Discount houses are active in making a market in these bills, thus giving them liquidity and enhancing their attraction to investors.
3. *Local authority bonds.* These have longer maturity and are therefore not liquid assets.

Not all local authority debt is purchased by the financial institutions in the UK monetary sector (although the proportion of the local authority debt held by the monetary sector institutions is about 50 per cent); industrial and commercial companies, personal sector and overseas investors also invest in local authority debt.

The sterling commercial paper market

In response to the interest expressed by a number of companies in issuing short-term debt securities in sterling, the Bank of England notified the public in April 1986 that such securities may be issued under the title 'sterling commercial paper' (SCP). SCP represents short-term negotiable borrowing by companies and can be sold directly to investors in the money markets, thus by-passing the banking overdraft and bill acceptance facilities. SCP is equivalent to a CD issued by a company.

The framework laid down by the authorities for the issue of SCP in April 1986 was replaced by a new framework in March 1989. Under the new framework the following arrangements have been established.

(a) *Issuers:*
  (i) UK and overseas companies with net assets of at least £25 million and whose shares are listed on the Stock Exchange are permitted to issue SCPs. Public sector entities cannot issue SCPs. Issuers can get an authorised bank or a company meeting the net asset requirement to act as guarantor to their SCP.
  (ii) Institutions authorised under the Bankers Act 1987, building societies authorised under the Building Societies Act 1986 and insurance companies authorised under the Insurance Companies Act 1982.
  (iii) International organisations which are exempted from the Banking Act 1987 and of which the UK is a member.
  (iv) Overseas public sector bodies.
(b) *Description.* An issue of SCP must carry two statements, namely:
  (i) that it is issued under the 1987 Banking Act (Exemption Transactions) Regulations (this is to avoid issuers becoming deposit-takers);
  (ii) that the issue does, or does not, carry the guarantee of a bank.
(c) *Disclosure.* If SCP is issued without a prospectus, then the issuer should make known to purchasers that the issuing company is in compliance with its obligations under the Listing Regulations of the Stock Exchange.
(d) *Minimum amount.* The issue must be transferable and should be issued in minimum amounts of £100,000. Previously it was £500,000, and its reduction to £100,000 will broaden the range of potential issues of SCP, as will the reduction of *assets* of the issuer from £50 million to £25 million.
(e) *Maturity.* SCP should have a maturity of up to one year but not less than seven days.
(f) *Monitoring.* Issuers should notify the Bank of England of the total amount of the SCP they propose to issue, details of the maturity, the name of guarantor if relevant, and

full description of the intended uses of the funds raised and, within a short specified time after the issue, the amount of the issue that has been purchased.

(g) *Management of issues.* Issuers may issue SCP directly to investors, or they may use a bank as an intermediary.

(h) *Interest payments.* Interest on SCP can normally be paid without deduction of income tax, and the issue and transfer of SCP will be free of stamp duty.

SCP is issued at a discount to face value and the discount rate is linked to London Inter-bank Bid Rate. It is negotiable and can be traded in the secondary market. It represents a major source of short-term funds for financially strong, highly rated companies. Investors in SCP, i.e. purchasers of the paper, tend to be large institutions such as insurance companies and bank trust departments; because of its relatively low risk and short maturity − often sixty days − it can be regarded as a close substitute to Treasury bills, CDs and other first-class money market instruments. It is an alternative to traditional bank loans and acceptance credits, and it does not have to be issued as a counterpart to a specific transaction.

There is also a thriving market in US dollars and eurocurrency commercial paper.

The SCP market extends the range of financing options available to UK companies and provides a means of by-passing the banks and the conventional securities exchanges. The attraction of this form of finance is its cost: funds can be obtained at lower interest rates for smaller fees than either banks or the securities market can offer. This is another form of securitisation and *disintermediation* (a company borrowing from another company rather than from a bank) with the banks losing on the loan front but earning more fee income. The SCP market also points to the potential advantages of disintermediation: both lenders and borrowers gain some benefit on interest rates.

The finance house market

The major finance houses have been 'recognised' by the Bank of England as 'Other British Banks' in its *BEQB*, but there are many other finance houses which still operate to meet the needs of the consumer demand by offering hire purchase facilities for consumer durables. Due to the tight monetary policies during the past two decades, including a credit squeeze applying to instalment buying facilities, a major proportion of finance houses' funds has been channelled to meet the needs of business companies, largely through their three main services, i.e. factoring, leasing and hire purchase. They are involved in both retail and wholesale banking activities.

As BFIs, the proportion of capital and reserves to borrowed funds differs widely in the balance sheets of individual finance houses. However, their *liabilities side* shows that the main sources of their funds are loans and deposits from the banking sector, discounted bills and deposits from business companies and individuals. Since finance houses are considered by the public as being less secure than banks and building societies, they have to offer higher rates to attract funds from corporate and personal sectors. The *major asset* item in their balance sheets is the provision of funds for hire purchase transactions, mainly for cars, to households and firms. It is a comparatively small secondary market. Most of the larger finance houses now form part of much larger banking groups.

The inter-company market

The development of the inter-company market (in 1969) was a device to get around severe credit restrictions during the 1960s. This market is another example of disintermediation, where surplus companies lend to deficit companies. It is a comparatively small secondary market, and its significance has been reduced by the advent of SCP market.

Summary

The sterling 'parallel' or 'secondary' markets in London comprise, chronologically, local authority, finance house, inter-company, certificates of deposit, inter-bank and SCP. In connection with these markets as a whole, three points are of significance.

1. They do not work in isolation from each other; lenders and borrowers are interwoven.
2. They are largely uncontrolled markets; therefore any direct official control on lending and interest rates which is not uniformly applied to all financial institutions triggers off disintermediation and 'round tripping' (see p. 72). This upsets the validity of the monetary statistics and loosens the hold of any official restrictions imposed via monetary policy.
3. It is both valid and useful at least for the time being, to distinguish between the discount and parallel markets.

The currency certificate of deposit market

This is one of the two secondary money markets operating in London designated in currencies other than sterling; the other is the eurocurrency market. Like the sterling CDs, currency CDs may only be issued by institutions authorised to accept deposits under the Banking Act 1987 and the Building Societies Act 1986, or by the specifically 'exempt' institutions under the 1987 Act. At present currency CDs are denominated in US, Canadian and Australian dollars, yen, SDRs and ECUs. Like a sterling CD, a currency CD is an acknowledgement by a bank of a deposit in major currencies placed with it, for a specific period of time and at a fixed rate of interest. Like sterling CDs, currency CDs are negotiable and can be bought and sold easily on the currency CDs market. Main participants are discount houses, American banks, Canadian security companies, etc.

The eurocurrency market

Eurocurrency deposits are deposits taken by a bank in a currency other than that of the country where it is located (e.g. DM deposits with a bank outside Germany). The banks use these deposits to make loans on the international market. London is the most important centre for eurocurrency transactions. On the inter-bank eurocurrency market, banks borrow and lend wholesale funds on an unsecured basis from each other for periods as short as overnight or as long as five years, although most borrowing is for six months or less. Currency CDs have become the most important negotiable instrument in the eurocurrency deposit market. Loans are generally linked to LIBOR in the particular currency.

Although the term 'euro' stems from the origins of these markets in Europe, the eurocurrency market is not restricted to Europe but encompasses transactions in eurocurrencies carried out in several non-European locations, including the Caribbean (e.g. Nassau), the Middle East (Bahrain) and the Far East (Singapore and Hong Kong). The eurocurrency markets have become the largest international financial markets in the world and the major single centre of operations is London, which is why so many foreign banks have opened offices in London in the last twenty-five years. Any account of the British banking system must include a discussion of eurocurrency markets.

Reasons for the rapid growth of the eurocurrency markets

(a) Increase in international banking activity due to growth in world trade and to general internationalisation of the world economy.
(b) Large balance of payment imbalances; deficits for oil using and surpluses for oil producing countries. Surpluses were channelled to deficit countries via international banking (eurocurrency markets), in preference to the International Monetary Fund (IMF) machinery, due to the IMF conditions.
(c) Euromarkets have been unregulated and without costly restrictions (e.g. no reserve requirements), hence were able to offer favourable lending and borrowing terms — this factor has been at the heart of all other growth factors.

Prudential supervision of eurocurrency markets

The growth of these markets in the last three decades has led to concern about their supervision and prudential control. Lack of regulation has led to serious problems, e.g. the collapse of several banks (Bankhaus Herstatt in 1974 and Banco Ambrosiano in 1982) which were active in these markets, the difficulties of certain heavily borrowed less-developed countries (due largely to no-questions-asked large-scale lending), the rapid growth in international liquidity, and the vast pool of 'hot' money in eurocurrency markets destabilising exchange rates and domestic monetary policies of several countries.

A committee of bank supervisors from ten major industrialised countries was set up in 1975. This committee agreed that national supervisory authorities are responsible for the supervision of foreign branches of their countries' banks. Foreign subsidiaries, which are separate legal entities registered abroad, are the joint responsibility of the authorities in the parent bank country and the host country. In 1983, the committee issued a revised agreement in Basle (Switzerland), indicating more specifically which supervisory authority should be responsible for risks on the basis of a bank's global operations. The Bank of England, for example, now scrutinises the global balance sheet of all UK banks. The capital adequacy for common international standards, announced in 1987 and outlined in Ch. 10, means that bank supervisors now have to assess the capital adequacy of 'internally active' banks operating within their national boundaries.

Sources and uses of funds

A major attraction of the eurocurrency markets for participants is that both as depositors and borrowers they benefit from slightly more competitive interest rates than are available in corresponding domestic markets, reflecting lower transaction costs in eurocurrency markets and economies of large scale. The following are the main suppliers of funds to these markets:

(a) *Commercial enterprises* seeking liquidity and security for currency holdings, thus avoiding the need to convert into local currencies.
(b) *Official institutions*, including central banks, governments and international monetary organisations, holding foreign currency reserves, investing at good returns, in these markets.
(c) *Commercial banks* are also a source of primary funds, investing surplus resources in the markets. However, much eurocurrency business is transacted by banks on-lending primary deposits to other banks.

The categories of borrowers are broadly similar to the depositors: large multinational companies, government and government agencies. Companies borrow for normal trading purposes, e.g. to finance major projects overseas, or for direct portfolio investment, e.g. purchase of stocks and shares and Treasury bills. Central banks borrow on behalf of their national governments to finance shortfalls on the current account of their balance of payments and/or to offset outflows on their currency flows.

Eurocurrency interest rates

Eurocurrency rates are prices of currencies outside the jurisdiction of their respective national central banks; the prices in euromarkets are, like all prices in near-perfect markets, determined by the supply (eurocurrency deposits) and demand (eurocurrency loans) for eurocurrency funds.

The euromarket interest rates must be closely competitive with domestic interest rates, but they are not identical with domestic rates even where currencies and maturities are the same. Suppose the domestic interest rates in Germany rose above the eurodeutschemark rate in London, then the London eurodeutschemark rate will quickly rise to a competitive level to stop eurodeutschemark deposits flowing back to Germany to take advantage of the higher domestic deutschemark rates. Thus the relationship between the euro interest rates and domestic interest rates is such as to keep them both at the same level. Of course this relationship need not hold if there are exchange controls in operation preventing the free flow of currencies; consequently, in these circumstances, euro and domestic rates may differ substantially.

The following example shows the *relationship between euro rates and exchange rates*. Suppose the exchange rate of the deutschemark appreciated against sterling from, say, £1 = DM2.50 to £1 = DM2.30. A customer of a UK bank holding deutschemark deposits might find it profitable to sell his deutschemarks and buy cheaper sterling, and invest the sterling proceeds into sterling deposits at sterling deposit rates. To prevent this happening, the bank will have to increase the interest paid on deutschemark deposits to reflect the appreciation in the exchange rate of the deutschemark against sterling.

The difference between the spot (current) and forward rates generally reflects the differences between the eurodeposit rates between two currencies. Euromarkets are borrowing and lending markets, and *swap agreements* between banks are frequent. Suppose Bank X has eurodeutschemark funds and Bank Y has eurodollar funds; the eurodollar rate is 6 per cent per annum, and the eurodeutschemark rate is 5.5 per cent per annum, and the exchange rate between these two eurocurrencies is $1 : DM3. A swap arrangement between X and Y would operate something like this: X buys, say, $100,000 from Y for DM300,000, and at the same time agrees to buy back DM300,000 for $100,000 after one year. Under this swap agreement X will gain 0.5 per cent and Y will lose 0.5 per cent on interest rate differentials between dollars and deutschemarks. Clearly Y will not agree to be a party to this swap agreement without some compensation for the loss of 0.5 per cent interest. However, the compensation comes from the difference between the spot and forward rates: the forward dollar spot rate will buy a premium margin of 0.5 per cent per annum. Due to the differential between spot and forward rates of the dollar, both X and Y would earn the same amount of interest as they would have done with their original currencies had they not swapped, because the swap agreement, seen from Y's viewpoint, will mean that a forward discount margin will apply to his deutschemarks. Forward margins of premium and discount are completely interwoven, and it is the difference between eurocurrency deposit rates that determine the forward discount and premium margins on exchange rates: the larger the euro rate differential, the bigger the forward margins of premium and discount, and vice versa. Therefore the forward exchange rate does not necessarily equal the market's expectation of where the exchange rate is going. (A fuller discussion of interest rates and exchange rates is given in Chs 6 and 9 respectively.)

The Euro Commercial Paper (ECP) market

Trading in short-term fixed interest securities issued by countries, companies and banks is done in ECP market. As investors sought the relative safety of short-term markets after the share price collapse in October 1987, the ECP market had an extraordinary period of growth. It has the makings of a global, multicurrency pool of liquidity for better-quality borrowers to tap.

∎ The capital market

Whereas the money markets provide very short-term loans, the capital market caters for medium- and long-term loans. It serves the needs of industry and commerce, government and local authorities. Private sector firms borrow their working capital (current assets *minus* current liabilities) from the money markets, which used to be mainly via commercial banks; the role of banks as middlemen has now diminished, even for the workng capital requirements. Private sector firms raise their fixed capital by the issue of shares or sterling commercial paper bonds. The shares and bonds are taken up by individuals, insurance companies, pension funds and unit and investment funds. Government and local authorities borrow medium- and long-term capital by issuing new gilt-edged stocks and bonds. The main market place for lending and borrowing medium- and long-term capital in the UK is the Stock Exchange in London.

The Stock Exchange

The Stock Exchange (SE), now known as the International Stock Exchange (ISE), is a centralised market on which longer term securities are traded. The liquidity given to investors by this important secondary market increases the attraction of holding negotiable securities, making it easier for companies and others to raise money by issuing such securities. Since October 1986 there have been major changes which have affected ISE organisation (see below).

The ISE, as the main institution involved in medium-term and long-term capital raising, no longer has a centralised, physical presence in one place. Since the deregulation of the securities industry, the raising of share capital and longer term loan capital by companies involves a variety of institutions, such as issuing houses, underwriters, market makers and brokers. Many of the activities of these institutions are now provided by the 'in-house' operations of major clearing banks or foreign banks. Banks themselves now raise capital to meet their capital adequacy requirements.

The company securities

There is a wide range of company securities traded on the ISE. These can be divided into two main categories, *share capital* securities and *loan capital* securities. Ordinary (equity) shares are the main share capital securities, although some companies also issue preference shares with fixed dividend rights. Ordinary shareholders' dividend receipts depend mainly on the profitability of the company.

Loan capital securities generally take the form of long-term bonds (debentures) carrying a fixed rate of interest. The market value of the company bonds, like other fixed interest securities, is inversely related to the movements in the general level of interest rates.

The gilt-edged securities

In terms of market trading the *gilt-edged* market is by far the largest on the ISE. It mainly covers British government and government-guaranteed stocks but also covers stocks issued by local authorities and by certain other borrowers. British government stocks may be 'short-dated' (with up to five years to run), 'medium-dated' (five to fifteen years), 'long-dated' (over fifteen years) or 'undated' (with no fixed redemption date).

New issues of the central government stock are made by the Bank of England on behalf of the government. Nearly all issues of the stock are made by way of public offers but they are not underwritten. Any unsubscribed stock is taken up by the Bank and subsequently sold in response to bids from market-makers in gilts. The time this process takes varies according, among other things, to market conditions. During this period the stock is referred to as the 'tap stock'.

Eurobonds

Eurobonds are primarily sold outside the capital market of the country in whose currency they are denominated (e.g. a sterling bond is sold mainly to overseas investors). London is the chief centre for the eurobond market. For technical reasons eurobonds are normally quoted on the ISE but are only rarely dealt in there. Most secondary market transactions are arranged over the telephone, with banks and securities firms acting as market-makers.

Eurobonds are bearer securities. Governments, companies and other large-scale borrowers issue eurobonds as a way of raising medium- and longer-terms funds. Traditionally eurobonds were issued at fixed rates, though more recently floating rate bonds have become common.

Originally almost all eurobonds were denominated in dollars, but now many currencies are used, including the 'basket' currencies, i.e. Special Drawing Rights (SDRs) and the European Currency Unit (ECU).

▌ The 'Big Bang'

The ISE members were constrained in their ability to compete in the increasingly international capital markets by three main requirements under the SE rules:

1. The fixed minimum commission scales for the brokers restrained member firms' competition with one another, and with dealers in securities markets outside the London SE.
2. The single capacity system prevented the development of flexible methods of doing business.
3. The ownership rules, by preventing SE firms from becoming part of wider groupings and limiting their access to outside capital, prevented SE firms from developing new types of capital-intensive activities.

Technological innovation made distance unimportant and the leading financial markets became more closely integrated and competitive. Investors, particularly institutions, are beginning to look for an international spread of investments in liquid and efficient markets. The internationalisation of savings flows reflects the removal of exchange controls in the UK in 1979.

On 27 October 1986, the ISE abolished its minimum commission scales, permitted 100 per cent ownership of a member firm by a single non-member and dual-capacity trading systems were introduced in the gilt-edged and equity markets.

The 'Big Bang' is a colloquial term for the lifting of many prohibitions and restraints from, and the large-scale restructuring of, the *entire* securities industry. In short, the Big Bang is the deregulation of financial institutions connected with the UK securities industry, which acted as a trigger, not only for reshaping the structure of the SE, but also for a massive spate of takeovers and mergers, involving British clearing banks and merchant banks, stockbrokers and jobbers, foreign commercial banks and other non-bank financial companies.

This shake-up has created a new set of operators, centred on the *market-makers* who must quote, and deal in, their list of shares at all times. The lowest dealing prices are continuously quoted on the ISE wide screen through the Stock Exchange Automated Quotation system (SEAQ); this system creates a competitive and open market, with best terms available for all.

In the gilt-edged market there are now specialist institutions such as the Gilt-Edged Market Makers (GEMMs), who have replaced the 'old' jobbers, Inter-Dealer Brokers (IDBs), who deal only with GEMMs, acting as intermediaries assisting GEMMs to adjust their positions in gilt stocks, and Stock Exchange Money Brokers (SEMBs), who enable the various participants to balance their books by lending and borrowing stock and cash between GEMMs, major financial institutions and the discount houses. GEMMs, usually subsidiary companies of major financial groups, have various privileges: e.g. they enjoy the 'last resort' borrowing facilities from the Bank of England, and the deposits of commercial banks with them are considered highly liquid. GEMMs have to some extent reduced the 'unique' position of discount houses. GEMMs are important to the Bank in its gilt-edged stock selling activities, and that is why it monitors their capital adequacy and risk positions.

The 'Big Bang' in the UK was a link in a chain of international deregulation. The general ending of controls over international capital flows led to the globalisation of financial services, which, in turn, motivated large financial institutions to innovate and provide the new types of financial products demanded in the international financial markets. These innovative products have introduced new concepts, such as *securitisation* (large-scale *direct* borrowing and lending by companies). Banks and other financial institutions are fast becoming brokers and guarantors of the securitised assets, and thereby in large-scale off-balance sheet business, which leaves them with surplus liquidity for traditional lending to the personal sector, say, for house loans and consumer spending.

It could be argued that the chain reaction caused by the national and international 'Big Bang' has dissolved differences between the wholesale money markets and the capital markets in the UK: many large financial groups operate in both markets through subsidiaries. The distinction between short- and long-term capital is less clear cut now. Due to the availability of such products as swaps and options (see Ch. 11), companies raising long-term funds, in sterling and other currencies, can now exchange their fixed interest payments for floating rate payments based on short-term rates.

In the highly competitive and fluid environment both the risks and scope for conflict of interest will be increased, reinforcing the need to strengthen market regulation and *investor protection*. Since functions ranging from market-making to investment management and share recommendation will be under one conglomerate, conflicts of interest do exist.

To prevent such risks of insider trading there are self-imposed 'Chinese walls', the City's four *Self-Regulating Organisations* (SROs), and on top of the SROs is the *Securities and Investment Board* (SIB). A Chinese wall is the code intended to prevent corporate finance departments in the new conglomerates passing on confidential, price-sensitive information about their client companies to market-makers in the same group who could profit from dealing in the shares. SROs are specific to functions and will provide the day-to-day supervision of the specialised financial institutions. The SIB authorises and regulates investment activities directly or through SROs. It has the power to authorise financial groups to carry out investment business, and to prosecute those who are suspected of carrying out investment business without proper authorisation (see Ch. 10).

Financial Services Act 1986

This Act is a concomitant of the deregulation of the ISE. By establishing the SROs and SIB with professional members, it provides a system of regulation that is firmly based in statute, but which is essentially run by practitioners. A practitioner-run strong legal system, it is claimed, will be more flexible and will be able to identify malpractice more easily.

The Act is broad in *scope* and covers many aspects of the financial services industry. It has three basic objectives: (1) financial services should be provided in the most efficient and economic way; (2) the financial services industry must be competitive both domestically and internationally; and (3) rules and regulations must be responsive to international developments and not a cover for protectionism.

The Act *covers*: (a) all activities related to shares, debentures, options, gilts, unit trusts, long-term insurance contracts and futures; and (b) firms or sole traders who transact business in investment or who manage or give investment advice. It does *not* cover: (a) banking, which is covered under the Banking Act 1987; (b) building societies, which have their own Act widening their powers; and (c) insurance companies (except for selling life insurance contracts), which will continue to be supervised by the Department of Trade and Industry.

The approach to investor protection may not be effective where the parent of a conglomerate is a foreign securities firm outside UK jurisdiction. Therefore workable relationships are being established between the securities market regulations of different countries. The ISE has reached an agreement in principle with the International Securities Regulatory Organisation (ISRO) representing international banks and securities houses in London which may lead to a single regulatory organisation and single Recognised Investment Exchange (RIE) to serve both ISE members and ISRO members (see Ch. 10).

The response of London banks to the challenge of 'Big Bang'

The challenge

The essence of a *global* securities and investment market is the removal of national boundaries between national markets, products, customers and delivery systems. Surplus funds of companies and wealthy individuals no longer stay in demand deposits but rather in money market funds or investment securities which can be held for short periods due to international secondary trading markets.

The stakes in the internationalised securities and investment market are high: business is likely to gravitate towards the financial centres offering the lowest transaction costs, the most liquid markets, the widest range of financial instruments and services and the surest settlement and communication system. Over the 1990s banks will face three major challenges:

1. *The capital challenge*. Banks will need large amounts of capital to (a) finance new product development; (b) finance growth; (c) meet costs of involvement in capital market activities; and (d) strengthen capital ratios.
2. *The technology challenge*. During the 1980s the proportion of technology expense to total operating expenses has more than doubled and it is likely to account for an even higher proportion over the 1990s. Among the most profitable banks in the 1990s will be those capable of delivering products and services at the lowest cost.
3. *The culture challenge*. This is the toughest challenge, because it means a change in the way banks do business − banks are becoming businesses rather than institutions − which means developing a more market-driven culture without losing the reliability and meticulous attention to detail. Top bank managements are faced with the twin challenges of managing the basics of the business of banking, particularly profitability and balance sheet strength, and, at the same time, restructuring the business to manage the sea change in the deregulated financial services market.

The response

Deregulation, which started as a trickle, has quickly turned into a flood. All kinds of new competing financial institutions have entered the market, and the lines between their activities have become increasingly blurred, so much so that it is becoming harder and harder to define a bank. Banks in the UK have responded eagerly to the challenge and opportunity to enter the new securities and investment market in London. Among the contenders there are various distinct groups: the 'Big Four' clearers, who are seeking to emulate the 'universal banks' of the continent; the London merchant banks, who are aiming to develop their capital market connections; a number of continental banks, who are building up their presence in the City; and a selected number of American commercial banks, who are building a global investment capacity.

To some extent the motivation behind the banks' response is defensive. Corporate lending is sluggish; major companies can now borrow more cheaply than the banks themselves. So it makes sense for the banks to move more deeply into the securities business. Given the riskier environment into which banks are moving, appropriately the Bank of England has begun to keep a closer eye on their activities.

The Big Four clearing banks

Although the Big Bang is essentially about deregulating the Stock Exchange, it raises major strategic questions for the banks as they adjust to an era when financing through securities markets is becoming more popular than finance in the form of bank loans and overdrafts, and the banks' role as providers of credit has diminished.

The clearers have finalised their new investment banking operations − all of them substantial and capitalised to the tune of several hundred million pounds. In the case of Barclays, National Westminster and Midland Banks, these have been constructed round acquired stockbroking and jobbing firms. Barclays Bank have acquired de Zoete & Bevan and Wedd Durlacher Mordaunt to create *Barclays de Zoete Wedd*. Midland Bank have acquired S. Montagu, Greenwell and Smith Keen Cutler to form *Greenwell Montagu*.

National Westminster Bank have acquired County Bank, Fielding Newson-Smith and Bisgood Bishop to constitute *County Securities*. Lloyds Bank have, in order to cut costs, developed such a business internally and have produced *Lloyds Bank Stockbrokers*. The two 'casualties' of the Big Bang among the clearers have been Greenwell Montagu; due to unacceptable losses, they have withdrawn as market-makers in equities and Lloyds Bank have ceased to be market-makers in gilts.

The investment banking operations of all four clearers are broadly similar: they combine securities issuing and trading with corporate finance, asset management and stockbroking services. Three clearers are primary dealers in the gilt-edged market.

The clearers are well equipped to become the major suppliers of investment services in Britain's high streets. But the move into the securities market poses several managerial and cultural problems for them. The clearing banks are unionised, bureaucratic and slow-moving, very different from the hire-and-fire, payments-by-results attitude of the ISE firms.

The merchant banks

Although the new investment banking operations of the clearers are *really* new to them and will test their mettle, the merchant banks, on the other hand, are probably mentally better equipped to cope with the ISE changes. For the UK merchant banks, the move into the securities markets will pose a much less extreme culture clash. But they lack the great capital resources of the clearers. To go seriously into the securities market, they have had to raise large new sums in capital and to increase their managerial staff considerably. Several of the merchant banking groups may feel that they need to tie up with clearing banks in order to gain the financial and personnel resources to compete in the global securities markets.

The foreign banks

With the deregulated ISE, the City is destined to play a leading role in the world-wide market in securities and other financial investments, as it already does in the field of international banking. And this can only enhance further its attraction to foreign banks as a base for their international activities. At present the City has a bigger representation of foreign banks than any other international centre. And, in spite of the cost of running a London operation and efforts by other centres to pull in international banking, London is likely to remain a dominant force. The *attractiveness* of London for foreign banks, in *this* context, is for three main reasons: (1) London is in a time zone conveniently overlapping New York and the Far East; (2) English is the language of international banking; (3) London has a pool of experienced talent, both in dealing in financial instruments and in producing new ideas in financing techniques.

The Bank of England has, however, made it clear to foreign banks operating in London that they will be expected to adhere to UK standards, whatever the situation may be on their own domestic markets.

The discount houses

It is possible that their privileged position as the buffer between the Bank of England and the rest of the banking system may be affected by the Big Bang, which is reshaping other financial institutions.

The eight discount houses − only four of which are independent institutions − have been looking at new businesses themselves, e.g. commodities broking, leasing, insurance, money broking and gilt dealing.

The other four discount houses which have been taken over by larger institutions (three of them foreign), are all being used by their parents as the short-term money market dealing arms of much larger capital market operations.

Summary

(a) *Deregulation* of the UK financial services industry has removed the barriers to foreign competition in domestic markets and to the ability of borrowers and investors to participate in foreign markets. In other words it has led to the 'globalisation' of financial services markets.

(b) The *Big Bang* has allowed the formation of commercial banking groups which, through their major investment subsidiaries, have entered into non-traditional areas such as mortgage finance, estate agency, insurance broking, unit trusts, and so on. On the other hand, building societies are now themselves allowed into banking operations, such as unsecured consumer credit and other financial services. Thus the roles of BFIs and NBFIs are being further blurred. However, although individual BFIs and NBFIs do now have a wider range of financial services, it is still important to maintain a reasonably clear conceptual difference between the various activities.

(c) At the company level, the trend towards '*securitisation*' – replacement of bank loans by marketable securities – is on the increase. The sterling commercial paper provides a recent domestic example of securitisation. Soon mortgage-backed securities will be on offer in the UK.

(d) *Disintermediation* is replacing intermediation (typically by a bank), as borrowers and lenders find that the traditional advantages of intermediation are being overcome by the greater availability of information and increased liquidity; some investors see large companies as being no more risky than a bank. The banks are now increasingly acting as guarantors of debts, and since such transactions are off-balance-sheet they incur reduced capital/liquidity costs. Their fee income is increasing but interest earnings are declining.

(e) The *jurisdiction* of commercial banking remains the province of the Bank of England. The overriding aim of banking supervision, under the 1987 Banking Act, is the protection of bank depositors. Building societies will continue to have their own regulatory framework under the Building Societies Act 1986, which has widened their powers. Investment business will be subject to the Financial Services Act 1986 and its SROs will be overseen by the SIB whose powers will derive from the Secretary of State for Trade and Industry. However, the trend towards financial service conglomerates means that supervision will overlap: banks and building societies wishing to do investment business will have to register with one or more of the SROs.

▊ Insurance and commodities markets

A variety of other financial markets are to be found in the City. The *Lloyd's insurance market* and the *commodity markets* are very important organised financial markets. Members of Lloyd's are individuals who group together into syndicates to underwrite (insure) various risks. Each syndicate is managed by an underwriting agent who deals with brokers wishing to place business on the Lloyd's market. On commodity markets a large number of commodities are traded for spot (immediate) or future delivery. These markets assist businessmen to make sure of future supplies of raw materials they require.

∎ The financial futures

A *financial futures contract* is an agreement to buy or sell a standard quantity of a specific financial instrument (e.g. a bond or a currency) at a future date, at a price agreed between the parties. The London International Financial Futures Exchange (LIFFE) operates the financial futures market in London.

There are seven contracts traded on LIFFE. Three of them are related to movements in interest rates, the other four cover specific currency movements against the dollar, namely sterling, deutschemarks, yen and Swiss francs.

The main role of LIFFE is to allow people to *hedge* against movements in interest and exchange rates. It enables people to look into known exchange rates or interest rates for transactions which they know they have to undertake later. The delivery period to which contracts relate can be up to fifteen months. Members of LIFFE include banks, stockbroker-dealers, and money brokers. Apart from hedging, LIFFE can be used for *speculative* purposes.

∎ The foreign exchange

London is an important foreign exchange market. In a foreign exchange market one currency can be bought and sold in terms of another currency. The organised foreign exchange market in London is almost exclusively a market between banks. The foreign exchange markets in other major centres throughout the world are in close contact with each other through very fast means of communication, which means that the *arbitrage* operations (profiting from the inconsistencies between exchange rates) are quite common (see Ch. 9).

∎ Instruments used in the financial markets

The instruments used in the bill market include 'bills', which are short-term securities issued by borrowers (government – Treasury bills; companies – commercial bills; local authorities – local authority bills) to obtain short-term finance. The lenders (bill holders) keep the bills as 'near' money assets.

(a) *Treasury bills* are issued by the Bank of England on behalf of the government in *amounts* ranging from £5,000 to £1 million (the minimum *tender* is £50,000), usually for a period of ninety-one days. There is no interest on Treasury bills and therefore these are issued below par and repaid at par; the capital gain is in lieu of interest rate. The discount houses agree to cover the entire weekly issue; the sale proceeds provide the short-term funds needed by the central government.

(b) *Commercial bills* become eligible bills for discount in the bill market and for re-discount at the Bank of England when accepted by an eligible bank – mainly UK commercial banks and the larger overseas banks. 'Accepting' literally means guaranteeing for a fee that the bill will be paid at maturity. Bills of exchange accepted by banks are called 'bank bills' and are easily marketable before maturity at the 'finest' rates, i.e. the person selling or discounting a bank bill receives a higher price for it.

(c) *Local authority bills* are 'receipts' issued by the borrowing local authority needing funds in advance of its yearly council tax inflow. To obtain large sums quickly, from seven days to a year, the local authorities operate through bill brokers and merchant banks. These bills are quickly marketable. Discount houses play an important part in making local authority bills liquid. (*The above three instruments are used in the Bank of England's open market operations [OMOs]*.)

(d) *Sterling Commercial Paper* (SCP) is a short-term fixed interest security issued by the UK and overseas commercial companies. It can be resold on the SCP market. The term of the SCP is between seven days and one year.

(e) *Certificates of Deposit* (CDs) are bearer certificates stating that a certain amount in sterling (or certain other currencies) has been placed with a particular bank or building society for a given period and at a particular rate of interest. The CD is a negotiable instrument and can be resold in the secondary CDs market. The term of the deposit is between three months and five years.

(f) *Certificates of Tax Deposit* (CTDs). A CTD is issued by the Inland Revenue acknowledging that money has been placed with it as an advance payment of a tax liability. The minimum purchase is £5,000 and it cannot be redeemed against PAYE liabilities. Therefore CTDs are most commonly used by companies with corporation tax liabilities. CTDs earn interest until applied to tax payments. Their issue smooths out the inflows of corporation tax receipts. In recent years they became significant instruments of financing the Public Sector Borrowing Requirement (PSBR).

(g) *Gilt-edged Securities* are British government fixed-interest securities of varying periods of maturity. Like all fixed-interest securities, their market value is inversely related to the movements in the general level of interest rates. They are easily negotiable on the gilt-edged market.

(h) *Stocks and Bonds* are longer term fixed-interest securities issued by local authorities and private sector companies. Company bonds can be bought and sold on the International Stock Exchange.

(i) *Equities* are ordinary shares which give the holders the residual ownership of the assets and earnings of a company. They have no fixed rate of return, and can be bought and sold on the International Stock Exchange.

(j) *Eurobonds* are issued in various capital markets and in different currencies to raise long-term funds.

(k) *Euro Commercial Paper* (ECP) is a short-term, eurocurrency-denominated, fixed interest security.

(l) *Note issue facilities (NIFs)*. A NIF is a medium-term legally binding commitment under which a borrower can issue short-term promissory notes in its own name; the underwriting banks are committed either to purchase any unsold notes or to provide standby credit facilities. For non-bank borrowers the promissory notes issued are known as Euronotes.

(m) *Floating Rate Notes (FRNs)*. FRNs are variable rate eurobond issues on which the interest rate is adjusted at six-monthly intervals in line with the appropriate reference rate in the London eurocurrency market for deposits in the currency of the note or bond, and is set normally half per cent above the six-month rate. FRNs are usually issued in denominations of $1,000 each, but may range from $100,000 to $500,000 each.

▌ The role of the Bank of England in the financial markets

The role of the Bank is three-fold and ensures that:

(a) the liquidity of the banking system is in balance;
(b) the short-term interest rates are in line with the monetary policy stance;
(c) the National Debt is so managed as to achieve certain specific monetary objectives.

Government transactions with the rest of the economy usually total several hundred million pounds in each direction each day. A net flow of funds *from* the government to the banks is reflected in the accumulation of operational deposits of the clearing banks at the Bank; a net flow from the banks *to* the government results in a drain on them. Through its open market operations (OMOs) in the money markets (buying and selling eligible commercial and Treasury bills) which are conducted mainly through the discount houses as intermediaries, the Bank offsets shortage or surplus of liquidity caused by these flows.

The Bank can use its OMOs not only to remove the liquidity shortage or surplus in the markets, but also to influence the levels of short-term interest rates.

If the amount of eligible bills the Bank sells exceeds the amount required to offset the liquidity surplus, money supply will decrease. If the amount of bills it buys exceeds the amount required to offset the liquidity shortage, money supply will increase.

If the Bank offsets the liquidity shortage (or surplus) at its bill dealing rates, which are higher or lower than the current level of short-term market interest rates, it will result in raising or lowering the marginal cost of funds to the banking system, which, in turn, will raise or lower the level of short-term money market rates.

The National Debt is the total of outstanding debt of the central government. It can be divided into marketable debt (e.g. gilt-edged securities) and non-marketable debt (e.g. National Savings Certificates). The Bank, as the manager of the National Debt, aims in its debt management to achieve three main objectives:

1. to influence the level of money supply and the structure of interest rates in line with the current monetary policy;
2. to ensure a stable market for government debt; and
3. to minimise the interest costs of the debt.

(a) The marketable debt is of great importance to almost all financial institutions: it provides an excellent balance between safety, liquidity and yield (rate of return). If the M4 private sector purchases it by drawing on its bank and building society deposits, then there will be no increase in the money supply (see Ch. 5). But it is not always possible to sell the entire marketable stock to the M4 private sector when the existing debt matures and/or the government needs additional borrowing. When the demand is weak, the Issue Department of the Bank can take up the unsold stock and, at a later date, when demand is strong, offer it to the market at acceptable prices.

(b) If demand for government securities is to remain stable, fluctuations in the gilt market need to be moderated. The authorities are willing to accept more fluctuations in interest rates − though reserving the right to intervene in the market if the market falls too much − to emphasise that the control of money supply has been the prime target of monetary policy. However, more recently the control of the money supply as a prime target of monetary policy seems to have lost its emphasis.

(c) In refinancing the maturing debt, the Bank does not wait until the stocks reach final maturity date; instead it buys stocks when they come on the market any time within the year to final redemption, thus avoiding large refinancing problems and the consequent disturbance in the gilt market. The new stock is taken up by the Issue Department of the Bank and then fed to the market as conditions permit. This technique is known as the 'tap' issue of the stocks, and avoids depressing the gilt market by the sale of large amounts of gilts immediately. As a rule, the Bank attempts to refinance the maturing stocks and Treasury bills by long-term debt (the process is known as 'funding') to reduce the frequency of debt refinancing.

Variations in government revenue and expenditure directly determine the size of the *budget deficit*. The budget deficit determines the level of the government's borrowing requirements. If the Bank directly sold *more* gilt-edged stocks than warranted by the budget deficit (along with deliberately increased sales of National Savings securities) to the M4 private sector, then bank and building society lending would be depressed – and so would the money supply – for longer periods.

The Bank can order commercial banks to place with it non-operational, but interest bearing, *special deposits*, with a view to mop up surplus liquidity in the market. It can release the accumulated special deposits to the banks to offset an expected shortage of liquidity in the banking system.

In order to depress consumer spending and to improve the balance of payments, the Bank can impose *qualitative lending controls* on the banks, which would restrict lending to personal customers and property companies but would encourage lending to manufacturing and exporting businesses.

∎ Recent examination questions

The following questions have been asked in the recent exam question papers. After you have read and *understood* this chapter, you should be able to answer them. Try first to answer these questions in point form, before checking your points with the outline answers given below.

Question 1

To what extent is it now valid or useful to distinguish between the discount and parallel markets in London?

Question 2

Assess the role of the so-called 'parallel' sterling London money markets in the present-day UK financial system.

Question 3

Discuss the significance of the following in the UK financial system:

(a) the inter-bank market;
(b) commercial (eligible) bank bills;
(c) the International Stock Exchange, including reference to the changes introduced by 'Big Bang'.

Question 4

(a) Describe in detail the way in which the Bank of England currently seeks to influence rates in the money markets.

(b) To what extent do the Bank's operations influence changes in commercial banks' base rates?

Question 5

What factors have contributed to the rapid growth of the eurocurrency markets in recent years? To what extent has this growth been a cause of concern to the world's monetary authorities?

Question 6

(a) Identify the main borrowers and lenders (other than developing countries) in the eurocurrency markets.

(b) What advantages do the eurocurrency markets have over domestic markets for the corporate and financial institutions?

▮ Outline answers

Answer 1

(a) Briefly describe the role of the two markets, highlighting the essential differences (lending in the discount market is secured) and similarities (both deal in wholesale short-term funds) in their present-day function.

(b) Show that it is both valid and useful, *at least for the time being*, to distinguish between them by explaining the following exclusive aspects of the discount market:
   (i) Through it the Bank provides its 'lender of last resort' facility.
   (ii) The Bank's daily operations through it influence the short-term interest rates and offset the net financial flows between the government and the banking system.
   (iii) It provides the vital buffer between the Bank and the commercial banks.
   (iv) It underwrites the weekly Treasury bill tender.
   (v) It maintains the secondary market in bank CDs, and is prominent in the short-dated gilt-edged market.

(c) Point to changes in recent years affecting the special position of the discount market:
   (i) Blurring of traditional boundaries between it and the parallel markets.
   (ii) Its significance as a market where banks adjusted their liquidity, which to a large extent is now replaced by the inter-bank and CDs markets.
   (iii) The deregulation of financial institutions may remove its exclusive position as the buffer between the Bank and the banking system.

Answer 2

(a) Parallel sterling London money markets are specialised short-term money markets. (Discount market and eurocurrency market are *not* included.)

(b) Chronological order: local authority, finance house, inter-company deposits, inter-bank and CDs, sterling commercial paper.

(c) In order of size: inter-bank first.

(d) These markets provide:

    (i) liquid assets for participants: banks (including clearers and accepting houses), local authorities, building societies and companies (companies are able to buy and sell CDs);

    (ii) profitable lending opportunities for participants;

    (iii) LIBOR (London Inter-Bank Offered Rate) plays a significant role in the inter-bank market in:

        – determining the cost of market-related borrowing by the banks' corporate customers,

        – calculating the internal cost of funds charged to banks' branches by their head office, and

        – determining the level of base rates.

(e) Parallel money markets play no direct role in the Bank of England's implementation of monetary policy.

Answer 3

(a) *The inter-bank market:*

    (i) It provides commercial banks with the opportunity to lend and borrow *wholesale* funds, short-term and unsecured.

    (ii) It is significant as a market which allows *day-to-day liquidity positions to be adjusted*, enabling banks' surplus funds to be employed profitably, and marginal funds to support additional business to be raised.

    (iii) The lending rate in this market is LIBOR, which is important as a determinant of base rates. Many commercial loans are directly linked to LIBOR.

(b) *Eligible bank bills market:*

    (i) EBBs are commercial bills which have been accepted by eligible banks.

    (ii) Bank of England deals mainly in EBBs in its OMOs to influence short-term interest rates. Such dealings are normally in Bands 1 and 2 of the band structure.

    (iii) If there is a cash shortage in the market, the Bank will provide relief by purchasing EBBs from the discount houses at rates which are consistent with interest rate policy.

(c) *The International Stock Exchange:*

    (i) It constitutes the capital market where long-term securities can be traded.

    (ii) It enhances the attraction of the primary market, enabling companies to raise equity and long-term loan funds.

    (iii) 'Big Bang' deregulated the securities industry. It abolished minimum commissions, replaced jobbers and brokers by dual capacity and removed barriers to the entry of banks and overseas investment houses.

Answer 4

(a)   (i) The Bank of England, dealing *predominantly* through eligible *commercial bills*, influences the short-term interest rates (basically seven-day rates), leaving longer-term rates to be determined by the market forces.

    (ii) The Bank also deals in Treasury bills and local authority bills.

    (iii) If a net shortage of cash seems likely, due to the net flow *from* the banks to the government, the Bank will undertake to offset the shortage by buying eligible commercial bills from the discount houses.

(iv) Discount houses offer bills to the Bank at their own prices; if the short-term interest rates implied by these prices are compatible with the Bank's interest rate objective, it will accept the discount houses' offer prices. If not, the discount houses are forced to make new offers which are consistent with the monetary policy on interest rates.

(v) The bill market operations of the Bank (OMOs) are conducted in maturity Band 1 (up to 14 days to maturity) and Band 2 (15–33 days to maturity). If there is a scarcity of short-dated bills, the Bank may provide funds to the banks by the sale and repurchase of certain securities for fixed periods and at fixed rates (REPOS).

(b) (i) Commercial banks' base rates follow the trend of *all* money market rates (particularly the LIBOR) because they determine the marginal cost of a large proportion of their funds.

(ii) But the base rates do not automatically respond to sharp day-to-day movements in the money market rates.

(iii) If the market rates are higher than the banks' base rates, 'round-tripping' or arbitrage could occur and harm banks' profitability.

(iv) Round-tripping is a process whereby large bank customers borrow under existing overdraft limits from their banks at base rate plus one, and on-lend the borrowed funds at higher rates in the money markets.

(v) The Bank also undertakes *direct intervention* in the market to relieve the liquidity shortage and also to influence short-term rates by lending directly to the discount houses (no buying and selling of eligible bills is involved) and to banks via REPOS.

Answer 5

Reasons for the rapid expansion of international banking in euromarkets are: increase in international banking activity due to growth in world trade and to general internationalisation of the world economy; large balance of payments imbalances – surpluses channelled to deficit countries via international banking (in preference to IMF machinery, due to IMF conditions); euromarkets are unregulated and without costly restrictions (no reserve requirements, etc.), hence can offer favourable lending and borrowing terms. Growth in euromarkets has slowed dramatically due to world recession and heavy indebtedness of Less Developed Countries (LDCs). Lack of regulation of euromarkets has led to problems, e.g. the extent of mismatching of lending and borrowing, capital inadequacy, etc.

Rapid growth in euromarkets leads to rapid growth in international liquidity, hence the concern about the possible inflationary effects.

A vast pool of 'hot' money in euromarkets potentially destabilises both exchange rates and domestic monetary policies.

Note: The main point is the lack of restriction, which has been at the heart of all these other growth factors. This is now changing.

Answer 6

(a) *Main lenders:*
   (i) central banks;
   (ii) governments;

(iii) commercial banks;

(iv) international organisations (e.g. IMF).

Main borrowers (the borrowers are at other times the lenders):

  (i) national governments (to finance balance of payments deficits);

 (ii) central banks (to defend the exchange rate of national currency);

(iii) commercial banks (to provide for their own needs and needs of their customers and other banks);

(iv) multinational companies (to finance international operations and takeovers).

(b) *Advantages over domestic markets:*

  (i) Availability of large amounts of wholesale funds.

 (ii) Surplus currency funds can be invested without conversion costs.

(iii) Availability of expertise in multicurrency capital raising and risk hedging.

(iv) Some tax advantage in dealing offshore.

 (v) Marginally lower lending and borrowing costs due to the large scale and highly sophisticated nature of eurocurrency markets.

(vi) For some banks and financial institutions these makets are still the only way to cross institutional boundaries, e.g. in Japan and the USA, where national laws prevent it.

▌ A tutor's answer

An essential element of the MFS syllabus is the relationship between domestic interest rates, eurocurrency market interest rates and the exchange rate. The following question seeks to test your understanding of this relationship. Prepare a brief outline plan for your answer, and then write according to the plan so that you answer the whole question.

Question

Examine the relationship between rates of interest for a currency in the domestic money markets and the euromarkets. Other things being equal, what effect would a change in domestic interest rates have on:

(a) the spot foreign exchange rate;

(b) the forward exchange rate?

Answer plan

(a) The close link between the two markets.

(b) Euromarkets enjoy a marginal cost advantage.

(c) Relative interest rate levels determine exchange rate movements.

(d) Interest rate differentials and the forward premiums/discount on currencies.

(e) Forward cover cost equalises the interest rate differentials.

Specimen answer

If there are no exchange controls, then there is no fundamental difference – apart from location – between currencies in domestic money markets and the euromarkets. The two markets are closely linked, and interest rates in the eurocurrency markets will closely follow the trends in national rates.

However, euromarkets possess a marginal cost advantage over the domestic markets. The absence of compliance costs of reserve asset and liquidity requirements, plus the economies of large scale associated with purely wholesale transactions, mean that, for any given loan maturity, prevailing eurocurrency rates will be slightly lower for borrowers and slightly higher for depositors than will be the case in domestic markets.

(a) Changes in domestic rates will influence the exchange rate, because relative interest rate levels are a major determinant of exchange rate movements. Therefore, other things being equal, an increase in domestic rates would exert an upward pressure on the country's current, or spot, exchange rate.

(b) The spot rate is the basis of all forward exchange rates. To ascertain the foreign forward exchange rate of a currency, the 'discount' is added to, or the 'premium' is subtracted from, its spot rate.

The forward premium or discount generally reflects the difference in the interest rates ruling in the inter-bank market for the currencies being exchanged. Currencies with lower interest rates (the stronger currencies), say DM, normally stand at a premium against currencies with higher interest rates (the weaker currencies), say sterling. Therefore a buyer of DM, to be delivered a few months hence, will find that his sterling will buy less of DM in a few months' time than it buys today. Similarly, if his stronger sterling (lower interest rate) will buy more of the weaker drachma (higher interest rate) in the future than it buys today, the drachma will be quoted at a discount in the foreign exchange markets.

Forward exchange rates generally reflect interest rate *differentials*; and the cost of covering forward the risk of exchange rate movement equalises the interest rate differentials, because the differentials directly determine the cost of covering forward. If this were not so, arbitrage would be triggered. Therefore if any part of the relationship between domestic interest rates and the exchange rate changes, the forward margin is automatically adjusted. Thus if a country's domestic interest rates rise, other things being equal, the forward premium on it narrows or the forward discount widens, depressing its forward exchange rate. (See Ch. 6 and p. 161 for further discussion of interest rates and exchange rates.)

■ A step further

Due to the deregulation of the financial institutions and markets connected with the UK securities industry, the UK financial system is in a state of flux. It is vital that you understand the reasons behind the changes and that you keep abreast of the changing scene as it develops.

In this connection, you will find the articles listed below (to which I am indebted) of especial relevance: 'Change in the Stock Exchange and regulation of the City', *BEQB*, December 1985; 'Changes in the structure of financial markets: a view from London', *BEQB*, March 1985; 'The City after the Big Bang' and 'The global financial village', *Banking World*, October 1986; and 'UK banking' (a *Financial Times* survey, 2 October 1986).

With regard to the euromarkets: they are the products of their time; they evolved because there was need for them and because conditions favoured their development; but their unregulated nature is cause for concern. It has led to international debt and banking problems in which there are several distressed, overborrowed countries and distressed, overlent banks: if these problems are not resolved, either by the international banks on their own, or in partnership with the IMF — which has assumed an important intermediary role — the consequences of bank failures could be catastrophic.

To keep abreast of changes in this area of the MFS, you should regularly study: the Bank of England *Quarterly Bulletins*, *The Economist*, *Finance and Development*, a quarterly publication of the IMF and the World Bank, *Banking World*, the Chartered Institute of Bankers' *Examiners' Reports* and *Updating Notes*. The excellent BIS publication, *A Guide to the International Monetary Systems*, will give a good understanding of the fundamentals of international liquidity and eurocurrency markets. The *Signpost* article in *Banking World* (March 1986, pp. 55–7) is worthy of careful study.

CHAPTER 5

The Money Supply

Syllabus requirements
- Money supply as an important indicator.
- Credit-creation multiplier.
- Constraints on the growth of bank deposits.
- Causes of changes in money supply, in particular:
    - (i) the Public Spending Borrowing Requirements;
    - (ii) public sector debt sales;
    - (iii) overfunding;
    - (iv) bank and building society lending to private, public and overseas sectors;
    - (v) external transactions.
- Causes of distortion in money supply.
- Interrelationship between changes in money supply and bank balance sheets.

▌ Getting started

In Chapter 2 we saw how difficult it was to give one all-embracing definition of money, and we considered the reasons for such difficulty. We also noted that in most money-using economies, money supply, or money stock, has two types of definition: the narrow and the broad definitions.

Under the *narrow* definition, the money supply of a country is comprised solely of the means of payment, i.e. the total money available to the public for immediate spending. This money is made up of the notes and coins (the cash) in *circulation* and the sight deposits held by the public in financial institutions: it is often referred to as 'spending' money. The distribution between cash and sight deposits depends entirely on public preference and the degree to which the financial system has developed. When a sight deposit holder cashes a cheque at his bank, the amount of deposits held by the bank is reduced and the amount of cash in circulation with the public is increased. The cash in *tills of the banks* is excluded from spending money because it is not directly available to the non-bank public for spending.

The *broad* definition of money supply comprises not only the spending money at the disposal of the non-bank public, but also 'near' money assets, because these can be converted with no or little difficulty and financial penalty into spending money. For money supply control purposes, monetary authorities may use either narrow or broad money definitions or some combination of both.

The quantity of money in a country is determined both by the actions of the M4 private sector (consumers and businesses), and by the decisions and actions of the commercial banks and other financial institutions, central bank and the government.

The growth rate of the money supply is an *important indicator* to the authorities of its likely impact on the monetary policies, as expressed by Fisher's equation ($MV = PT$). If the money supply rises too fast in relation to the volume of goods and services, inflationary pressures begin to build up in the economy. Inflation has serious consequences for the level of interest rates, savings, profits, wages and employment. On the other hand, insufficient money supply growth will adversely affect economic growth, commercial activity and employment. Thus the rate of growth of the money supply must be such as will encourage 'real' economic growth. It is for these reasons that the authorities place much emphasis on controlling the rate of growth of money supply in pursuit of their broader economic objectives (see Ch. 7), notably economic growth without inflation.

▌ Essential principles

Money creation by commercial banks

Sight deposits with commercial banks (and building societies, in the UK) form a major part of the real or spending money in a country with a developed banking system. Cash, which forms a very small part of the total spending money, is provided by the central bank. If the banks and building societies could increase the volume of sight deposits without causing a reduction in the amount of cash in circulation they would increase the quantity of spending money in the UK.

The banks and building societies are in fact able to do this, for two main reasons.

1. Sight deposit holders have full confidence in the ability of banks and societies to pay cash on demand. Therefore the public accepts payments by cheques, and other means provided by banks and societies, because it is both more convenient and safer than receiving payments in cash.
2. Whenever a bank or a society makes a *loan* to a customer, somewhere in the banking and building society system a *deposit* of equal value is created. When the banks and societies are increasing the supply of loans (their assets), their deposits (their liabilities) are also increasing by an equal amount. Not only do these loans increase the purchasing power in their own right but they also, in turn, provide a base for further loans, i.e. for credit creation.

Suppose there is only one bank in a community, and the public, with absolute confidence, deposit their surplus cash in that bank. Customer A deposits £100 cash, which is surplus to his immediate spending needs, with the bank, which credits A's account. The bank's liabilities (A's deposit) and assets (£100 in the till) have increased by the same amount. Let us assume that the bank, as a matter of policy, keeps 10 per cent of all deposits in cash or near-cash assets to meet customers' withdrawals of cash. The bank can on-lend £90 from A's £100 deposit to, say, customer B. The bank then credits B's current account and debits B's loan account with £90; once again the bank's liabilities and assets have increased by the same amount. Most probably, B has borrowed £90 to repay a debt for purchasing goods or services, say, from C. C accepts B's cheque for £90 with confidence, and deposits it in his account at the bank. The bank's liabilities and assets are not affected by this transaction, because the credit of £90 is now in C's account and the debt of £90 is still in B's loan account. The bank is now able to advance £81 (£90 less 10 per cent liquidity cushion) to, say, customer D.

The process of receiving deposits, on-lending them (less 10 per cent) and creating more deposits can continue until the total amount of deposits, or spending money (low-powered money), created by the bank on the basis of A's £100 cash deposit (high-powered money) reaches £1,000; i.e. the bank has increased the narrow money supply by a multiplier of 10.

The *credit creation multiplier* measures the amount of new deposits created from the original deposit. It can be measured by the following formula:

$$\frac{\text{Total value of new deposits created (say, £1,000)}}{\text{Total value of original deposit (say, £100)}}$$

The fact that in real life there are several banks (and building societies) does not invalidate the credit creation principle. Although the assets and liabilities of the *individual banks* connected with the process of the above £1,000 credit creation may increase by larger or smaller amounts, the liabilities and assets of the *banking system as a whole* will increase by £1,000.

When in response to a greater demand for cash by the public the central bank issues, via commercial banks, an additional supply of cash (high-powered money), most of the additional cash will 'seep' back into bank and building society deposits, enabling them to start the credit creation process. Banks and building societies create money by lending. Each loan creates a new bank/building society deposit, and money is the sum of cash in circulation *plus* all bank and building society deposits.

▌ Can banks and building societies create money indefinitely?

The credit creation process is triggered when there is an injection of 'high-powered' funds from the monetary authorities into banks and building societies. The banks and building societies receive high-powered money deposits when the authorities borrow from them to finance the government's borrowing requirements, the redemption of maturing government stock held by the M4 private sector and the return of special deposits held by the Bank of England, to the banks.

Assuming that an injection of high-powered money has increased the deposits of banks and building societies, their power to create credit in terms of low-powered funds is limited due to the following considerations.

Cash leakages

Internal

Suppose, in the above example, B needs some cash, and therefore deposits not £90 but £80. This will reduce the bank's ability to create credit, as will a purchase of government securities by B.

External

If there are no foreign exchange restrictions, then bank customers can transfer funds overseas, perhaps to earn a higher rate of return. Such transfers of funds overseas reduce the credit creation multiplier.

Customer demand for loans

If the economy has been suffering a long period of recession, then the level of business profits will be low and the level of unemployment high. Consequently, the demand for loans by the corporate and personal sectors would be low. Banks and building societies are seriously hampered in credit creation if the M4 private sector *does not want to borrow*. They could lower interest rates charged to borrowers and attempt to attract demand for loans. Other things being equal, a decrease in interest rates increases the demand for loans by the M4 private sector, especially by business firms, because lower borrowing costs increase their profitability. Conversely, an increase in interest rates contracts demand for loans by firms and households; they will defer such purchases as can be deferred until borrowing costs come down.

Self-imposed constraints

Banks and building societies will not knowingly risk their depositors' funds or their own surplus resources if there is a likelihood that the loans they give may become bad debts. They may not lend, especially in times of economic recession, to firms which are on the verge of bankruptcy. Therefore credit creation may not take place to the extent that the demand for loans at the prevailing interest rate would allow.

Liquidity cushion

To maintain the confidence of the M4 private sector in their ability to pay on demand, and to avoid a 'run' on themselves, prudent banks and building societies keep a cash-reserve-to-deposit ratio in cash and near-cash assets. They must keep a proportion of their assets in liquid (cash in tills) and near-liquid (CDs, short-dated gilts, Treasury bills) form. The higher this liquidity ratio, the smaller the credit creation multiplier. In addition to a self-applied prudential liquidity ratio, the central bank may impose on the commercial banks' liquidity its own prudential requirements, e.g. they may be obliged to maintain a *specific* reserve-to-deposit ratio in liquid or near-liquid form. Such official constraints on the banks' liquidity would curb their ability to create credit. Banks in the UK are required to maintain 0.35 per cent of their deposit liabilities with the Bank of England; this cash ratio is non-operational and non-interest bearing.

Government policy

Money supply in developed economies is ultimately under the control of the monetary authorities. If the authorities fear that the credit creation is exceeding the desirable level, they may restrict the ability of the banks and building societies to lend. This may be done by asking banks and building societies for some form of deposits at the central bank that will reduce their ability, and indeed desire, to lend, or it may be done by direct instruction.

■ Profitability versus safety

Commercial banks are business organisations. They market financial services to make a profit from which they can meet their running and capital costs and to distribute dividends to their shareholders. Like most other commercial enterprises, they usually aim to maximise profits. In theory, maximising profits requires that they should on-lend all the deposits they take at the highest rate possible; this might mean lending to the riskiest borrower for the longest period of time! However, in practice banks cannot neglect the safety of their deposits. Sound banking demands a fine balance, which *both* maximises safety for their depositors' funds and maximises dividends for their shareholders. Banks resolve the dilemma of safety versus profitability by maintaining a prudent liquidity cushion in the form of cash in tills, operational deposits with the central bank, loans to money markets on a call or short notice basis, first-class commercial bills, government short-dated bills and CDs issued by other banks and building societies. After the liquidity cushion portfolio is satisfactorily constructed, banks make advances. Making advances is traditionally a bank's major activity and the interest on them is its traditional source of profit. Banks may also buy long-term, fixed interest government securities, partly for security and partly because they produce a higher income than near-money assets and the possibility of capital gains.

▌ Useful applied material

M0 includes notes and coins and the operating balances held by banks with the Bank of England. Other measures of money — M2, M4 (and liquidity outside M4) — include various types of deposits held by the public with banks and building societies, and other financial holdings with varying degrees of liquidity. Recent research in the Bank suggests that private sector *wealth* is a more important determinant of broad money holdings than are changes in people's incomes.

Even though targets are not set for broad money, the analysis of M4 trends plays an important part in the Bank's assessment of financial and economic developments. M4 can be analysed either in terms of its *components* — cash and deposits — or of its *counterparts*, which represent the other side of banks' and building societies' balance sheets (and must, as an accounting identity, total the same). These counterparts include banks' and building societies' lending to the M4 private sector and their transactions with the public sector and with overseas residents. Note that the exam questions frequently seek the counterpart analysis of changes in M4.

Counterparts of M4

A *change* in M4 equals:

(a) sterling lending by banks and building societies to the M4 private sector;
(b) *plus* the PSBR;
(c) *minus* public sector debt sales to the M4 private sector;
(d) *plus/minus* external flows (i.e. external finance of public sector debt and external transactions of banks and building societies);
(e) *minus* the change in sterling net non-deposit liabilities of banks and building societies (see p. 86: Answer 6).

▌ Factors which cause changes in the broad money supply (M4)

A very large proportion of the money supply in the UK is made up of bank and building society deposits. Therefore *anything* which affects these deposits affects the level of broad money supply. The following are the major influences which affect bank and building society deposits.

Lending by banks and building societies to the M4 private sector

Since every loan creates a deposit, therefore all sterling lending by banks and building societies to *this* sector increases money supply in its own right; at the same time, it enables especially banks to operate the credit creation multiplier, thereby increasing the money supply still further.

The Public Sector Borrowing Requirement (PSBR)

The UK public sector comprises the central and local governments and the public corporations (mainly nationalised industries). The total public sector expenditure includes spending on goods and services, interest payment on National Debt, grants to industry and financing of losses of nationalised industries. The total public sector receipts include tax revenue, repayment of grants, interest received, profits of nationalised industries and, more recently, the sale proceeds of the public sector assets, i.e. privatisation proceeds.

The levels of public sector expenditure and revenue, and any excess of expenditure over revenue are normally announced in the annual budget. The budget deficit, i.e. the excess of public sector expenditure over public sector revenue, is called the PSBR, and, as *committed* expenditure, it has to be financed almost at once by borrowing by the central government.

The PSBR can be financed from the following *four* main sources, and it makes a great deal of difference to the growth of the money supply from which source the PSBR is substantially financed.

Borrowing from the M4 private sector

This sector does not hold operational balances with the Bank of England, it holds sight deposits with banks and building societies. The government borrows from this sector by the sale of its securities: gilts, National Savings products, etc. The large institutions in this sector (e.g. pension funds, insurance companies) and individuals purchase government securities by sending their cheques, drawn on their deposits with banks and building societies, to the Bank of England. The payments by this sector for its purchases of public sector debt will reduce the deposits of banks and building societies; i.e. the money supply will be decreased by the same amount that the public sector spending will increase it. Hence the level of money supply will change little.

Borrowing from the UK bank and building society sector

When this sector lends to the public sector, either directly or by the purchase of government securities, then its operational deposits with the Bank of England decrease by the same amount as its holdings of claims against the government increase. Hence, at this point, no change occurs in the money supply. However, as the borrowed sum is spent by the public sector, it creates new bank and building society deposits, *without* any offsetting leakage; therefore the money supply *increases*; and it will increase further, as a second round effect, when this sector pivots the credit creation multiplier on its new deposits.

Borrowing from the Bank of England

This is an orthodox way of financing the PSBR. Sales of government debt to the Bank will *increase* the money supply, because when the sums borrowed are spent by the government the high-powered money deposits of banks and building societies will increase and that will, of course, enable the credit creation multiplier to be operated and for the money supply to *increase*.

Sales of government securities to overseas residents

If overseas residents already hold sterling deposits with banks and building societies in the UK, then the money supply will *not increase* directly: overseas residents' sterling deposits are not included in M4. If sterling was held overseas then there would be a *secondary expansion* as the credit creation base of banks and building societies is increased.

The stance of the UK monetary policy

The stance of the monetary policy (see Ch. 7) has a bearing on the banks' and building societies' ability to lend and create deposits. If the monetary policy is *contractionary* (i.e. aims at making money more expensive and difficult to obtain), it may require banks and building societies to keep a cash-to-deposit ratio, and may also place qualitative (lending priorities) and quantitative (lending and interest rate ceilings) restraints on the banks' and building societies' lending activities which will *reduce* the money supply, unless the banks and building societies are able to obtain reserve funds from uncontrolled sources and can find ways of lending without transgressing the official requirements. An *expansionary* policy, on the other hand, by making money cheaper (lower interest rates) and easier to obtain (no constraints on bank and building society lending), *increases* money supply.

Financing the external account balances

The official financing of the balance of payments *deficit* or surplus (see Ch. 8) affects the money supply figures. Financing a deficit broadly means that money is leaving the country, hence causing a *reduction* in the money supply. Conversely, financing a balance of payments *surplus* broadly implies that money is coming in which, when spent, will increase the bank and building society deposits and therefore will *increase* the money supply.

Increase in banks' and building societies' non-deposit liabilities

These liabilities include their share capital and reserves. The net non-deposit liabilities of a bank or building society equal the total of its capital and reserves *minus* its land, buildings, capital equipment and the like. Since in any balance sheet, liabilities and assets must always be equal, an *increase* in the net non-deposit liabilities, e.g. increase in reserves, of banks and building societies reduces their deposit liabilities, and that *reduces* money supply.

Investment returns overseas

If the returns from overseas investments are perceived to be higher than those available in the UK, some deposit holders in the UK may be encouraged to invest overseas. This may cause a semi-permanent *reduction* in money supply until the interest rates offered in the UK become competitive with overseas rates.

Bank and building society lending to overseas sector

If money lent overseas finds its way into the UK private sector's sterling deposits, the money supply will *increase*. If it stays overseas the money supply will *decrease*.

Overfunding

Sales of government debt to the non-bank and non-building society sector in *excess* of the PSBR will reduce the deposits of banks and building societies, and that will *decrease* the money supply.

Privatisation

The net revenue from the sales of public sector assets *reduces* (not finances) the PSBR, and consequently the money supply may be reduced. Privatisation proceeds have, however, distorted the value of the PSBR as a statistic.

▋ Changes in money supply and banks' balance sheets

The connection between changes in money supply and banks' liabilities and assets is of considerable significance and must be clearly understood.

A large proportion of increases in sterling bank lending (banks' assets) ends, in due course, in the sterling deposits with the banks (banks' liabilities). This provides the banking system with a larger deposit base upon which to pivot the banking multiplier which increases bank deposits even further. Since the sterling bank deposits of the UK non-bank private sector are included in the broad monetary aggregates, increases in sterling bank deposits increase the broad money supply.

As the bank lending increases, banks hold larger amounts in their tills and in operational balances with the Bank of England. Since both these banks' assets are included in the narrow money aggregate M0, an increase in bank lending increases the narrow money supply too.

Thus the policy implications of the above analysis are that if the authorities wish to control the narrow and broad money aggregates, they must find effective means to control the growth of sterling deposits held with the UK banks by the UK non-bank private sector.

▋ Recent examination questions

The following six questions should give you an idea of the types of questions that may be set on the 'Money Supply' section of the MFS syllabus. First try to identify from the text the main points you would use to answer these questions. Then spend ten minutes or so planning your answer to each question before turning to the section on 'outline answers' below.

Question 1

Outline the main ways in which a government can finance a budget deficit. How might the need to finance a rising deficit affect commercial banks?

Question 2

Discuss in detail the main factors which cause changes in the money stock.

Question 3

Explain in detail how an increase in government borrowing influences:

(a) the money supply;
(b) conditions in the money markets.

Question 4

What effects do changes in a country's money stock have on its commercial banks?

Question 5

(a) What is meant by the term 'Public Sector Borrowing Requirement' (PSBR)?
(b) Assuming the PSBR is zero, discuss the factors which could generate an increase in a country's money supply.
(c) Can the credit creation process be carried on indefinitely?

Question 6

(a) Define the measure of money supply known in the UK as M4.
(b) Discuss in detail the main factors which cause M4 to grow.

■ Outline answers

Answer 1

(a) Budget deficit may be financed by borrowing from:
    (i) the M4 private sector (issue of notes and coins, marketable debt, non-marketable debt);
    (ii) the banking and building society sector (sale of short-dated marketable debt);
    (iii) the central bank (against the issue of new gilt-edged securities);
    (iv) the overseas sector (direct currency borrowing, sale of government debt).
(b) Effects on commercial banks of:
    (i) borrowing from the M4 private sector and/or overseas residents with bank deposits outside the UK: deposits of the banking system will fall first (temporary reduction in liquidity), then restored after the government spends the borrowed money;
    (ii) sales of additional debt to the banking and building society system together with the government spending the borrowed funds: banks' liquidity increases and so does their potential for lending;
    (iii) rising budget deficit creates competition for the available funds, which raises interest rates, affecting the banks' lending and profits.

Answer 2

(a) *Increase in PSBR* increases money supply, unless funded by the sales of government securities to the M4 private sector.
(b) *Increase in bank and building society lending to the private sector* will increase money supply, and vice versa.
(c) *A deficit in the balance of payments* broadly reduces money supply (money flowing out) and a *surplus* increases money supply (money flowing in).
(d) *Overfunding* will decrease the money supply.

Changes in interest rates, quantitative and qualitative controls and reserve ratios will influence bank lending, which will affect money supply.

Answer 3

(a) If the government borrows from the:
  (i) banking and building society system – money supply will increase;
  (ii) M4 private sector and overseas in foreign currency – money supply will change very little.
(b) If borrowing is from:
  (i) bank and building society sector – liquidity will increase and put a downward pressure on very short-term interest rates;
  (ii) M4 private sector – the liquidity effect is neutralised, and the operational balances of banks with the Bank of England are first reduced, and then increased by the same amount.

Beware the common fault: government borrowing does not *automatically* mean higher interest rates. An increase in PSBR means that money supply goes up and, in the first instance at least, interest rates will *fall*.

Answer 4

Bank deposits are a major part of the money stock.

(a) Increase in the money stock will increase bank deposits.
(b) Increased deposits enables increased lending; increase in profitability of retail banks (no change in interest rate is assumed).
(c) Profitability of wholesale banks will fall as margins of bid and offered interest rates narrow.
(d) Increase in the money stock may lead to economic growth (if there is spare capacity) and a consequent increase in consumer spending.
(e) Increase in consumer spending and imports provides an opportunity for increased bank lending and services.
(f) If the increase in the money stock is excessive, then interest rates may fall and diminish retail banks' profits.
(g) If the money stock decreases, the above effects will be reversed.

Answer 5

(a) PSBR = total public sector expenditure *minus* total public sector receipts. PSBR must be financed by borrowing.

(b) (i) If PSBR is zero, money supply will still grow as a result of:
  - bank and building society lending to the M4 private sector;
  - net external inflows;
  - underfunding;
  - decrease in non-deposit liability of banks and building societies.

  (ii) Extra lending by banks and building societies is the most important contribution to money supply growth.

  (iii) The ability of banks and building societies to create money means that the authorities often take steps to restrain bank lending.

  (iv) External flows: bank and building society lending in sterling to the overseas sector: money supply will increase if the money lent is spent in the UK;
  - current account position: surplus increases money supply, deficit decreases it.

(c) Factors which restrict the credit creation process by banks and building societies:
  (i) a proportion of their assets must be kept liquid or near liquid;
  (ii) there may be leakages from the system (e.g. internal, into gilts; external, overseas);
  (iii) insufficient demand for loans by M4 private sector (e.g. due to recession);
  (iv) restriction on lending may be imposed by the authorities.

Answer 6

(a) M4 essentially consists of notes and coins in circulation with the public and M4 private sector's holdings of:
  (i) sterling sight and time deposits with banks;
  (ii) sterling CDs issued by banks and building societies;
  (iii) building society shares and deposits.

(b) The *counterparts* analysis shows that:
  a *rise* in M4 equals PSBR
  less public debt sales to non-bank non-building society sector (M4 private sector)
  plus bank and building society lending to the M4 private sector
  plus/minus external flows
  minus increase in sterling non-deposit liabilities of banks and building societies.
    The above analysis makes the following likely:
  (i) M4 will grow to the extent the PSBR is financed by public debt sales to banks, building societies and the Bank of England.

  (ii) The creation of deposits via the credit multiplier through bank and building society lending is an important potential contribution to M4 growth, which is significantly influenced by the interest-rate policy; lower interest rates tend to generate a larger growth in M4.

  (iii) M4 can grow as a result of external flows, e.g. government borrowing in sterling held overseas by overseas residents; current account surplus. Again, the interest policy will bear on the extent of M4 growth.

  (iv) A decrease in sterling non-deposit liabilities of banks and building societies will cause M4 to grow.

▌ A tutor's answer

The following question deals with various aspects of money supply. The specimen answer is intended to help you establish the scope of the question, so that you write relevant information when faced with similar questions in an examination.

Question

Define the measure of money supply in the UK known as M4. Explain how M4 would be directly affected by each of the following:

(a) Increased sales of gilt-edged securities by the Bank of England.
(b) The payment by companies of value-added tax.
(c) An increase in sterling bank lending to the overseas sector.

Answer plan

(a) Briefly define M4 and state its components (PSBR funding irrelevant here).
   (i) Who purchases? Only the direct effects of purchases asked.
   (ii) Are current accounts of companies reduced?
   (iii) Are there matched increases in lending and deposits?
(b) Explain only the direct effects; avoid second-round effects.
(c) Keep asking: does a direct effect cause changes in the *components* of M4?
(d) *Stop* once the effects are technically and correctly explained.

Specimen answer

M4 is an official monetary aggregate in the UK which measures the 'broad' money in the country. It comprises 'real' money (immediate purchasing power) *plus* 'near' money (real money, once removed).

   The Bank of England definition of the M4 aggregate includes the following components:

(a) notes and coins in circulation with the public,
(b) *plus* M4 private sector interest-bearing and non-interest bearing (sight) sterling bank and building society deposits,
(c) *plus* M4 private sector sterling time bank and building society deposits,
(d) *plus* M4 private sector holdings of bank certificates of deposit,
(e) *plus* M4 private sector holdings of building society shares and deposits and sterling certificates of deposit,
(f) *less* building society holdings of bank deposits and bank certificates of deposit, and notes and coins.

Public sector sterling bank and building society deposits are excluded from M4's composition because such deposits are both small and unlikely to influence economic behaviour.

(a) The *direct* effect on M4 of an increase in sales of gilt-edged securities by the Bank of England (these sales are *not* meant to finance a PSBR) will depend upon who purchases them. If the purchasers are the UK *M4 private sector*, then M4 will be reduced. This will happen because when the M4 private sector make payment to the Bank of England for their security purchases, they will draw cheques on their sight deposits with banks and building societies. This will reduce the private sector's non-interest bearing sterling sight deposits with banks and building societies. This, in turn, will reduce M4 because these deposits are a component of M4. If the *banking and building society sector* purchases the gilt-edged securities, then there will be no change in M4. The reason for this is two-fold:
   (i) Banking and building society sector purchases of securities reduce the operational

deposits of the banking and building society sector with the Bank of England; but the banking and building society sector's operational deposits *are not* a component of M4.

(ii) Bank and building society sector purchases of securities do not affect the bank and building society deposits of the UK *M4* private sector, which *are* a component of M4. The purchases of gilt-edged securities by *overseas residents* will reduce their sterling sight deposits with banks and building societies, but these deposits are not included in the components of M4. Hence M4 will not be affected.

(b) If the companies pay VAT by drawing cheques on the credit balances in their sterling sight deposits with banks and building societies, then M4 will be reduced: 'companies' are a part of the UK M4 private sector, and UK M4 private sector sterling sight deposits with banks and building societies are a component of M4. However, if the companies paid their VAT bill by increasing bank and building society borrowing, say, by overdrawing their sterling sight deposits with banks and building societies, then M4 will remain unaffected; the increase in bank and building society lending is offset by a reduction in bank and building society operational deposits, so that sterling deposits remain the same.

(c) An increase in sterling lending to the overseas sector has the same effect as any bank and building society lending, i.e. a rise in bank and building society deposits. If a rise in bank and building society deposits is 'matched' by an increase in the sterling deposits of overseas residents, then M4 will be unaffected, simply because overseas residents' deposits are not a part of M4. If, however, the overseas residents have increased sterling borrowing in order to meet their commitments to the UK non-bank and non-building society public, say, in respect of export credits, or the purchase of a business, then the UK private sector sterling deposits with the banks and building societies will increase, and so will M4.

▌A step further

Once again, as with 'Money', your best source for money supply figures and definitional changes is the *BEQB*. Articles on money supply matters appear often in the quality newspapers, *Signpost* articles in *Banking World* and in the *Updating Notes* and *Examiners' Reports* (published by the Chartered Institute of Bankers); these are of extreme importance not only to keep abreast of the latest changes in the topic of money supply, but also to see an analysis of the reasons for, and the expected effects of, such changes. More important than the statistics of money supply are the *principles* underlying the concept of money supply.

The recent change in broad money definitions was discussed in a *Signpost* article in the January/February 1990 issue of *Banking World*.

CHAPTER 6

Interest Rates

Syllabus requirements
- The determinants of:
  (i) the general level, and
  (ii) the pattern of the interest rates.
- The role of interest rates.
- The significance of LIBOR, overnight rates, base rates.
- The term structure of interest rates.
- The distinction between 'real' and 'nominal' interest rates.
- The relationship between domestic and international interest rates and exchange rate.

▮ Getting started

In money using economies, money creates claims because it is an asset, a store of value, as well as a means of exchange. Therefore those who lend money expect to be recompensed for handing over their claims for the period of the loan to those who borrow money. The recompense is the interest rate. It is expressed as a rate per cent per annum because it is a convenient way of calculating and comparing the cost of borrowing money. Thus one commonly used definition of the interest rate is that it is a 'price' at which money is lent and borrowed.

Borrowers borrow money because they are short of funds to meet their current needs for goods and services, whereas lenders lend funds which are surplus to their current needs for goods and services. Therefore the interest rate can also be defined as the 'price' the lenders expect (and the borrowers pay) for exchanging current claims for greater future claims to goods and services.

In modern economies the principal lenders are often those at one stage removed, since most of their funds are obtained from others. Individuals lend to banks and other financial institutions by depositing their savings with them, or lend to businesses and the government by directly purchasing their securities and bonds. Banks on-lend much of their deposits to individuals, firms and countries as overdrafts and term loans. Building societies lend most of their accumulated deposits from the public to house buyers. Finance houses lend funds out of their accumulated borrowings to finance the hire purchase transactions of the public. Insurance companies collect premiums for various kinds of insurance policies they sell to the public, and then lend or invest significant proportions of their receipts in government and company securities. Firms use their surplus funds to make deposits with banks or to lend to the government by purchasing government debt or lend to other firms against their promises to repay. Governments borrow huge sums of money from anyone who is willing to purchase their securities, and in turn lend a portion of their borrowed funds to nationalised and other industries, to foreign governments and other borrowers. Virtually all of this lending and borrowing activity is linked by the receipt and payment of interest rates.

High interest rates encourage savings but may discourage investment. The cost of credit, which is dependent on the level of interest rates, significantly affects spending, exchange rates and economic activity of a country. The Bank of England uses its control over short-term interest rates to achieve monetary policy objectives.

∎ Essential principles and useful applied material

Determinants of changes in the general level of interest rates

Although no single theory of interest provides a complete explanation of the determination of the *level of interest rates*, yet the following points can be identified as influencing that level.

(a) *Real and nominal rates of interest*. The real rate can simply be defined as the nominal rate (the rate actually paid) *if* there is no inflation over the term of a loan. In the *long term* the real rate will be determined by the 'fundamental factors', such as: (i) the rate of return which the private sector borrowers hope to achieve when undertaking capital investment; and (ii) the attitude of lenders to foregoing spending today in favour of higher spending tomorrow. However, once inflation is introduced then other factors will also affect the long-term rate of interest, at least as regards the nominal rate: it must be high enough to yield an amount which (i) would compensate lenders for the *expected* fall in the value of money, and (ii) would compensate lenders for the uncertainty over the course of future inflation, i.e. a risk premium.

The major problem with this approach is that it is not possible exactly to allocate the split between nominal rate, real rate and the *expected* change in inflation rate.

To overcome this problem, the general practice is to deduct the *current* inflation rate, as measured by, say, the RPI over a given period from the *nominal* interest rate to arrive at the *real* rate. The real rate would be *positive* where the nominal rate exceeds inflation rate, and *negative* when the reverse is the case. This practice is fair enough for short-term rates but is misleading for long-term rates because it makes no allowance for the risk and uncertainty concerning the *expected* rate of inflation.

In the UK, with the introduction of index-linked gilt-edged securities, it is possible to measure the real rate with some precision on securities of different maturities. For instance, if the rate of return on long-term index-linked gilts is, say, 3.25 per cent, and the rate of return on similar non-index-linked securities is, say, 9 per cent, then after allowing for a premium for uncertainty (say 1.75 per cent) it could be estimated that over a period of twenty years the inflation rate would average around 4 per cent per annum.

Note: a fall in inflation, nominal rates unchanged, raises the real rates.

(b) *Government borrowing requirements*. A large increase in government borrowing to finance current spending will push up interest rates if there is no parallel increase in private sector savings. This will occur even with an inflation rate that is stationary.

This point has been well illustrated by the huge US budget deficit, which has attracted, via relatively higher US interest rates (until recently), much of the private savings of the free world and has pushed up real rates of interest around the world.

(c) *Term structure of interest rates*. When lenders/investors are uncertain about future interest rates they may wish to hedge their bets; this introduces a new dimension into interest rate calculations and gives rise to the *term structure* of interest rates. It makes sense for investors to attempt to arrange their portfolio of investments so that the *expected* return on a series of short-term investments during a certain period *equals* the return on long-term investment over that period. If short-term rates are *below* long-term rates, this broadly implies that short-term rates are expected to rise; and of course vice versa. However, since future rates cannot be predicted with absolute certainty, allowance has also to be made for a *risk premium*. Therefore both *inherent uncertainty* of future interest rates, and the investors' *own perception* of the risk involved in that uncertainty, will be important in determination of the level of interest rates.

(d) *Defence of exchange rate.* The authorities may counter any excessive downward pressure on the exchange rate, caused by a perceived weakness of the national currency, by deliberately raising the level of short-term rates. This will help attract large amounts of interest-sensitive, overseas short-term capital into the country, thereby helping ease the downward pressure by increasing the demand for the national currency.

(e) *Market expectations.* If the market believes that the authorities are succeeding in their counter-inflationary policies, and that a relaxed monetary policy is in the offing, then these expectations will help bring about a fall in the level of interest rates. For instance, lenders/investors will no longer seek such a high nominal interest rate to cushion them against future inflation. Of course, interest rates will tend to rise if market expectations are for a 'tighter' credit policy.

(f) *Supply and demand of loanable funds.* The level of interest rates will rise when the demand for loanable funds increases *relative to* the supply of loanable funds, and of course vice versa.

(g) *The level of interest rates overseas.* Provided there are no exchange controls, the level of other countries' interest rates, other things being equal, will affect the level of domestic interest rates (see (b) above).

Interest rates in the UK

In most countries the monetary authorities determine the level of short-term interest rates; in the UK the unique position of the Bank of England as lender of last resort to the banking system, almost exclusively through the discount houses, ensures its dominating influence on the determination of the level of short-term interest rates. It can raise or lower the *marginal cost of funds* to the banking system by raising or lowering its dealing rates in its OMOs relative to the prevailing money market rates. The Bank uses its dominance over short-term rates of interest: (a) to control changes in bank lending and therefore changes in money supply; (b) to curb inflationary pressures; and (c) to influence exchange rate movements. If the Bank chooses to raise the level of short-term rates, its activities will *override* any free market forces in the supply and demand of loanable funds, i.e. the short-term rates will be determined *administratively* and not by the market forces.

If the *short-term* rates are totally determined by the *monetary authorities*, and the *long-term* rates primarily by the *fundamental factors* relating to the real rate of interest and the expectations regarding future inflation, then there may still be a problem of reconciling the levels of short with long rates. For example, if the authorities *pushed up* the short rates, this could lead to less bank lending and a higher exchange rate, both of which could in turn lead to lower future inflation, and therefore *lower* long rates; but the theory of the *term structure* of interest rates suggests that a rise in short rates directly points to a rise in long rates in order to compensate long-term investors for the higher short rates currently available (see below).

Broadly speaking, it is true that any uncertainty surrounding future inflation and future interest rates will be *outweighed* by the movement of short rates, i.e. a rise in short rates will usually lead to a rise in long rates, though perhaps not to the same extent. Nevertheless there are times when short rates rise and long rates fall. This happened, for example, in the UK during the first three months of 1986; short rates rose but the long rates actually fell. The rise in short rates was administratively engineered in order to shore up the sharply falling exchange rate of the pound caused by the slump in oil prices. The fall in long rates was due to an improved inflation outlook (due to the fall in oil prices!) and to the market expectation that the rise in short rates would be temporary. Indeed, the short rate fell by mid-March 1986, and fell again later in 1986 and were lower than long rates. During 1989, long rates were generally lower than short rates (14 per cent), largely because the money markets accepted that the high short rates, after causing the inflation rate (over 8 per cent) to come down, would fall, i.e. the high short rates were temporary.

The level of *short rates* is therefore the *pivot* of the interest rate system. Other rates do not in general move too far from the level of short rates. Since the monetary authorities can totally control the level of short rates, it might appear that it is the monetary authorities who, directly or indirectly, determine the *general* level of interest rates, both short- and long-term rates. This is not entirely so. For instance, the sudden reduction in the Bank of England's money market dealing rates in April 1986, should have led to a reduction in long rates. However, due to the strong market expectation that long rates would not fall and might even rise, the long rates did not fall. The reason for this anomaly was the market expectation that the UK inflation rate would probably rise and a belief that UK interest rates would not remain out of line with overseas interest rates, which were themselves expected to rise. This anomaly illustrates the point that the monetary authorities' ability to engineer drastic changes in interest rates is largely limited to short-term rates.

The determinants of the *general level* of interest rates may be summarised as follows.

(a) The short-term interest rates are influenced by:
    (i) the stance of the short-term monetary policy objectives;
    (ii) the extent of credit creation by the financial institutions;
    (iii) the defence of the exchange rate by the authorities;
    (iv) the level of interest rates in other countries, provided there are no exchange controls, other things being equal.
(b) The longer term interest rates are influenced by:
    (i) the longer term stance of the monetary policy;
    (ii) the expected rate of domestic inflation;
    (iii) the market belief in the efficiency of the official anti-inflationary policy;
    (iv) the expected rate of return on investment at home and overseas.

Significance of the 'real' interest rate

Their importance relates to the following considerations:

(a) *The cost to corporate borrowers.* Positive real rates increase companies' costs by being higher than RPI. Negative real rates decrease their costs and encourage borrowing.
(b) *The attitude of lenders.* When the real rates are negative, i.e. when the nominal interest rate is lower than the current rate of inflation, lending is discouraged; it is encouraged when the real rates are positive.
(c) *The international comparisons.* Other things being equal, and assuming no exchange controls are in operation between countries, comparatively higher domestic real rates will encourage the inflow of overseas funds, which, in turn, will influence the domestic exchange rate and balance of payments position (see Chs 8 and 9).

∎ The way the Bank of England fixes short-term rates

You studied earlier how the Bank of England, while performing its lender of last resort role, ensured that the level of short-term rates was in line with the stance of monetary policy. Now you'll see once again in some detail how the mechanism functions, and this will strengthen your comprehension of this very important part of the syllabus.

The Bank of England as the central bank of the UK has aimed to keep the *short-term* (up to one month) interest rates within a narrow *unpublished* band, but to allow market forces in the money markets a greater role in determining the *longer-term* rates. This policy helps shape the structure of money market rates.

The control of the Bank over the very short-term rates is assured, for three main reasons:

1. It offsets, at its own terms, shortages (or surpluses) of liquidity in the money markets via the discount houses; in this way, it can control the marginal cost of funds to the banking system. In theory, the Bank is not expected to act as the lender of last resort to the banking system, yet in practice it does; it has to, for it cannot abdicate its responsibilities as the central bank!

2. In its open market operations, the Bank buys and sells eligible commercial bills and Treasury bills in the discount market in four bands, according to the maturity of the bills. The bands where the Bank's control is the strongest are Bands 1 and 2, i.e. bands in which bills have maturities of up to fourteen days and thirty-three days respectively. Bands 3 and 4 include bills with longer maturities; in these bands the Bank's direct influence is less strong. Changes in the Bank's dealing rate in Bands 1 and 2 are taken by the money markets to mean that the Bank intends to bring about a change in the marginal cost of funds and therefore in the general level of short-term money market rates. Clearly if the Bank makes short-term funds more expensive to the banking system, the banks in turn will charge more for overdrafts and short-term loans. Thus, despite the suspension (not abolition) of the Minimum Lending Rate (MLR) in August 1981, the Bank exerts the key influence on the level of short-term rates in the money markets. The interaction between the bill operations of the Bank and market expectations is the main determinant of the level and structure of short-term rates in the UK, and it plays an important part in determining long-term rates in the money markets.

3. Occasionally cash shortages can be relieved by direct lending to discount houses at the Bank's own lending rates. Also the Bank may enter into agreements of sale and repurchase of gilts (REPOS) at fixed rates and for fixed periods with the commercial banks to relieve liquidity shortage (during January and February, the tax-gathering season) and to influence the level of short rates and stabilisation.

With the more aggressive deposit-gathering stance of the building societies, the clearers have come to rely increasingly on funds from the money markets, e.g. wholesale deposits, in recent years. Still more recently, clearers have themselves been collecting higher interest bearing retail deposits. Therefore bank base rates will have broadly to move in line with the money market rates. In fact, after December 1973, the clearers even geared the advances made to certain corporate customers to market rates rather than to base rates. Using market rates such as the sterling London Inter-Bank Offered Rate (LIBOR) as the basis for setting interest rates on term lending is of benefit to the banks; it gives them the opportunity to match their lending rates and conditions with those for the wholesale deposits they obtain through the inter-bank market. Non-bank financial institutions, who, like banks, obtain wholesale funds, apply a similar criterion in on-lending for longer terms. Thus, although the Bank openly fixes the short-term rates, yet the direction given by it to short-term rates permeates right through the whole spectrum of interest rates in the monetary system.

∎ The effects of changes in the general level of interest rates on banks

The effects of a fall in interest rates

(a) It will reduce both the cost of funds acquired by banks and the interest received by them from advances. However, if the demand for advances is interest-elastic, the total advances might rise substantially; increased advances will create increased deposits in the banking system as a whole and may improve the banks' profitability.

(b) It will squeeze the net return (the 'endowment' effect) of the non-interest bearing deposits of the retail banks considerably, thus reducing their profitability. On the other hand, their profit margins on fixed-rate lending would be increased. Now that the banks, under competition from the building societies, have begun to offer some interest on current accounts, the endowment effect of the 'free money' has declined considerably.

(c) Building societies have been slow to reduce their interest rates on deposits; *banks* have been relatively quicker to reduce their deposit rates as the level of interest rates falls, and have therefore tended to lose retail deposits to building societies as interest rates fall.

(d) Banks might widen the margin between interest paid and interest received as their interest receipts fall, in order to maintain acceptable profitability margins, and might also increase service and commission charges.

(e) A fall in interest rates would increase the capital value of the banks' fixed interest investments; banks might realise the capital gains by selling some of these investments.

(f) The loan repayment burden of banks' customers is reduced when interest rates fall; therefore there will be fewer bad debts and the banks will probably reduce their bad debt provisions and thus release additional resources for lending.

(g) To ward off the adverse effect of falls in interest rates, banking groups may actively encourage lending at fixed rates via their subsidiaries, e.g. hire purchase companies.

The effects of a rise in interest rates

By and large, the effects on banks of a rise in interest rates would be exactly opposite to those of a fall in interest rates:

(a) Higher loan and deposit rates of the banks might suggest that their profit margins would remain unchanged, but for retail banks margins improve because of the endowment effect of non-interest bearing deposits (now reduced). On the other hand, their profit margins are reduced on fixed rate lending.

(b) Higher price of loans may reduce loan demand of the banks' business customers; although in practice necessity overcomes price, at least in the short term. The demand for loans for capital goods, and more particularly working capital, tends to be interest-inelastic, and therefore, provided that profit margins are maintained, the loan demand for capital goods by the banks' private sector business customers is unlikely to change. The same is true of public sector investment expenditure.

(c) Banks are in competition with non-bank financial institutions, chiefly building societies, National Savings and the government, for the savings and deposits of the public.

Whether the banks' deposit inflow would increase or decrease would largely depend upon how well the banks' interest rate structure compared with that of the other financial institutions and with that offered on government securities. Apart from the banks' large and sophisticated corporate depositors, most of the other depositors tend to be sluggish in switching their deposits between financial institutions.

(d) High interest rates tend to depress the economy by depressing demand in certain sectors of the economy, e.g. in the consumer goods industry. The more the economy becomes depressed, the lower are profits and the greater becomes the significance of the interest rate bills for business firms; this may lead to more bad debts for the banks (as has been the case since 1989), who would probably have to increase their bad debt provisions, which reduces their profitability.

(e) Relatively higher rates in the UK would tend to act as a magnet for large short-term capital flows from abroad and this would raise the exchange rate of the pound. It would benefit the UK's currency inflows under floating exchange rates provided overseas rates remained unchanged. However, interest payable on foreign capital would eventually produce an increase in net currency outflows on invisible account (see Ch. 8). The rise in the exchange rate would reduce the sterling value of overseas residents' deposits and of the earnings of the overseas subsidiaries of the UK parent banks, thus reducing their profitability. A higher exchange rate would also reduce the competitiveness of UK exports and import substitutes, tending further to depress the economy as in (d) above.

▮ Banks' base rates

The clearing and other deposit-taking commercial banks cater for the major proportion of the borrowing needs of the public, other than house purchase. Although the rates payable by customers are a matter for negotiation, most lending banks quote a 'base rate' and grant overdrafts at a fixed margin over this rate.

There are three main determinants of the banks' base rates:

1. Marginal cost of raising funds in the inter-bank and CDs markets (the wholesale markets). The shorter-term market rates (overnight or seven-day rates) are more volatile and fluctuate daily and sometimes several times during a day. The three-month money market rates are more stable, and banks use them for setting their base rates. Small day-to-day fluctuations in the three-month rate do not trigger base rate changes. Banks usually charge their blue-chip customers base rate *plus* 1 per cent for loans and overdrafts, but for personal customers the rates charged can range from 3 per cent to 8 per cent over the base rate, depending upon the credit rating of the borrowers.

2. When the more volatile shorter term market rates and the banks' base rate move sufficiently apart, banks' corporate customers can take the 'arbitrage' profits, i.e. they borrow cheaply from their banks and on-lend at a higher rate in the wholesale markets, or make 'round-tripping' gains by borrowing to their overdraft limits and then on-lending the borrowed funds back to the banks at higher market rates. Arbitrage has led to the growth in LIBOR-linked lending by the banks, which causes the base rates to change much more quickly. LIBOR-linked lending enables banks to match their lending rates and conditions with those under which they themselves borrow wholesale funds.

3. The Bank of England can, through its OMOs, influence the level of short-term rates

in the money markets. If the bank causes market rates to move by as much as 0.5 per cent then banks' base rates will usually move in line.

▌ The pattern of interest rates

Although many of the interest theories assume that there is *one* rate of interest, which moves up or down, this is, in reality, both incorrect and misleading. You have only to look at the daily, and especially the weekend, newspapers to notice the wide pattern of interest rates. For example, the sterling money rates prevailing in London are shown in Table 6.1. The three most important sets of rates are those under 'Interbank', 'Bank Bills' and 'Sterling CDs'. The double-barrelled quotation of rates (in some newspapers) displays the spread between the bid (deposit) and offered (lending) rates. Where there is a single rate, it is the offered rate.

The existence of so many interest rates broadly reflects variations in the risk, supply and demand considerations, expectations of future rates, needs of investors and borrowers, credit rating of borrowers and maturity of loans. Lenders are willing to accept lower interest rates from those borrowers who minimise lending risks.

The lending risks

The *lending risks* may take the following forms:

(a) *The risk of default.* The borrower may become unable to repay the loan. For this reason, for three-month money, Treasury bills (government IOUs) are considered safer by lenders than, say, bank deposits; therefore Treasury bills offer a slightly lower rate of return than do bank deposits. Similarly, banks offer a slightly lower interest on savings deposits than do finance houses. Borrowers' credit-rating is crucial.

(b) *The loss of liquidity.* That is, how quickly, conveniently, and without significant loss in income and/or capital value the lender can convert his lending (e.g. bond, bank and building society deposits, share certificates) into cash. The longer the loss of liquidity, the higher normally will be the rate of return. For example, banks offer a higher rate on *term deposits* than on *seven-day deposits*, and building societies offer higher returns on *deposits* which have a *penalty clause* for immediate withdrawals than for *normal share deposits*. The concern with the liquidity aspect of lending is reflected in the preference of lenders for relatively short-term lending. However, money is borrowed, especially by business firms, for relatively long periods of time. Consequently there is a greater supply of short-term funds, but a greater demand for long-term borrowing; hence, short-term lending usually earns a lower rate of interest, and borrowers wanting longer term loans have to offer higher rates to overcome the lenders' reluctance to part with liquidity for longer periods.

(c) *Fall in market value.* The market value of the asset held by the lender may fall. A major reason for this lending risk, especially for fixed interest lending, is rapidly rising inflation. In times of a rising inflation rate, the longer the maturity period of a loan, the greater the lending risk. Therefore in such times lenders expect to receive a rate of interest which is higher than the *expected* rate of inflation; or alternatively that their lending should be index-linked; index-linked securities yield positive, real rates.

(d) *Capital loss considerations.* Suppose that the general level of interest rates is 10 per cent per annum, but that it is expected to rise. An investor buying a £100 bond with

Table 6.1 London money rates

March 26	Overnight	7 days' notice	1 month	3 months	6 months	1 year
Inter-bank offer	$7\frac{1}{4}$	$6\frac{1}{8}$	6	6	$5\frac{7}{8}$	$5\frac{7}{8}$
Inter-bank bid	5	$5\frac{3}{4}$	$5\frac{7}{8}$	$5\frac{7}{8}$	$5\frac{3}{4}$	$5\frac{3}{4}$
Sterling CDs	–	–	$5\frac{15}{16}$	$5\frac{27}{32}$	$5\frac{27}{32}$	$5\frac{27}{32}$
Local authority deposits	$5\frac{3}{4}$	$5\frac{7}{8}$	$5\frac{7}{8}$	$5\frac{7}{8}$	$5\frac{3}{4}$	$5\frac{3}{4}$
Local authority bonds	–	–	–	–	–	–
Discount market deposits	$6\frac{1}{2}$	6	–	–	–	–
Company deposits	–	–	–	–	–	–
Finance house deposits	–	–	$5\frac{7}{8}$	$5\frac{7}{8}$	$5\frac{27}{32}$	$5\frac{25}{32}$
Treasury bills (buy)	–	–	$5\frac{9}{16}$	$5\frac{1}{4}$	$5\frac{1}{4}$	–
Bank bills (buy)	–	–	$5\frac{11}{16}$	$5\frac{5}{8}$	$5\frac{1}{2}$	–
Fine trade bills (buy)	–	–	–	–	–	–
Dollar CDs	–	–	3.01	3.06	3.17	3.39
SDR-linked deposit offer	–	–	$4\frac{7}{16}$	$4\frac{7}{16}$	$4\frac{3}{8}$	$4\frac{3}{8}$
SDR-linked deposit bid	–	–	$4\frac{5}{16}$	$4\frac{5}{16}$	$4\frac{1}{2}$	$4\frac{1}{4}$
ECU-linked deposit offer	–	–	$7\frac{15}{16}$	$7\frac{5}{8}$	$7\frac{1}{4}$	$6\frac{11}{16}$
ECU-linked deposit bid	–	–	$7\frac{11}{16}$	$7\frac{3}{8}$	7	$6\frac{7}{16}$

Note: London clearing banks' base lending rate: 6% since January 1993.
Note how rates vary, both between markets and over different periods.
Source: *Financial Times*, 9 July 1993.

a 10 per cent per annum yield will expect to receive £10 every year until the bond matures for repayment. Suppose, later on, that the general level of interest rates rises to 20 per cent per annum; this will cause the *market price* of the 10 per cent per annum bond to fall to £50: because an investor investing £100 in 20 per cent per annum bond will earn £20 per year. An expected (or actual) rise in interest rates means a fall in the market price of fixed interest lending, i.e. a capital loss or depreciation; conversely, an expected (or actual) fall in interest rates will cause the market price of fixed interest lending to rise, i.e. it will benefit from a capital gain or appreciation. Therefore if investors expect interest rates to rise in the future, they will require higher rates than currently available to compensate for the probable capital loss.

Lenders may, however, be willing to accept a lower rate of interest for longer term lending if they strongly expect a substantial *fall* in the general level of interest rates, in the hope of making a gain on the capital value of their lending.

The current and future tax positions, therefore investment needs, of lenders/investors also influence acceptable interest rates.

∎ The term structure of interest rates

This means the level of short- and long-term rates and the relationship between them. This relationship can be seen in the movements of the normal money market curve, i.e. the *yield curve* (Fig. 6.1). A yield curve is the relationship between yields on *similar* financial assets with *different* terms to maturity. Its steepness shows that generally the *longer* the term to maturity, the *higher the yield, because lenders require a larger compensation for a more sustained loss of liquidity, a higher lending risk and greater uncertainty.*

Yield curve 1 is the normal money market yield curve, which slopes upwards signifying that, other things being equal, lenders lending for longer terms require larger compensation for longer loss of liquidity, higher lending risks and greater uncertainty. They are *not* expecting any future interest rate changes.

The 'other things being equal' assumption is upset, chiefly, by the role of *expectations*. If the expectation of the majority of lenders is that the future rates will *fall*, then long rates will be below short rates, as shown by **yield curve 2**; here the long rates will tend to approximate to the *average* of expected future rates, as shown in the example below.

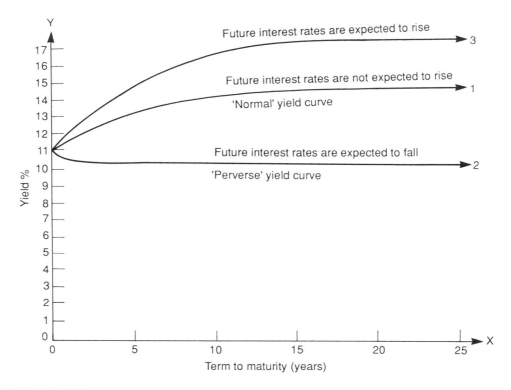

Fig. 6.1 Yield curves

Suppose the current market rate is 11 per cent per annum, but is expected to fall over the year as follows: after three months to 10.5 per cent p.a., after six months to 10 per cent p.a. and after nine months to 9.5 per cent p.a. A bank makes a loan of £500,000 to a business customer for one year. What rate per annum should the bank charge to the customer, taking into account the expected fall in rates over the year? The following schedule shows the bank's interest earnings for each quarter, during the year (compound interest considerations which would be relevant in an actual case of this kind, are ignored, to keep the calculations straightforward).

Interest earned for the first quarter:
$$= \frac{£500,000 \times 0.25 \times 11}{100} = £13,750.$$

Interest earned for the second quarter:
$$= \frac{£500,000 \times 0.25 \times 10.5}{100} = £13,125.$$

Interest earned for the third quarter:

$$= \frac{£500,000 \times 0.25 \times 10}{100} = £12,500.$$

Interest earned for the fourth quarter:

$$= \frac{£500,000 \times 0.25 \times 9.5}{100} = £11,875.$$

Total interest earned for the whole year = £51,250.

The average of the four short-term rates:

$$= \frac{11 + 10.5 + 10 + 9.5}{4} = 10.25 \text{ per cent.}$$

The bank will charge a rate of 10.25 per cent per annum to the customer. Thus, although the current short rate (three months) is 11 per cent per annum, the longer rate (one year) is lower at 10.25 per cent per annum; this is because future interest rates are expected to fall over the year. If, after one year, future interest rates are expected to stabilise at 10.25 per cent, then the yield curve will become horizontal at 10.25 per cent, as in yield curve 2.

If current short rates are higher than long rates, this could be due to several reasons:

(a) Future interest rates are expected to fall.
(b) The high short rates are expected to be temporary; perhaps the need of banks and other financial institutions for funds to balance their books at the end of each financial year and half-year has pushed short rates up temporarily.
(c) The monetary authorities have raised short-term rates in response to general economic developments; e.g. to control inflation, or to deal with a downward pressure on the exchange rate, the authorities may deliberately raise short-term rates temporarily, in order to encourage the inflow of short-term currency flows and to discourage the outflow of funds.
(d) The belief that the authorities will succeed in curbing inflation soon, hence the expectation that a relaxed monetary policy, with lower interest rates, will follow.

Yield curve 3 reflects a situation in which the expectation of the majority of lenders is that interest rates will *rise*, and therefore the capital value of lending will fall; hence long rates will be much higher than short rates to compensate both for the lengthier loss of liquidity as well as the possible capital loss.

In Fig 6.1, the gradients of the three yield curves flatten out and become parallel to the X axis. The reason for this is that the uncertainty element in the minds of lenders/investors becomes the same for a loan maturity of twenty years as for a loan maturity of, say, twenty-five years. Therefore the interest rate for the two maturities will probably be the same. After very long periods the length of the term loses its effect on interest rates.

To maximise the returns from lending, lenders will, other things being equal, switch between longer and shorter loans/bonds according to their expected yields over the period for which they wish to lend. There is no further gain to be made by such switching when the yield on long loans is equal to the average of the expected yields on short loans during the period in question (as shown by the above calculations). If lenders then begin to expect a rise in future rates, they would prefer to lend short term so that on maturity they may lend the repayments at higher rates. Conversely, if they begin to expect future rates to fall, they would prefer to lend long at fixed rates in order to make capital gains as the level of interest rates falls.

While the short-term interest rates in the UK rose sharply during 1989 (to 14 per cent), longer term rates increased much less. As a result the yield curve had been downward sloping for most of 1989, and later into the 1990s, reflecting the expectation that short-term rates would not stay high for too long.

∎ The patterns of interest rates in the UK

The following factors can be identified as affecting the various individual interest rates which together constitute the general pattern of interest rates *in the UK*:

(a) In the case of long-term gilt-edged securities, it is their respective supply and demand which strongly influence the interest rates offered by the authorities. The supply of these securities is linked to the government's borrowing requirements and to the nature of the monetary policy in terms of 'funding', i.e. the extent to which a given PSBR is being supported by long-term borrowing as opposed to short-term borrowing. A large increase in the issue of long gilts tends to raise the level of long rates to induce investors to take up the extra stock. Conversely, if the monetary policy is to bring down the long rates, the government will refrain from issuing long-term gilts.

(b) Lending to the government can be regarded as being free of the risk of default as compared with long-term lending to private sector companies. Therefore private sector companies must offer a higher rate than that available from gilt stocks to compensate lenders for the higher default risk.

(c) When there is a cash shortage in the money market, the discount houses offer eligible bills for sale to the Bank of England. The rate at which the Bank purchases them sets the pattern of short-term rates in the UK. Sometimes, when the cash shortages are very large (e.g. during January and February, the tax gathering season), the quantity of eligible bills the discount houses can offer for sale may be insufficient fully to relieve the shortages. This may require the Bank to enter into purchase and resale (REPOS) agreements of certain financial assets of the commercial banks directly. The cost of the purchase and resale agreements will affect the level and pattern of the UK interest rates.

The authorities do not, as a rule, intervene directly in the money markets, and the money market rates, especially the *inter-bank* rates, can sometimes depart from the Bank's dealing rates. The main driving force for the level of inter-bank rates tends to be expectations over the future course of interest rates. Thus if the three-months inter-bank rates rise above the Bank's dealing rates, it will be expected that the Bank will sooner or later have to raise its own dealing rates. Nevertheless, it is the Bank of England that is the predominant influence over the level of short-term rates, for reasons discussed earlier.

(d) The bank base rates are pitched at a level broadly equal to the marginal cost of funds (as determined by the Bank's dealing rates); this cost generally corresponds to the three-month rate prevailing in the inter-bank market, i.e. three-month LIBOR, because it is more stable than the overnight and seven-day rates.

The level of the banks' retail deposit rates offered to depositors is traditionally set below the money market rates. This allows a margin for covering the cost of running large branch networks and for covering the higher administrative cost of raising relatively small retail deposits compared with raising large wholesale deposits in the money markets.

The level of banks' retail lending rate charged to customers is linked to the banks' base rates, and makes an allowance for banks' profit margins or for the riskiness of the borrowers.

(e) The main competitors of the banks for retail deposits are the building societies. The behaviour of building society interest rates is broadly determined by the demand for mortgages and the supply of retail deposits. Unlike banks, building societies were, until recently, unable to raise cheaper wholesale funds in the money markets. Therefore the building societies have tended to pay rather more for retail deposits than the banks, causing the banks' share of retail deposits to decline steadily over the years. The banks have therefore had to depend increasingly on wholesale deposits in the money markets, especially in the inter-bank and CDs markets.

Since 1985, however, the competitive situation between the banks and the building societies has changed dramatically, in at least two respects:

1. *Both* the banks and the building societies now pay interest to depositors 'gross'; this exposed further the banks' relatively poor retail rates of interest compared with building society rates. To redress the balance the banks responded aggressively by introducing very competitive 'high interest rate' deposit accounts.

2. The building societies, like the banks, are now able to borrow cheaper wholesale funds, subject to a ceiling of 40 per cent, on the money markets. Also they can provide, in competition with the banks, up to £15,000 of unsecured consumer finance. Therefore it is the level of *money market rates* which should now impose the limits on the rates of interest that both the banks and the building societies will pay for retail deposits, but with two *qualifications*. First, the retail deposit taking institutions, e.g. banks, building societies, finance houses, unit and investment trusts, might be willing to pay more to ensure a stable retail deposit base, in preference to being too dependent on the more volatile money market wholesale funds. Second, these institutions might accept the payment of high retail deposit interest rates in the hope of a profitable trade-off in terms of selling other financial services. This element of cross-subsidy is especially significant in the context of those current accounts on which interest is not paid, but where free banking can be enjoyed in lieu of interest.

The trend of the pattern of interest rates, due to increasing innovation and competition in the financial system, is towards a narrowing of interest rate differentials among the various financial institutions; retail deposit rates are now moving up towards wholesale rates; even the growth of free banking is a move towards narrower interest rate differentials as the current account holder is getting the equivalent of a higher rate of interest.

Retail borrowing rates are subject to similar competitive forces; these rates generally reflect three *additions*, over and above the cost of funds: (1) a margin which covers the administrative costs, *plus* (2) a margin which allows for risk, *plus* (3) a profit margin. The banks have reduced the rates they charge on endowment mortgages, thus bringing these rates closer to the rates charged by building societies.

∎ Recent examination questions

The following six questions give an indication of the types of questions you will need to answer on interest rates. You could usefully spend ten minutes or so on each question, trying to identify the main points you would use in your answer, before turning to the outline answers below.

Question 1

(a) What is meant by the term 'yield curve'?
(b) Examine:
  (i) the factors which, in normal conditions, produce higher rates of long-term rather than short-term maturities;
  (ii) the relationship between short-term interbank rates and commercial bank lending rates.

Question 2

(a) Why and how does the Bank of England intervene in the money markets?
(b) Discuss the view that the level of mortgage rates is primarily determined by the rates at which the Bank of England deals in fourteen-day bills of exchange in the money market.

Question 3

Discuss the factors which affect the level and pattern of money market interest rates in the UK. To what extent do changes in money market rates lead to changes in commercial banks' base rates?

Question 4

Analyse the effects of a rise in a country's interest rates on:

(a) the personal sector;
(b) the corporate sector;
(c) the commercial bank;
(d) the capital account of the balance of payments.

Question 5

(a) What is meant by 'real' rates of interest and how are they calculated?
(b) Why have real rates remained high in most major economies for the greater part of this decade (the 1980s)?

Question 6

Why, in practice, are there so many different rates of interest in a country such as the UK?

■ Outline answers

Answer 1

(a) A yield curve shows in its slope the relationship between yields on *similar* assets with *different* terms to maturity.

(b) (i) *Liquidity preference*. Longer-term rates will be higher than short rates because lenders/investors require greater compensation for longer loss of liquidity.

Risks involved. Greater risks of default, and capital erosion by inflation are involved in lending long term.

Expectations of an increase in interest rates. These expectations will intensify, the longer the gap between short-term and long-term maturity. Lenders will therefore prefer to lend short (increasing supply and depressing rates) while borrowers will prefer to be locked in for long periods at the prevailing low rate (increasing demand and rates at the long end).

(ii) Short rates in the inter-bank and CDs markets represent the banks' marginal cost of funds. This affects:

- the rate charged to market-rate related loans;
- the level of rates on lending linked to base rates.

Answer 2

(a) *Why*.

(i) To influence very short-term interest rates.

(ii) To smooth cash flows between the government and monetary sector.

How

(i) If a shortage is likely to develop, the Bank will indicate to the discount house its willingness to buy (mainly) eligible commercial bills.

(ii) The houses offer bills at prices of their own choosing.

(iii) If the interest rates implied in these prices are in line with the monetary policy (*i.e. within the undisclosed band*), the Bank will accept the prices offered, otherwise the houses are forced to make offers of higher rates.

(iv) These OMOs of the Bank are usually conducted in Bands 1 and 2 (fourteen days' and thirty-three days' bill maturity).

(b) (i) The factors affecting the *general level* of interest rates (inflation expectations *plus* a margin to give lenders normally a positive return) are also the most important determinants of *mortgage rates*.

(ii) *Long rates* are also influenced by the demand/supply of long-term funds (market forces) and changes in short rates (a change in short rates engineered by the authorities gets translated into movements along the entire interest-rate spectrum).

(iii) Since the Bank can influence short rates by its OMOs, there is close relationship between this rate and the level of mortgage rate.

(iv) In practice, a significant change in Bank's dealing rate will be quickly reflected in the same directions of mortgage rates.

Answer 3

Two-part question; make sure you answer both parts.

1. (a) The Bank of England exerts the major influence in the determination of short rates:

    (i) Controls marginal cost of funds to the banking system through its operations in the bill market, via discount houses.

    (ii) Interaction between the Bank's bill operations and money market expectations is the chief determinant.

(b) Long rates greatly influenced by the above two points.

2. Bank base rates depend upon the following:

(a) Wholesale rates in the inter-bank market (LIBOR), because of less dependence on traditional retail deposits and more on wholesale funds. Base rates move in line with short-term (up to three months) money market rates.

(b) The extent of competition for deposits.

(c) The monetary policy directives.

(d) The rate of inflation – positive returns.

(e) The rates in overseas financial centres.

Answer 4

(a) Effects on the *personal sector*:

    (i) Mortgage payments will be increased.

    (ii) Customer spending may be discouraged (borrowers are not normally concerned with the interest element in total repayment costs).

    (iii) Savings may be encouraged, by those who can afford to save, i.e. those with high incomes.

    (iv) Distress borrowing tends to be interest-inelastic.

(b) Effects on the *corporate sector*:

    (i) Capital investment by companies would be discouraged, particularly if higher rates were seen as a part of the package to deflate the economy, adversely affecting business prospects.

    (ii) Corporate costs will increase, but not significantly as interest costs are a small part of total costs.

(c) Effects on the *commercial banks*:

    (i) Profitability of retail banks is enhanced because of the 'endowment' effect; but this may be offset by a reduction in loan demand, increased provisions for bad debts, reduced profits on fixed rate lending.

(d) Effects on the *capital account of the balance of payments*:

    (i) Capital inflows may increase, provided overseas interest rates remain unchanged.

    (ii) Capital inflows would be mainly through portfolio investment (e.g. to purchase Treasury bills).

    (iii) Such inflows are largely short term and are often called 'hot money'.

Answer 5

(a)   (i) The real rate of interest is the rate actually paid (nominal rate), adjusted for inflation.

    (ii) The real rate is positive where the nominal rate exceeds inflation rate; negative if the reverse is the case.

    (iii) The real rate may increase either due to increase in the nominal rate or a decrease in the rate of inflation.

    (iv) It can be calculated by deducting the rate of inflation as measured by the RPI over a given period from the nominal rate of interest.

(v) Since investors and borrowers are influenced by the future, rather than the historical, rate of inflation, the *expected* rate of inflation should be used in calculating the real rate of interest.

(b) (i) The need to curb inflation has meant restrictive monetary policy stances.

(ii) Lax fiscal policies in many economies, e.g. the US economy, have meant large budget deficits, which have had to be controlled by tight monetary policies for much of the period.

(iii) The strength of the dollar, coupled with high interest rates until recently (to finance the budget deficit), have necessitated high real rates of interest in other major economies to prevent serious falls in their exchange rates.

Answer 6

Reasons for so many interest rates:

(a) Risk element: e.g. Treasury bills considered safer than bank deposits, therefore offer lower rate of return; the rate may become even lower if Treasury bills are in short supply.

(b) Time element: yield curve explanation: longer-term, higher rate.

(c) Size of loan: larger loans may attract lower rates.

(d) Cost of funds in the wholesale money markets.

(e) Type of currency involved, e.g. eurocurrency rates generally lower than sterling rates.

(f) Consumer Credit Act requires the publication of the true rate as well as the flat rate for personal loans.

(g) Floating base rates: to estimate the future course of interest rates, for term loans, to crystallise customer's repayments.

(h) Bank of England's bill dealing rate: determined administratively, not by the market.

(i) Status of the borrower, e.g. blue chip rate (base rate + 1) for blue chip customers only.

∎ A tutor's answer

A specimen answer is given below to a question on an aspect of interest rates which is of increasing importance. The answer plan is intended to help you assess the scope of the question. Try to plan an answer to the question yourself before turning to the answer plan, and the full specimen answer given below.

Question

Assess the likely effects of an increase in the general level of interest rates on:

(a) a country's economy;
(b) the commercial banks.

Answer plan

Effects of an *increase* only to be discussed:

(a) (i) deflationary effects;
   (ii) inflationary effects;
   (iii) balance of payments effects.

(b) (i) effects on profit margins;
   (ii) endowment effect;
   (iii) fixed interest lending effects;
   (iv) changes in banks' balance sheets;
   (v) competitive advantage and disadvantage;
   (vi) effects of a higher exchange rate.

Specimen answer

(a) Higher interest rates will tend to depress demand, output and employment levels because all these are to some degree sensitive to changes in interest rates.

Consumer spending is likely to be reduced for three main reasons: (1) higher cost of consumer credit; (2) higher mortgage payments; and (3) higher prices of consumer goods (assuming the consumer goods industry passes its own higher interest costs on to the consumers). The demand for consumer goods, due to more expensive loans and higher prices, will tend to decrease, which in turn will cause contraction of output and employment within the consumer goods industry. The increase in unemployment will reduce tax revenue and increase government spending, particularly on unemployment benefits. Government borrowing may increase.

The effect on the capital goods industry will be different, largely because the demand for capital goods tends to be interest-inelastic. Since a large part of capital expenditure comes from the public sector, and public sector expenditure of this type is highly insensitive to interest rate changes, capital expenditure will therefore be little affected by higher interest rates. Output and employment within the capital goods industry will, provided profit margins are maintained, remain largely unchanged by higher interest rates.

Higher interest rates will tend to attract short-term investment and speculative balances from overseas to take advantage of any interest rate differential. Assuming that the conversion of 'hot money' balances into the national currency is on a large scale, it will increase the exchange rate of the national currency. The higher exchange rate will raise export prices, making exports less competitive, and reduce import prices, making imports more attractive. If the elasticities of demand for exports abroad and for imports internally are sufficiently elastic, then not only will the balance of trade go into deficit, but also domestic output and employment will be reduced by the production of fewer exports and by the increased penetration of imports.

Higher interest rates will also increase the cost of export finance, which, in turn, will increase export costs and, possibly, export prices. However, this *direct* effect of higher interest rates on exports is likely to be less significant – interest costs are a small part of the selling price of exports – than the *indirect* effect of the higher exchange rate.

Higher interest rates, if *persistent*, will tend to increase the *headline* inflation rate, because of *higher mortgage costs*. On the other hand, higher interest rates will have a deflationary effect on aggregate demand, cutting consumption, investment and exports. This will 'weaken' both goods and labour markets, which would mean reduced profit margins and lower pay settlements, i.e. lower *underlying* inflation rate. Cheaper imports, because of the high exchange rate, and a reduced money supply, because of high interest rates, may again lead to lower inflation.

(b) A general statement that higher interest rates increase bank profits is incorrect. The banking system may be divided into wholesale banking and retail banking. *Wholesale banking* (e.g. merchant banking) will not be much influenced by an increase in interest rates, because it relies to a much greater extent on the *margins* between lending and borrowing rates for its profits, rather than on actual rates. Higher loan *and* deposit rates for the wholesale banks would mean that their profit margins would largely remain unchanged.

For *retail banks* (e.g. clearing banks), higher loan rates also mean higher deposit rates, and therefore the increase in the profitability due to higher lending rates is largely offset by higher deposit rates. However, the profit margins of retail banks increase from the 'endowment effect' of their non-interest bearing deposits, i.e. the increase in net returns on non-interest bearing current accounts, which are now rather rare. On the other hand, their profit margins would be reduced on fixed-rate lending. Also, due to a fall in the value of assets charged as security for bank advances, their capital value may fall as interest rates rise. Furthermore, the authorities may claw back a portion of the extra profit from the endowment effect by imposing a windfall tax. This may explain, in part, why some banks traditionally choose to reduce the margins between deposit and lending rates when interest rates are rising, and to increase them when interest rates are falling.

There will be several likely changes on a bank's balance sheet from an increase in interest rates. The higher price of loans may reduce loan demand to buy consumer goods, if not capital goods. However, 'distress borrowing', especially by businessmen, is interest-inelastic and will still take place, increasing the retail banks' profitability. An increase in interest rates results in higher interest rate bills for bank customers, especially large borrowers; this may cause an increase in the bad debt rate and the banks would have to increase their bad debt provisions, which will reduce profitability. The effect on banks' deposit taking *vis-à-vis* their competitors, especially building societies, would largely depend upon how well the interest rate structure of banks compares with that of their competitors. Building societies, unlike banks, have been slow to change their rates in response to changes in market rates, and it is likely that the banks' inflow of deposits may increase temporarily at the expense of building societies. Against this, an increase in interest rates slows down the growth of current accounts, since the opportunity cost of holding such accounts is more interest foregone. In fact, there may be a considerable switch from lower interest-free current accounts to interest-bearing accounts. If interest rates are expected to fall in the future, fixed interest government securities become more attractive, which may further curtail the banks' current accounts.

∎ A step further

Interest rates are an item of vital concern to banks. The *Financial Times* is an invaluable source of up-to-date data and information on the level, structure and pattern of interest rates. There are also many useful articles on interest rates and interest rate-related issues in the past editions of the *Financial Times*, which can be located via the *Financial Times Monthly Index*. The *Examiners' Reports* and *Updating Notes* published by the Chartered Institute of Bankers highlight those areas of interest rates which are most important to bankers. Articles in the quality financial press and in banking magazines will keep you abreast of major changes in this topic of the syllabus. The two-part *Signpost* article, 'Interest rates − theory and practice', in the May and June 1986 issues of *Banking World* is of particular importance. Be sure to read both parts of that article. *BEQB* provides an authentic guide to the movements in the yield curve, and the reasons for movements.

CHAPTER 7

Economic Policy

Syllabus requirements
- Aims of economic policy, problems in achieving them, and the extent to which they have been achieved.
- The intermediate targets of economic policy and the techniques of achieving them.
- The relationship of monetary policy with fiscal policy.
- General techniques of monetary control (portfolio constraints, interest rates, size of PSBR).
- The influence of monetary policy on the banking system.
- Principles of demand management through physical controls (prices and incomes policy) and fiscal policy techniques.
- The effectiveness of monetary and fiscal policies.

∎ Getting started

Monetary economics is one aspect of a much broader area of economic study, called 'macro-economics', and monetary policy, fiscal policy, exchange rate policy, and prices and incomes policy fit into the broader economic policy.

Monetary policy is a set of measures by which the authorities attempt to regulate the aggregate expenditure in the economy by influencing liquidity and the terms and availability of credit in the country.

There are of course other policies which the authorities may use, either singly or in combination, to regulate aggregate demand in the economy. The attempt to regulate the level of economic activity by influencing public receipts (i.e. taxes) and public expenditure, is called *fiscal policy*. Alternatively, the authorities may attempt to control the spending ability of the private sector directly, e.g. by pursuing a *prices and incomes policy*. The authorities may pursue an *exchange rate policy* and set a target against a particular currency to be 'shadowed' to ensure that exports are maximised and that inflation is not imported via high-priced imports.

The objectives of these policies are set within the broad framework of *economic policy*, so that their techniques may influence aggregate purchasing power and demand in a manner which is consistent with the broader economic objectives. Such broader economic objectives may be divided into internal and external objectives. Internal objectives generally include stable prices, a high employment level, rising economic growth and living standards, and a fair distribution of wealth among individuals, industries and regions of the country. External objectives include a stable exchange rate for the national currency, a satisfactory balance of payments and level of foreign currency reserves, and also the provision of aid to developing countries.

The dilemma that confronts the authorities is that achievement of some of these objectives may clash with the achievement of others. For example, the pursuit of high economic growth and employment may lead to inflationary pressures which may destabilise prices internally. Again, the maintenance of a stable exchange rate externally may become difficult if inflation internally is making exports less attractive overseas and imports more attractive than domestically produced import substitutes. It is doubtful whether *all* the economic policy objectives can be achieved simultaneously. Hence it is a question, for the authorities, of assigning priorities amongst the objectives: which of the objectives should be given highest priority will depend upon the needs of the economy at any given period of time.

In recent years, most governments in the free world have faced varying degrees of rising inflation rates, which have undermined the value of people's incomes, savings and profits. Hence the main objective for most governments has been, for several years, 'stable prices', to help money regain and retain its legitimate value, both internally and externally. The belief has been that stable prices will in themselves lead to a higher rate of economic growth, a higher level of employment and increased prosperity.

▌ Essential principles

Economic policy

The scope of macro (meaning 'large') economics concerns questions such as the following: What determines the general level of prices (e.g. the rate of inflation)? What determines the percentage of the overall labour force that is unemployed? What determines the total quantity of goods and services (national output) produced in a year? What determines the level of interest rates? What determines the rate at which the national currency exchanges for other currencies? What determines the country's balance of payments with other countries? Macro-economics is concerned not only with the *level* of, say, unemployment and prices, but also with the *rate* at which they change.

Since the Second World War, British governments have formally committed themselves to achieve the following *major* economic policy objectives: (a) substantially full employment; (b) a stable level of prices; (c) annual growth in the level of national output; and (d) a balance over time on the balance of payments. Other objectives of the economic policy are concerned with the redistribution of income through the government expenditure and taxation system, and with the structure of industry – e.g. should there be more or less public ownership?

The dilemma that confronts the authorities is that achievement of one objective may clash with the achievement of another. For instance, the pursuit of a high level of economic growth and employment may lead, via increased expenditure and rising wages, to inflationary pressures which, in turn, may destabilise prices internally. Or the maintenance of a stable exchange rate externally might become difficult, since the raising or lowering of interest rates internally could adversely affect domestic economic growth and employment. It is doubtful whether *all* the economic policy objectives can be achieved simultaneously. Therefore, it is a question of the authorities assigning priorities among the objectives, depending upon the perceived needs of the economy at any given period. For instance, in the early 1960s it was full employment; in the late 1960s and 1970s, it was the eradication of balance of payments deficit; in the 1980s it was the control of inflation, reduction in taxation and privatisation.

There are two major economic policy disagreements among economists: First, should economic policy be *specific* or *detailed*? With specific policies the authorities select a very few highly aggregated economic variables – such as the exchange rate, money supply, government expenditure — and try to control them, intervening very little in other areas. Detailed policies imply a plethora of devices aimed largely at achieving broad economic objectives. Such a policy may include a prices and incomes policy, minimum wage legislation, interest rate manipulation, regulation of private industry and trade, exchange rates, and controls and subsidies. Under a detailed approach to economic policy, the government will involve itself in all aspects of the economy. Second, should there be *rules* or *discretion* in the implementation of economic policy? The government announces a set of rules and targets publicly and commits itself to them, never deviating (the 'U-turn') from them. On the other hand, with discretion the government's intervention is responsive to current developments in the economy, and the policies are adjusted in the light of current economic events at the authorities' discretion, with no stigma attached to the policy alterations.

Very generally, those economists who favour specific policies also favour rigid rules, and those who favour detailed policies also favour discretionary intervention.

Economic policy instruments

Governments have at their disposal a number of instruments of economic management to aid them in implementing the policy objectives of their Monetary Policy, Fiscal Policy, Prices and Incomes Policy, and Exchange Rate Policy.

Since 1985, the stability of the exchange rate of the pound sterling, especially against the US dollar and the German mark, had been assigned an elevated position among the economic policy objectives. However, the flare-up in the inflation rate since between 1988 and 1992 has led to the unique prominence of the interest rate policy, or rather, a high interest rate policy, to depress domestic spending and demand for credit, and thereby to reduce inflation, balance of payments deficit and bring the economy down to a 'soft landing', i.e. bringing the level of spending down without severe recession. However, the prolonged high interest rates have seriously hurt the UK commerce and industry, and the adverse balance of payments is showing no signs of improving. The high interest rates caused the mortgage rates to stay at high levels and that, in turn, *caused* the headline inflation to remain high.

Conduct of economic (monetary) policy

Let us assume that the authorities in a 'free' economy decide that the control of inflation is the *broad economic objective* that has highest priority, and that to achieve it the major *monetary policy objective*, a subset of economic objective, is to be the control of expenditure. In the achievement of particular monetary policy objectives, central banks play a pivotal role.

In a free economy, the central bank cannot use monetary policy to control expenditure directly: there is no physical rationing under 'free' economies in normal times. Instead it tries to control expenditure by using indirect methods, such as setting intermediate monetary targets, e.g. controlling the rate of increase in money supply. To control the increase in money supply it sets operating targets on the banking and financial institutions, e.g. reserve asset requirements to reduce the credit multiplier. To accomplish its various operating targets, the central bank employs a range of monetary instruments, e.g. open market operations or imposing its own interest rates.

There are therefore various stages in the conduct of monetary policy, which are invariably interlinked:

Instruments → Operating targets → Intermediate targets → Monetary policy objective; and of course vice versa

While the central bank has complete control over its own *instruments*, which in turn exert control over *operating targets*, yet thereafter its control becomes gradually weaker. It cannot, for instance, fully control the *intermediate targets*, e.g. the growth of money supply, because the growth of money supply in a free economy depends on the behaviour of banks and their customers. For instance, the central bank has no control over how much credit bank customers demand or banks provide at a given level of interest rate. The link between the *intermediate target* and the *monetary policy objective*, e.g. the control of expenditure, also depends upon the behaviour of the general public: it is the general public which decides how much will be spent from a given amount of money supply available within the economy.

Thus the main issue in monetary policy is how far the things that the central bank *can* control enable it effectively to influence the things it *cannot* control wholly. The more reliable the links between the various stages of the monetary policy, the more successful will the central bank be in achieving the various objectives of monetary policy. We have assumed, for the purposes of analysis, that the *economic policy objective* is to *control expenditure* (in order to control inflation). The central bank should then choose as the *intermediate target* that monetary variable which is most reliably linked to expenditure and upon which the central bank can exert most influence.

∎ Economic policy targets

There are five main variables from which the central bank, observing the above criteria, may choose intermediate targets in order to control expenditure: (1) the money supply; (2) credit; (3) interest rates; (4) exchange rates; (5) expenditure.

The money supply

The monetarists think that money supply is a good intermediate target. They believe that increases in money supply will, via the 'transmission mechanism', increase expenditure, some of the new money being used to buy goods and services, which increases expenditure directly, and some being invested in safe securities, such as first-class fixed interest bonds, which increases expenditure indirectly. Buying bonds increases the market prices of such bonds but lowers interest rates: lower interest rates increase investment and consumption expenditure. Hence, the monetarists argue, the central bank should choose the growth in money supply as the intermediate target when it seeks to control expenditure.

There are some problems in making money supply growth the intermediate target for controlling expenditure.

A problem arises with regard to how interest-elastic is the demand for money. Suppose firms decide to increase investment while money stock is stationary; this will raise interest rates which, in turn, will lower the demand to hold money and increase its velocity of circulation. Therefore higher levels of both income and expenditure will be possible with no increase in money stock.

The extent to which the change in velocity upsets the relationship between money, income and expenditure will depend upon how interest-elastic is the demand for money. If the demand for money is, as monetarists believe, interest-inelastic, then any change in interest rates will cause a small change in velocity, so that money, income and expenditure may still have quite a close relationship.

In any case, the central bank could reduce the *rate* of monetary growth to compensate for any increase in velocity. This, however, would involve the central bank in doing two very difficult things: first, *estimating* fairly closely the extent of the reduction in the demand for money (increase in velocity), and second, judging whether this reduction is temporary or likely to continue. If it misjudges, it could make things worse rather than better by reducing the rate of money supply growth. Besides, cutting the rate of monetary growth will not have its full effect on expenditure until the private sector has had time to adjust its expenditure pattern to it. The danger then is that, if the level of private sector expenditure does not decrease to the expected level fairly quickly, an impatient central bank may *further* reduce money supply so that, in due course, the twin action of a double reduction of money supply growth may create undesirable fluctuations in expenditure.

Thus, for money supply to be a useful intermediate target, it is essential that the velocity of circulation of money is reasonably stable. This in turn will depend upon whether the demand for money is interest-elastic or inelastic. The velocity of circulation of money will be more stable the more interest-inelastic is the demand for money.

Assuming that the monetary authorities do decide to make money supply an intermediate target, they then will need to make further decisions in respect to the following:

(a) *Which monetary aggregate* should they choose as a target? Most central banks monitor a range of narrow and broad monetary targets, which include a widening range of financial assets on the liquidity spectrum. Each central bank would choose that monetary aggregate as a target which is most closely related to expenditure and over which it has the most control.

(b) Having chosen the monetary aggregate, should the authorities *publicly announce it*? If the public believed that the central bank would be able to achieve the target, and that this achievement would cut inflation, then the public, including trade unions, might accept lower future money incomes without anticipating a fall in their 'real' incomes and therefore in their standards of living. Business firms would then require lower price increases to achieve a particular level of 'real' profitability. These are some of the advantages of publicly announcing the targets and their growth rates. However, a disadvantage of such announcements would be to curtail the authorities' flexibility of action. The authorities would not be able to change the targets for the monetary aggregate without being accused of making a 'U-turn', even though changes in economic conditions might require such changes in targets.

(c) Should there be *point* targets or target *ranges*? While precise point targets reduce uncertainty in the minds of the public, they are also very difficult to achieve, especially during a fluctuating economic climate. Therefore, it would probably be more realistic to set a target range, e.g. 0–4 per cent per annum growth rate in the targeted monetary aggregate; this would also allow some flexibility of action to the authorities.

Credit

In modern economies, credit (bank and building society lending in the UK) and money are closely linked. An increase in bank and building society lending usually leads to an increase in bank and building society deposits and therefore an increase in the money supply. As modern economies become more and more 'cashless', the role of bank and building society lending (including credit cards) becomes crucial to aggregate expenditure in the economy.

The volume of bank and building society lending is, however, determined not only by the banks and building societies but also by the overall demand for credit in the economy. The immediate effect of a rise in total credit will be to increase bank and building society deposits, but some of the increase in deposits may disappear if the borrowers substitute, say, government bonds for their bank and building society deposits; in this case, government accounts with the central bank will increase and the banking sector's balances with the central bank and their share of total deposits will fall by the same amount. It is when the public buy more of other financial assets, using their bank and building society deposits, that the total stock of bank and building society deposits will be reduced. The volume of bank lending will also be determined by the amount of competition from *non-bank and non-building society lenders*.

Is credit (bank and building society lending) a good intermediate target? Although money supply and credit are closely linked, and a rise in credit is one of the ways in which money supply and therefore expenditure may increase, yet there is no reason why money supply and credit should grow at the same time or at the same rate: if banks and building societies increase lending to the public, but at the same time the central bank sells securities to the public, then there is no increase in money supply, even though credit has increased.

Some economists argue that credit is a better intermediate target than money supply in controlling expenditure, because households and firms rarely borrow unless they wish to spend. Therefore, an increase in credit should have a predictable effect on expenditure, and the control of credit should, more predictably, control expenditure. However, *if* credit is taken as an intermediate target of economic policy, then *all* credit should be the basis for the control of expenditure by the authorities, i.e. bank and building society credit, including debit and credit cards and unused overdraft *plus* funds borrowed by the public from other non-bank financial institutions, in order to avoid disintermediation.

Interest rates

If the authorities knew reasonably well what level of expenditure would result from a given level of interest rates, then interest rates would be a good candidate for the intermediate target. However, the problem with interest rates as a target is that it is the *expectations* of businessmen which determine expenditure by firms, not interest rates. If business expectations of future demand and profitability rise considerably, then firms will increase their borrowing of investment funds, no matter what the level of interest rates. Even if the authorities do stabilise interest rates, the level of expenditure may fluctuate widely at any given level of interest rates, due to sudden changes in business expectations. Furthermore, 'distress borrowing' of the non-bank public, and the government's borrowing to fund the PSBR, are interest-inelastic. Rising inflation encourages borrowing irrespective of interest rates, since the 'real' value of debt becomes gradually less, especially if the loans are used to buy goods which rise in price rapidly, e.g. houses. Therefore interest rates may have a poor correlation with credit and/or money supply, and therefore an unreliable link with expenditure. A prolonged period of high interest rates would certainly reduce expenditure, and therefore inflation, but would seriously harm economic growth, employment and exports, and would cause recession in the economy.

Exchange rates

The exchange rate is the price of domestic currency in terms of foreign currencies. In those economies in which international trade accounts form a relatively high proportion of economic activity, changes in exchange rates can cause considerable disturbance in the domestic economy. For example, a fall in exchange rate will make exports more, and imports less, competitive, which will stimulate domestic economic activity; if the exchange rate rises, the reverse will happen, and domestic economic activity will be depressed.

If the country has a fixed exchange rate as its intermediate target, but has a higher domestic inflation rate than that of its trading partners, then the competitiveness of its exports will suffer, leading to pressure for a devaluation of its exchange rate to such an extent as would neutralise the inflation rate differentials.

While the authorities, by intervening directly (through buying and selling domestic currency) or by manipulating domestic interest rates, can influence the exchange rate of the domestic currency, a country's foreign currency reserves, its ability to borrow currency overseas or the advantages of interest-rate manipulation, are not limitless. Hence direct official intervention can only be to a limited extent; and manipulation of interest rates beyond certain levels may have dangerous effects for the economy. This could happen if external pressures lead to higher domestic interest rates than domestic economic conditions might warrant.

Expenditure

The authorities could choose expenditure itself as an intermediate target to control inflation; however, if they did so, two major problems would confront them. First, there is a time lag, often of up to two years, before expenditure by households and firms responds fully to changes in monetary policy; impatient authorities might change the economic policy *before* the full effects of the current economic policy measures on expenditure levels had become apparent. Second, since current information on the growth of expenditure is not readily available, the authorities could be seriously handicapped in their economic policy decisions for lack of up-to-date information on expenditure growth.

▮ Instruments and methods (techniques) of monetary control

The two main components of money supply are cash (notes and coins) and deposits with banks and non-bank financial institutions. Central banks do not normally control the supply of cash in circulation; this is determined by the preference of the public for cash or deposits; there can, for instance, be large seasonal variations in the public preference for cash or deposits. Central banks, however, attempt to regulate the growth of total deposits in several ways, but especially the growth of bank deposits, because these deposits constitute a significant proportion of the total money supply.

The following methods or techniques (instruments) are commonly used by the central bank to control the level of deposits with financial institutions.

Direct controls

This technique places direct restrictions on bank lending or deposit growth. There are two instruments of direct control: lending ceilings and direct interest rate control.

Lending ceilings

The central bank instructs the commercial banks (and any other financial institutions under its jurisdiction) not to lend above a prescribed ceiling, say 6 per cent per annum. Since the commercial banks have to abide by the direct instructions of the central bank, the main advantage of this instrument is that bank lending, and therefore bank deposits, will not increase beyond 6 per cent per annum. This is called 'quantitative' ceilings. As against this advantage, there are two serious disadvantages:

1. Unless the lending ceilings are applied uniformly to *all* lending, the borrowing public could quite easily switch that part of its borrowing requirements which is *in excess* of the bank lending ceilings to uncontrolled non-bank lending institutions; then disintermediation, with all its distorting effects on money supply measurement, would occur.
2. Competition and innovation among banks would be inhibited to the detriment of bank customers.

Qualitative guidance

Priority lending to certain sectors of the economy (e.g. manufacturers and exporters), and restraints on lending to other sectors (e.g. property companies, households) are advised.

Direct interest rate control

On the assumption that the public's demand for funds is interest-elastic, the central bank imposes differentials and ceilings on interest rates paid on deposits and charged on lending to influence public borrowing and saving according to money supply growth targets; setting a higher rate to decrease bank lending and to increase deposits, and a lower rate to achieve the reverse. Direct interest controls can, however, cause several complications:

(a) Unless interest rate control is uniformly applied to all lending institutions, 'round-tripping' or arbitrage could be triggered: if controlled rates are below uncontrolled rates, then the non-bank public could borrow cheaply at controlled rates and lend the borrowed sum, at a quick profit, at uncontrolled rates. Round-tripping leads to a misallocation of funds.
(b) The size of the PSBR is determined by the government's tax revenue and spending policy; *public sector borrowing* is largely interest-inelastic, therefore insensitive to interest rate controls.
(c) *Private sector borrowing* is not always interest-elastic. The possibility of profitable investment may be related more to business expectation than to the level of interest rates. 'Distress' borrowing (e.g. the need for working capital) is also largely unrelated to interest rates. Also note that people often prefer to use the much more expensive credit card rather than bank borrowing because of convenience and 'no-questions-asked' spending.
(d) Direct interest rate control has a delayed, or lagged, effect on bank lending: this is because the expenditure commitments of firms and households take time to adjust to changed interest rates. It may therefore be just when the non-bank public has begun to adjust its borrowing requirements in line with the objective of controlled interest rates that the central bank may decide to alter the level of the controlled rates again.
(e) Rigid interest rate control may clash with other economic policy objectives, e.g. a rigidly

applied high interest rate policy may militate against the need to increase investment in order to counteract rising unemployment and to avert recession.

Borrowing ceilings

Restrictions may be placed on the quantity of deposit liability which the controlled institutions may raise from a particular source (e.g. no more than 40 per cent from the wholesale markets).

Indirect controls

Open market operations of the central bank

Open market operations are a two-way weapon in the armoury of the central bank. On a day-to-day basis the technique is used to smooth out fluctuations in liquidity in the money market. This means the central bank selling high-quality, money market instruments to mop up excess liquidity, and buying these instruments to relieve any liquidity shortage in the market. This type of open market operation will be applied at the existing interest rate level. However, if the authorities wish interest rates to rise, then the central bank will do so by altering the *cost of 'last resort'* assistance to relieve the liquidity shortage of controlled institutions by buying money market instruments at a rate *higher* than is consistent with the existing interest rate level. Sometimes the central bank may deliberately create a shortage of liquidity in the money market by selling excessively attractive government and money market instruments, and then relieve the shortage at its own terms; this will raise the level of money market interest rates.

Cash-to-deposit ratio and reserve asset ratio requirements

Both these requirements place constrains on the controlled institutions' asset structures. If the central bank requires them to maintain, say, a 20 per cent cash-to-deposit ratio, it will clearly reduce their ability to lend by 20 per cent. If the central bank now requires that a portion of their cash-to-deposit ratio should be kept in specified reserve assets, the banks will either have to curtail lending by raising lending rates, or bid for more deposits (by raising deposit rates or converting their non-reserve assets into reserve assets) if the reserve asset ratio falls below the required level. The effect of imposing these requirements is to reduce the credit multiplier.

Call for special deposits

The central bank may instruct controlled institutions to deposit a specified percentage of deposits as 'frozen' funds, i.e. these interest bearing deposits cease to be a part of their liquid funds, and are therefore not available for lending and credit creation.

Supplementary Special Deposits ('Corset')

In addition to operating on commercial banks' reserve assets, the central bank can control the money supply by acting on *banks' liabilities*, via Supplementary Special Deposits (SSDs). If a bank's, say, quarterly average of interest-bearing liabilities exceed a *specified* percentage, a *non-interest bearing* Special Deposit becomes payable to the central bank (central bank's corset). Corset technique makes it less profitable for the banks to bid for deposits beyond a certain level.

▌ Fiscal and monetary policies

Fiscal policy implies management of aggregate demand in the economy by varying the size and the content of public revenue (i.e. taxes) and government expenditure, and making good any deficit by borrowing. Fiscal policy establishes the size of the PSBR or PSDR (Public Sector Debt Repayment) by determining the level of 'government' revenue in relation to its expenditure. 'Government' includes central and local governments, *plus* nationalised industries.

The *chief objective* of fiscal policy is to regulate aggregate level of economic activity by varying taxation and government expenditure: reducing taxation to lower unemployment; increasing government expenditure to raise the level of economic activity.

The Public Sector Borrowing Requirement (PSBR) is the excess of government or public sector spending over government or public sector revenue. Monetary policy is responsible for financing PSBR or neutralising a PSDR, either by transactions with the non-bank and non-building society sector, or by transactions with the central bank and the commercial banks, or by transactions with overseas residents. If it is financed mainly by *banks* and *building societies* in the UK in exchange for government securities, then they will be able to use these securities to increase their deposits, and the money supply will increase. On the other hand, if the PSBR is financed by the *M4 private sector*, then there will be no net impact on the money supply growth, but the yields (interest rate returns) on the government bonds (securities) will have to be raised sufficiently high to attract the public to buy the government bonds. High interest rates will tend to curb investment and consumption expenditure. Thus, fiscal policy measures cannot be implemented independently of monetary policy measures. However, monetary policy can be implemented by the authorities independently of fiscal policy: the central bank can alter its lending rate and/or issue instructions to commercial banks on their lending activities, thereby putting into motion the desired changes in the growth of the money supply and in the general level of interest rates. Since the monetary policy is responsible for financing the PSBR or neutralising the budget surplus, the fiscal policy's budget deficits and surpluses provide the essential link between monetary and fiscal policies.

▌ Prices and incomes policy

This policy generally refers to the government's attempt to control wage and price rises either by freezes or by voluntary and statutory norms, in order to control inflation, reduce foreign trade deficit and maintain high levels of employment.

The UK government employs nearly a third of the UK work force, hence a control of wage-push inflation is crucial to curbing inflation. However, voluntary and statutory norms disrupt established patterns of wage differentials and relativities, which is not acceptable to some unions. Incomes policies tend merely to defer rather than control large wage and price increases, because once the policy period has ended the unions and the firms try to make up the lost ground.

▌ Useful applied material

Economic policy in Britain

By 1973, control over the growth of money supply became the main objective of the monetary authorities. In 1976, the official practice of announcing targets for money supply growth was started, and since then the authorities have tried gradually to reduce the rate of growth of money supply. Successive governments attached greater importance to the intermediate target of controlling the growth of money supply, believing this to be vital in containing inflation. This gave monetary policy the prominence previously accorded to fiscal policy. The policy of monetary control was designed to limit private sector demand in the economy, particularly by influencing private sector expectations as to future inflation; hence the monetary targets were publicly announced in advance.

However, the target ranges were frequently exceeded. The reason for this lies in the difficulty confronting the monetary authorities in controlling money supply. If the Bank of England were to use changes in interest rates to control money supply, then it had to estimate fairly precisely the total demand for credit by the private sector at various levels of interest rate. Again, if the exchange rate is too high and attracts short-term capital in flows, then domestic interest rates will need to be lowered; but lowering interest rates will increase money supply! Yet again, the level of interest rates required to keep the exchange rate at a particular level may well be different from the level of interest rates required to meet the money supply growth target. Since changes in the exchange rate have significant effects on the rate of domestic inflation and on economic activity, the authorities gave priority to the control of the exchange rate during the 1980s, at the expense of monetary targets. There was no official exchange rate target in the UK economic policy; however, since the January 1985 sterling crisis, when sterling fell sharply, the exchange rate has been assigned an elevated role in the UK economic policy, and since March 1986 has become an instrument of monetary policy. And in October 1990, the UK joined the Exchange Rate Mechanism (ERM) and the sterling exchange rate became all important until September 1992.

In the Budget for 1987/88, the Chancellor stated that *no* target range would be set for the growth of the broad money aggregate: this marked the end of an era which began in 1976 when sterling M3 (the then broad money aggregate) was first targeted and, during the early years of the Medium Term Financial Strategy (MTFS) (see below), was assigned a central role in the anti-inflationary battle. The authorities believed that there was a reasonably *close* relationship between the behaviour of sterling M3 and the inflation rate. In the event, the inflation rate was progressively reduced to around 4 per cent but the inflation success seemingly owed little to the behaviour of sterling M3. In every one of the past years, until it ceased to be targeted, the growth of sterling M3 exceeded the inflation rate and the increase in money incomes. The formal abandonment of sterling M3 targeting was, therefore, an official recognition of the fact that the path of broad money targeting had not been a good guide to the course of inflation in the 1980s.

The absence of a target range for broad money growth, however, should not detract from the way in which broad money and credit behaviour are strong influences on both the authorities' and the financial markets' assessment of overall monetary conditions.

The conduct of monetary policy has become increasingly complex in recent years, which has unavoidably led to a pragmatic approach. The appropriateness of the policy stance therefore takes such indicators as the exchange rate, M0 (which is still formally targeted, its 1993/94 target range is 0−4 per cent), growth of demand in the economy, wage and inflation prospects as well as broad money and credit behaviour into consideration.

Funding policy

Funding policy relates to the role played in controlling the money supply by the authorities' transactions in government debt instruments such as gilt-edged securities. In recent years the authorities have pursued a *full* funding policy, ensuring that the impact of government financial activities on the money supply is neutralised, i.e. the public sector as a whole does not inject liquidity into the economy, nor does it extract liquidity from it. In the early 1980s funding policy was deliberately used to reduce money supply growth – by *overfunding* the PSBR. Since then the PSBR has been replaced by a budget surplus (until 1990) and an accompanying Public Sector Debt Repayment (PSDR) programme. The intention has been to off-set the contractionary impact on the money supply of a budget surplus by repurchasing gilts from the private sector.

The authorities' objectives when conducting gilt sales or repurchases with the M4 private sector are not confined simply to neutralising the impact on the money supply of a budget surplus or deficit, the authorities also consider the effect on the domestic money supply of the direct intervention on the foreign exchanges. In 1989, for example, the UK's official reserves of gold and foreign currencies fell by over $14 billion, reflecting considerable Bank of England action to support sterling. The effect of such intervention is to drain liquidity from the system, and in order to neutralise this additional repurchases of gilts from the M4 private sector were necessary. The reverse is of course also true. When the Bank of England intervened to prevent sterling from appreciating in 1988, the authorities neutralised the accompanying monetary increase by gilt sales.

The authorities are committed to their full funding policy, but with two exceptions: (1) neutralising intervention on the foreign exchanges would not necessarily be undertaken in the course of one year, but over a period; and (2) Treasury bill operations would, for technical reasons, be excluded from the funding equation. This move has assumed additional significance since the Treasury bill issue was raised significantly in 1989 to absorb liquidity from the system. This keeps conditions in the money market tight so that, in subsequent operations to relieve shortages of cash, the authorities can purchase eligible gilts at rates of interest of their own choosing and consistent with the monetary policy.

Targeting of M0

A 'target' is an economic variable which, unlike an economic policy 'instrument' (e.g. interest rates), is beyond the direct control of the authorities. A target is significant because it shows how the changes in instrument setting are affecting the ultimate policy objectives, and whether the policy is on course.

Suppose the authorities, in order to slow down the growth of *total spending in the economy* (i.e. Money Gross Domestic Product), raise the interest rates. It will take months before the government's statisticians confirm the decline in money GDP. Therefore any monetary aggregate whose growth relates closely to the level of money GDP, and for which weekly and monthly figures are available, provides the authorities with an invaluable guide to setting interest rates in the short and medium term.

The authorities found the broad money aggregates, especially M3, unreliable in this respect, in that although M3 rose rapidly, the rate of inflation actually fell quite considerably. Hence the authorities suspended, at least until the pace of financial innovation in the UK (which largely caused the erratic behaviour of M3) has subsided, the targeting of broad money, leaving M0 (narrow money) the only targeted monetary aggregate.

M0 was introduced as a target in 1984, initially alongside M3, and since 1987 has been the only targeted monetary aggregate. M0 is basically notes and coins in circulation with the public. If the public's demand for notes and coins for spending increases they draw upon their sight deposits with banks and building societies. The Bank of England refills banks' tills with newly-issued notes and coins, and debits the banks' operational deposits with it by an equivalent amount. Thus the relationship between aggregate spending (money GDP) and notes and coins in circulation is simple and straightforward; as the money GDP increases, so does the M0, and M0 will only remain within its target range so long as money GDP is on course. When the money GDP goes off course, M0 statistics provide the authorities with early warning, thereby telling them to raise or lower interest rates.

Raising the interest rates would encourage the public to economise on spending by transferring funds from non-interest bearing sight deposits to interest-bearing savings deposits, and thus the M0 will get back within its target range. M0 is like a 'thermometer' which gives accurate, early warning to the authorities of the 'temperature' money GDP has reached, so enabling them to change instrument settings so that the policy remains on course. In February 1990, M0 rose by 6.5 per cent, 1.5 per cent above its 1989/90 target range, thus signalling the authorities not to relax on the high interest policy.

▌ Medium Term Financial Strategy (MTFS)

Broadly speaking, the government employs fiscal policy in support of its monetary policy objectives, e.g. reducing public sector borrowing and spending in order to reduce money supply and thereby interest rates. The government has sought to restrain the public sector's demand for funds in order to achieve its monetary targets at lower interest rates, and thus to encourage more domestic investment and output in the private sector. The combined objectives for money supply *and* public sector borrowing were first established in 1980, and are known collectively as the Medium Term Financial Strategy.

The basic aims of MTFS are to reduce inflation by reducing the growth of total spending power in the economy, as measured by the cash value of UK national output, to transfer more resources to the private sector via a balanced budget, to keep the growth of M0 (narrow money) within the range of 0–4 per cent in 1993/94, and to base decisions about interest rates on a continuous assessment of all monetary conditions. The reasoning underlying the MTFS objectives is that a higher PSBR requires higher interest rates to finance it and that public sector borrowing tends to be interest-inelastic, whereas private sector borrowing trends to be more sensitive to higher interest rates. Therefore the higher interest rates required to meet the increased needs of the public sector borrowing requirement 'crowds out' private sector expenditure; this arrests economic growth and employment.

In the early 1980s, the authorities emphasised control of the money supply through the MTFS. Targets for narrow and broad money aggregates were set each year and publicly announced with the objective of reducing public expectations of future inflation. More recently, partly due to the changes in the financial markets, only M0 has been targeted. The broad measures have been allowed to grow strongly.

The MTFS also set a target for reducing the PSBR over a number of years, starting from its 4 per cent of Gross National Product level in 1980. The fiscal years from 1987/8 to 1990 saw the replacement of a PSBR by a PSDR, indicating the success of the government's aims in this area; albeit assisted by large privatisation receipts.

However, upward pressure on prices has not been relieved by the reduction in public sector spending; by the middle of 1990, the inflation rate had climbed up to very nearly

10 per cent. The authorities maintained that a huge increase in the private sector consumption, due to high wage settlements and large increases in borrowings from banks and building societies, fuelled inflation to double figures. Hence the authorities' determination to keep the interest rates as high and for as long as is necessary to bring down the private sector spending, which will bring down inflation to zero. The authorities have been criticised for using a one-club approach in tackling the problem, and that in addition to raising the interest rates, they should affect bank lending by imposing credit 'ceilings' and calls for special deposits, and even applying the 'corset' (supplementary special deposits) on the banking system. The authorities claim that under the present liberalised financial markets, with no exchange controls, the UK households and companies could easily borrow from overseas lending institutions. The UK authorities have no control over those institutions.

▌Current monetary control techniques in the UK

The monetary policy in the UK is designed, in the main, to control money supply, interest rates and the exchange rate of the pound sterling. Until 1980, the authorities used several control techniques, such as reserve asset ratio requirements, quantitative and qualitative controls on bank lending, Minimum Lending Rate (MLR) changes, open market operations, calls for special deposits and supplementary special deposits. Of these control techniques, only open market operations, the possibility of resurrecting the MLR, calls for special deposits and 'qualitative guidance' (requests by the Bank of England to banks that they give priority in lending to certain sectors of the economy, and restrain lending to other sectors) have survived the 1981 changes (see p.127).

Open Market Operations (OMOs) involve the buying and selling by the Bank of England of eligible commercial and Treasury bills to influence: (a) the cash and liquidity base of the banking system and therefore the capacity of banks to lend; and (b) directly the level of short-term interest rates and indirectly the structure of longer term interest rates. Short-term interest rates are an essential instrument of UK monetary policy. Changes in interest rates have a reasonably quick and direct effect on narrow money, as they do on the exchange rate. Their effect on broad money, however, is more complex and much more delayed.

If the objective of OMOs is to *affect the growth of bank advances* in order to control the growth in money supply, then the Bank relieves the liquidity shortage in the market at a bill dealing rate which is higher than the current money market rate. In this way the Bank is able to control the marginal cost of funds to the banking system. The level of short-term (up to three months) inter-bank rates broadly corresponds to the marginal cost of banks' funds. However, since the Bank in its OMOs continues to deal primarily with the discount houses, its bill dealing rates can be out of line with inter-bank rates; the difference between the two rates represents the marginal cost of funds to the commercial banks. The level of banks' base rates tends to move in line with money market rates. A rise in the banks' base rates, the authorities believe, would lower the demand for bank lending and, in turn, would curb the growth in money supply.

If the objective of the OMOs is simply to *relieve any shortage or surplus of liquid funds* in the money market, then the Bank buys and sells money market instruments at a bill dealing rate that is equal to the existing level of short-term interest rates.

If the authorities wish to encourage the public to hold the public sector debt for a longer term, they will attempt to affect the *structure* of interest rates. While changes in the Bank's bill dealing rates will directly affect the level of short-term rates, these changes will also indirectly affect the structure of longer term rates; they will do this by affecting market expectations as to the movements in longer term rates, e.g. movement of short-term rates over the year (yield curve) will influence the one-year money market rate.

The OMOs are conducted by the Bank of England exclusively in the bill market via the discount houses, and in order to ensure an adequate supply of commercial bills – bills of exchange issued by commercial firms to finance short-term transactions – the authorities have increased the number of eligible banks to over 100, i.e. banks whose acceptances the Bank is prepared to purchase in its OMOs.

In times of acute shortage of liquidity in the market, the Bank enters into REPOS agreements with the commercial banks directly.

All institutions in the monetary sector are obliged to keep with the Bank 0.35 per cent of their deposits in non-operational and non-interest bearing deposits. This requirement is not meant to affect the assets of the banks – although it does; rather, it is meant to provide income for the Bank.

Under the 'dirty' floating exchange rate policy (i.e. the Bank intervenes in the market when it feels it to be necessary) pursued in the UK, the authorities seek to hold the exchange rate of sterling within a range which they believe to be in the best interests of the economy as a whole (currently the crucial rate is between sterling and deutschemark). To prevent the exchange rate falling dangerously low, the Bank of England will seek, by direct intervention (i.e. buying sterling on the foreign exchange market), to raise short-term interest rates respectively to reduce the supply of, and increase the demand for, sterling on the foreign exchange markets.

Monetary control in the UK has not been an unqualified success. As far as the *manipulation of interest rates* is concerned, via OMOs, the interest rate policy has suffered due to two reasons:

1. The Bank of England cannot control *both* the money supply and the price of money, i.e. interest rates, simultaneously.
2. The demand for bank advances, at least in the short run, is often interest-inelastic.

UK interest rates were above those in other major countries, making UK firms less competitive internationally. In 1993, however, the UK interest rates have been competitive.

The attempts by the Bank of England to ease the acute downward pressure on the *foreign exchange value of sterling* by raising the level of short-term interest rates has attracted excessive inflow of foreign speculative and investment balances into the country. This had an adverse effect on efforts to control the growth of money supply. Fluctuations in the exchange rate have caused uncertainty for UK exporters and importers. The balance of payments position has progressively deteriorated. Inflation reached an unacceptable level, until falling to below 3 per cent in 1993. The economic growth rate for the first half of 1989/90 was a mere annualised 1.5 per cent. During late 1990 and early 1991, it was negative.

The above analysis of the problems and after-effects of monetary policy which has sought to control interest rates, the money supply and the exchange rate, shows that the authorities cannot, in practice, achieve the intermediate monetary target of controlling all these variables *at the same time*, however much they might think otherwise.

On the positive side, the total national output growth has been until 1991 around 3 per cent, and the PSBR, as a percentage of the national output, has been steadily reduced, there was a balanced Budget for 1989–90, and since the 1987–8 Budget there has been budget surpluses. Unemployment steadily fell but since the middle of 1990 it has been rising rapidly, reaching 2,753,400 in July 1992. Economic growth became positive in 1993.

■ Recent examination questions

The following six questions have been asked in recent years on the topic of economic policy, monetary policy and its relationship with fiscal policy. Before looking at the outline answers, spend ten minutes or so trying to identify the main points to be used in your answer to each question.

Question 1

To what extent is a successful anti-inflationary policy necessarily associated with an increase in unemployment? Illustrate your answer with reference to the economic experience of the UK during the past decade.

Question 2

(a) Outline the principal goals of economic policy.
(b) Consider the extent to which monetary policy in the UK has been successful in achieving these economic goals in recent years.

Question 3

In the 1988 UK Budget the Chancellor of the Exchequer indicated that the UK no longer had a Public Sector Borrowing Requirement (PSBR) but a Public Sector Debt Repayment (PSDR).

(a) Explain precisely what the Chancellor meant by this statement.
(b) Discuss the impact a PSDR will have on:
    (i) interest rates;
    (ii) the market for gilt-edged securities;
    (iii) the money supply.

Question 4

How is the growth of the money supply affected by the following: (a) fiscal policy, (b) monetary policy and (c) exchange rate policy?

Question 5

Describe the following and discuss their role in the operation of monetary policy:

(a) gilt-edged securities;
(b) commercial (eligible bank) bills;
(c) the sale of public sector assets.

Question 6

In seeking to achieve the ultimate objectives of economic policy, the authorities can set *intermediate* targets.

(a) Discuss the *intermediate* targets that might be selected.
(b) List the techniques that could be used to achieve these targets.

■ Outline answers

Answer 1

(a) Explain *alternative* policies to control inflation:
  (i) Deflation: via monetary policy and/or fiscal policy.
  (ii) Prices and incomes policy: to control aggregate demand and expenditure.
  (iii) Import controls: their effects on balance of payments deficit.
(b) Discuss causes of inflation:
  (i) Cost-push: increased labour costs pushing up prices.
  (ii) Demand-pull: prices pulled up by too much money chasing too few goods.
(c) In the UK there has been some trade-off between inflation and unemployment.

Answer 2

(a) List clearly the traditional goals of economic policy:
  (i) Full employment; stable prices; slight surplus in the current account of balance of payments; reasonable 'real' economic growth rate; satisfactory and stable exchange rate; a more equal distribution of income between rich and poor people and between rich and poor areas.
(b) Explain the problems confronted by the authorities in achieving all goals simultaneously:
  (i) Inherent conflicts among goals: control of inflation leads to rising unemployment and unsatisfactory exchange rate.
  (ii) Monetary policy, like fiscal policy, is an integral part of economic policy, and is not easy to isolate for analysis.
  (iii) MTFS and its link with PSBR and money supply.

Answer 3

(a) (i) A PSBR is the *excess* of central government nationalised industries and local authorities expenditure over revenues. This has been the situation for many years in the UK, certainly since the Second World War.
  (ii) The emergence of the PSDR implies the *reverse*, meaning that National Debt can be repaid from the excess of revenue accruing to the public sector.
(b) (i) A PSDR implies that the private sector borrowers are not 'crowded out'; there is less pressure for borrowing *long-term* funds, and long-term interest rates should fall, other things remaining unchanged.
  (ii) The gilt market will contract as the government requires to raise no funds to finance its activities, and repays existing debt.
  (iii) – Reference to the *counterparts* analysis shows that the sector from which gilts are purchased is crucially important. Bearing in mind that the government has withdrawn funds from the system. To the extent that gilts are purchased from the private sector (other than banks and building societies) there will be *no impact* on the money supply *once the cycle is completed*.
    – Purchases from banks and building societies will *reduce* the money supply.
    – Purchases from overseas residents, e.g. from sterling held overseas, will *reduce* the money supply.

Answer 4

(a) *Fiscal policy*. Money supply growth is affected by changes in taxation and revenue which establish the size of the budget deficit or surplus: increase or decrease, respectively.

(b) *Monetary policy*.

    (i) By transactions with M4 private sector: no net impact on the money supply.

    (ii) By transactions with central bank and commercial banks: increase in the money supply (in case of PSBR), decrease in the money supply (neutralising budget surplus).

    (iii) By transactions with overseas residents: money supply will increase, if sterling was held overseas (PSBR), no change in money supply if the destination of sterling is overseas (PSDR).

    (iv) By indirect controls on bank lending (e.g. raising interest rates) or direct controls on bank lending (e.g. special deposits, corset).

(c) *Exchange rate policy*. Direct intervention to support exchange rate will automatically affect the money supply: it will increase if sterling is being sold; it will decrease if sterling is being bought, *unless* the effects on money supply are neutralised by OMOs. Increase in gilt sales when selling sterling; increase in gilt purchases when buying sterling.

Answer 5

(a) (i) To finance the PSBR, the authorities can sell gilts to the:
- M4 and building society private sector;
- banking and building society sector;
- Bank of England;
- overseas sector.

    (ii) Sales to the M4 private sector together with the increase in PSBR have no effect on money supply, therefore keep monetary expansion under control.

(b) (i) Commercial bills accepted by eligible banks become eligible bills, eligible for sale by the discount houses to the Bank of England to relieve cash shortages in the market.

    (ii) Dealing in eligible bills dominates the Bank's money market operations to smooth liquidity fluctuations and to influence short-term interest rates; the Bank provides relief to the market by purchasing the bills at rates consistent with interest rate policy.

    (iii) Dealing is usually in Bands 1 and 2 of the four maturity bands, but also sometimes in longer-term bills, if considered appropriate.

(c) (i) Sale of public sector assets *reduces* the size of the PSBR, rather than finances it; therefore the amount of gilt sales is reduced by the amount of the net privatisation proceeds.

Answer 6

(a) Candidates for intermediate targets:

    (i) *Money supply*. Monetarists consider this as a very important target because of the close link between changes in the money supply and inflation. *Problem*: which definition of the money supply to target.

    (ii) *Interest rates*. Interest rates play a significant role in controlling other intermediate targets. By effecting changes in interest rates, the authorities hope to influence consumer spending and business investment. *Problem*: it will be months before interest rate changes take effect.

   (iii) *Credit*. There is a close relationship between the volume of credit and the level of expenditure because changes in credit cause changes in the money supply. *Problem*: unless *all* credit is targeted, disintermediation will result.

   (iv) *Expenditure*. A target might be set for the nominal GNP growth. *Problem*: too many factors affect the GNP growth. PSBR, as a proportion of the GNP, may be targeted.

   (v) *The exchange rate*. The connection between it and inflation and trade performance make it an obvious target: *Problem*: achieving the exchange rate target may militate against other objectives.

(b)   (i) The size of the PSBR and the sources of its finance.
   (ii) Direct intervention by the central bank to influence exchange rate.
   (iii) Manipulation of interest rates.
   (iv) OMOs.
   (v) Moral suasion.
   (vi) Reserve requirements.
   (vii) Direct control on lending:
      - special deposits;
      - quantitative;
      - qualitative.

▌ A tutor's answer

The following question deals with the theory and the practice of monetary policy. The specimen answer covers the full scope of the question. Try to make a relevant answer plan yourself before reading the specimen answer.

Question

(a) Outline the principal features of monetary policy as operated in the UK since 1979.
(b) To what extent have the overall goals of macro-economic policy been achieved in the UK since 1979?

Answer plan

(a)   (i) The ultimate objective of the monetary policy.
   (ii) The policy framework to achieve that objective.
   (iii) The implementation of the policy.
(b) An account of how monetary policy has fared in tackling:
   (i) inflation;
   (ii) economic growth;
   (iii) current account of the balance of payments;
   (iv) unemployment.

Specimen answer

(a) The main thrust of the monetary policy since 1979 has been towards securing a progressive reduction in monetary growth to contain and ultimately to eliminate inflation, thus providing a firm basis for economic growth. A steady decline in the PSBR as a percentage of Gross National Product, and in money supply growth, were projected for a number of years in advance, though these projections have been subject to upward revisions from time to time. Annual targets for various monetary and liquidity aggregates, and for the PSBR/GNP ratio have been adopted. Sterling's performance, as reflected by its exchange rate, has not been an explicit intermediate *target*. Rather it has become an increasingly important *indicator* of the success of monetary policy, particularly so from October 1985 onwards with the reduced emphasis on the behaviour of broad money. With UK's entry in the ERM (1990 to 1992), exchange rate was targeted.

The implementation of the policy has been achieved through: (i) controlling the size of the PSBR by expenditure cutbacks; (ii) Bank of England money market operations to influence the level of interest rates; and (iii) funding (or, for much of the period, overfunding), by selling public sector debt outside the banking system.

(b) The problem of *inflation* has been tackled very successfully over the past eight years, with the RPI falling from 18 per cent in 1980 to a little over 3 per cent in the first half of 1987. However, the inflation rate had risen to nearly 10 per cent by June 1990, but fell to below 3 per cent in 1993.

Economic growth in the period from 1983 to 1985 was restored to the long-term average of between 2 per cent and 3 per cent a year. This was near the EC average, but low by comparison with the USA and Japan. Economic growth, however, slowed down during 1986, but there was some resurgence in 1987, achieving a growth rate of around 2 per cent by August 1989. For 1990 and 1991, economic growth was mostly negative. By the middle of 1993 the growth rate was positive.

The *current account of the balance of payments*, aided by substantial oil revenues (except for the first nine months of 1986) had been in moderate surplus or near equilibrium from 1980 to 1985. It went into heavy deficit in March 1986, and performed rather badly until the rise in oil prices in the autumn of 1986. Britain, however, is currently a net importer of manufactured goods. By the end of 1992, the balance of payments deficit was approximately £20 billion.

The buoyant economic conditions during 1987−8 and increased government tax revenues and privatisation receipts resulted in the elimination of the PSBR and the emergence of a PSDR (Public Sector Debt Repayment) of over £14 billion in 1988−9.

In the twelve months to February 1989, M0 grew at 6.6 per cent per annum, a substantial drop from 8.1 per cent annual growth in January 1989. Since 1991, M0 has stayed within its target range.

In common with the experience of most other countries in Europe, and North America, the UK performance on *unemployment* has been disappointing. Despite the economic upturn between 1982 and 1985, the number out of work remained on a stubbornly rising trend, reaching over three million by August 1986. The unemployment figures rose to nearly three million during 1992. There are economists who maintain that a reflationary monetary policy will break the log jam rapidly and reduce unemployment. There are others who claim that reflation will merely result in an upsurge in price and wage inflation. The stance of the current UK monetary policy was slightly expansionary until about the autumn of 1988, when the inflation rate began to rise alarmingly and the brakes were applied on economic activity via the high interest rate policy. In August 1993 bank base rates were 6 per cent, and the PSBR for 1993/4 was £50 billion, suggesting an expansionary economic policy to alleviate the severe recession. UK joined the ERM in October 1990 and left it in September 1992, because the UK authorities could not keep the pound within the six per cent fluctuation margin.

∎ A step further

This chapter and the chapters on 'Money and Inflation', 'Money Supply', 'Interest Rates' and 'Exchange Rates' are closely connected. It is essential for you to understand this linkage in order to gain an overall understanding of domestic monetary economics. The Chartered Institute of Bankers' *Examiners' Reports, Updating Notes* and 'Signpost' articles in *Banking World* are extremely useful sources for keeping abreast of various movements in monetary policy, and also in topics linked to monetary policy. In this connection, a study of *A Guide to Monetary Policy*, published by the Banking Information Service, is strongly recommended. Bank of England *Quarterly Bulletins* (*BEQB*s) give the up-to-date official figures and facts of the UK economy.

CHAPTER 8

Balance of Payments

Syllabus requirements
- The structure of the balance of payments accounts in general and of the UK in particular.
- Recent influences on the UK balance of payments.
- Causes and effects of changes in the terms of trade.
- Method of correcting current account disequilibrium.
- Difference between 'financing' and 'correcting' current account imbalances.

▮ Getting started

A country imports those goods and services which it needs but is either unable to produce internally or which it can only produce at uncompetitive cost or of inferior quality. It pays for the imports of such goods and services largely by its foreign currency earnings from exports. The balance of payments of any country records the revenues and payments from *all* economic and non-economic transactions between its government, firms (including their foreign subsidiaries) and residents, and the governments, firms and residents of those countries with which it trades. The balance of payments is an account and, like any other account, it must balance.

The importance of the balance of payments position to a country is that if it has exported more goods and services than it has imported, then it is a creditor country and stands to receive payments in foreign currencies. These can be used to build up its currency reserves, to repay past overseas loans, to invest overseas and to give aid to less developed countries (LDCs). Conversely, if it has imported more goods and services than it has exported over a period of time, then it is a debtor country, and has to make good the deficit by drawing on its currency reserves, by borrowing overseas, by selling its valuable assets and foreign investment and even by accepting foreign aid. A chronic balance of payments deficit for a country suggests to the rest of the world that it is unable to pay its way in international trade and investment, which reflects badly on its government, firms and citizens.

A country's foreign currency and gold reserves are finite and its ability to borrow overseas or to raise funds in some other ways is not without limit. Therefore, a country with a continuous balance of payments deficit runs the distinct risk of being treated as a bad debtor by its trading partners, who may refuse to sell it the goods and services it needs. If this happens, then its economic growth will be badly hit and the level of employment and the standard of living of its residents will fall significantly.

It is therefore of utmost importance for the government of a country suffering from a prolonged deficit on its external account to take such measures internally as will encourage its exports and discourage its imports, so that the deficit on its balance of payments is rectified and it is once again able to pay its way in the world.

■ Essential principles

Terms of trade

Over a period of time, the terms of trade compare the relative changes in the prices of a country's exports with relative changes in the prices of its imports. The changes in export prices are expressed as a percentage of changes in import prices, and then presented as an index, with some base year as 100. The terms of trade index of a country is determined by the following formula:

$$\text{Index of terms of trade} = \frac{\text{Index of export prices}}{\text{Index of import prices}} \times 100$$

The indices for both exports and imports start at 100 at a common starting date. If the index increases, compared to a base year at 100, the terms of trade are said to have 'improved', i.e. a given quantity of exports will purchase more imports than before. Thus, if the index of export prices of a country has risen over a period of years from 100 to 119, and its index of import prices has fallen over the same period of years from 100 to 97, then the terms of trade of the country are said to have improved over the period by the ratio 119/97 x 100 = 122.68 per cent. Since the terms of trade index in the base year was 100, then, in the above example, the purchasing power of a fixed bundle of exports rose over the period by 22.68 per cent, i.e. 22.68 per cent more imports could be purchased at the end of the period than were purchased by the same fixed quantity of exports in the base year. Note that the terms of trade refer to the multilateral trade of a country and not to its bilateral trade.

Changes in the terms of trade, i.e. relative changes in the prices of exports and imports, affect the *values* of exports and imports. Since values are quantities multiplied by prices, the relative *elasticities* of demand for exports and imports will be vital in determining whether the total receipts from exports or the total payments for imports will rise or fall as export and import prices change. If the overseas demand for a country's *exports is elastic*, then, other things being equal, its total receipts from exports will be greater at *lower* export prices, i.e. when the terms of trade have 'deteriorated'. If the overseas demand for its *exports is inelastic*, then total receipts from exports will be greater at *higher* export prices, i.e. when the terms of trade have 'improved'. Similarly, if the domestic demand for its *imports is elastic*, then, other things being equal, its import bill will be greater at *lower* import prices, i.e. when the terms of trade have 'improved'; if the demand for its *imports is inelastic*, its import bill will be greater at *higher* import prices, i.e. when the terms of trade have 'deteriorated'. Clearly the terms 'improvement' and 'deterioration' must be treated with caution when applied to the terms of trade.

There are gains to be made by countries specialising in the commodities they are relatively most efficient in producing, and exporting the surpluses for imports. However, if the terms of trade deteriorate, then the *exchange* advantage can be less than before. This does not mean however that the gains from trade will necessarily grow just because the terms of trade 'improve'. For instance, a rise in the price of exports may − unless demand for exports is inelastic − be associated with a fall in the *volume* of exports. Any cut in the volume of trade will clearly diminish the gains from specialisation and trade.

Changes in the prices of exports and imports result from various factors affecting the conditions of supply and demand for goods which are traded on international markets. *Producers* of a good for which there is a world-wide inelastic demand may exploit their *monopoly* position and raise the price of the product several times over, thereby improving their terms of trade. On the other hand, the major *buyers* of certain products may exploit their *monopsony* (buyer's monopoly) position by deliberately withholding demand, thereby causing the terms of trade of the suppliers of such products to deteriorate.

Shortages of food and raw materials in industrialised countries, or increases in demand for such commodities via higher real incomes or population growth, will tend to improve the terms of trade of *primary goods producing* countries. On the other hand, technical progress may cause the terms of trade of primary goods-producing countries to deteriorate; for instance if the new information technologies economise on the need for raw materials in production.

∎ Protectionism and other direct controls

In order to protect home industries and employment against foreign competition and to become self-sufficient in essential goods, a country may seek to protect itself against imports. Import barriers may take any of the following forms:

(a) *Import tariffs.* When home products and foreign substitutes are equally priced, an import duty which is higher than any domestic excise duty is protective; it raises the price of foreign substitutes above the price of the domestic product, making home products more attractive.
(b) *Subsidies.* The government gives direct grants to home producers to reduce their unit costs and give them a price advantage over imported goods.
(c) *Export premiums.* Exporters are given rebates or refunds of taxation on exports to encourage the expansion of existing export industries.
(d) *Quotas.* A specified volume or value of imports is allowed during a *given* period.
(e) *Physical controls.* A complete embargo may be imposed on imports from certain countries.

Of the above protective methods, only import tariffs provide income for the government practising protection. In the UK, protection in one form or another has been practised since 1932. Protective measures are often 'hidden', in the form of credit guarantees, cheaper finance to exporters, import deposits and excessive documentation against imports.

Most trading countries accept that an international trade free from protection will benefit all participants. To free international trade from trade barriers, associations such as the General Agreement on Tariffs and Trade (GATT) have been set up. Although GATT, with over 100 member countries, has succeeded in reducing import tariffs to an appreciable extent, the aim of complete free trading among members still remains only an ideal.

Protection need not be confined to a single country, but may be extended to cover a group of countries, e.g. the twelve member countries of the EC enjoy free trade amongst themselves but have a protective wall around themselves and the rest of the world.

∎ Rectifying imbalances in the balance of payments

As we have already noted, no country can continue to have a balance of payments deficit year after year. However, no country may continue to have a balance of payments *surplus*, for at least two reasons.

1. It means that such a country is continuously selling more to the rest of the world, and buying less from it. This is likely to mean that the export earnings of *other countries*

in the surplus country's currency are less than is required; therefore they will become less and less able to buy and pay for the surplus country's exports. It may even be in the surplus country's own interest to work off its surplus by increasing its imports from the rest of the world.

2. If the surplus country refuses to increase imports, it may lead other countries to erect trade barriers against its exports via prohibitive import duties, stringent import quotas or even an embargo on its exports.

∎ Rectifying a balance of payments surplus

Under freely floating exchange rates (see Ch.9), the adjustment should be automatic via the market mechanism. The demand for the surplus country's currency will be high, because the rest of the world will need its currency to pay for their imports; this will push up the exchange rate of the surplus country's currency, making its exports expensive and its imports cheaper and more attractive. The higher exchange rate will, other things being equal, tend to eliminate the surplus and bring about an automatic equilibrium in its balance of payments. If 'other things' are not equal, e.g. there is inelastic demand for its exports, then the government of the surplus country will need to take deliberate policy action to discourage exports and the inflow of capital, and to encourage imports and the outflow of capital.

The following are possible policy measures which the government may take to correct a *surplus* on its balance of payments on current account.

(a) *Expansion of home demand.* This may be achieved by reducing taxes, lowering interest rates, lifting credit restraints and increasing public expenditure. The increase in home demand would divert export production to the home market and increase the level of imports, thus reducing surplus on visible trade. The extent to which resources switch to home demand will depend on the elasticity of domestic supply, i.e. how quickly domestic supply can meet increased home demand.

(b) *Allow its exchange rate to rise.* That is, let the exchange rate appreciate under floating rates, revalue under fixed exchange rates. Adjustment through the exchange rate mechanism involves changes in prices, so that the elasticities of demand for imports and exports will be crucial. If the demand for *imports* is elastic, then the total amount of foreign exchange paid out on imports will be greater at a lower domestic price, i.e. after appreciation (or revaluation) of the domestic currency; similarly, if the demand for *exports* is elastic, the amount of foreign exchange received for exports will be lower at the higher overseas price, i.e. after appreciation (or revaluation). The policy objective here is to increase total import payments and to decrease total export revenue.

(c) *Free imports from restrictions, and place restrictions on exports.* Import restrictions, such as import quotas, restrict the volume of imports; *removal* of such restrictions will markedly increase imports. By the same reasoning, placing export quotas, especially if the demand for exports is elastic, will quickly achieve a reduction in the volume of exports. However, some countries, e.g. those who produce and export oil, may prefer to place a tax on exports; this will not only reduce exports, but will at the same time benefit the National Exchequer.

(d) *Reduce net 'invisible' earnings.* This may be achieved by a variety of measures, such as giving grants to developing countries, or by encouraging residents to take holidays abroad and to send gifts to relatives and to charities overseas. Note that giving *loans* to developing countries will mean that interest on loans will increase the surplus on current account.

■ Rectifying a balance of payments deficit

A deficit country will need to adjust its current account and/or currency flows.

Adjustments on current account

Depreciation or devaluation of the exchange rate of the domestic currency

This means a fall in the exchange rate. Other things being equal, this will make imports expensive and therefore less competitive with domestic goods, and make exports more competitive in overseas markets. The extent of the reduction in imports and increase in exports will be determined by the relative elasticities of demand for imports and exports. If the price elasticity of demand for imports is elastic, i.e. if the percentage change in quantity of imports demanded divided by the percentage change in price of imports (consequent upon depreciation/devaluation) results in greater than one, then a rise in import price will cause a more than proportionate fall in the quantity of imports. The *value* of imports (quantity of imports × price) will then be less than it was *before* the depreciation/devaluation. If, however, the price elasticity of demand for imports is inelastic, then depreciation/devaluation will cause the value of imports to be greater than it was prior to the fall in the exchange rate. A similar calculation will derive the price elasticity of demand for exports. Note that the calculation of the *relative elasticities* of demand for imports and exports is vital in order to determine precisely the extent to which the exchange value of the national currency must fall in order to achieve the desired level of import reduction and export expansion.

The factors which determine the demand elasticities for imports and exports are:

(a) the availability of close substitutes in terms of price and quality; such substitutes tend to make demand elastic;

(b) the time scale; in the short term, both demand and supply tend to be less elastic than they are in the long term.

If the *sum* of price elasticities of demand for exports and imports is *greater than one*, i.e. elastic, then a fall in the exchange rate will improve the balance of payments (*Marshall-Lerner* theory). It will be some months before the fall in exchange rate has full impact: the *'J' curve effect* − falling to begin with then rising, i.e. the deficit may worsen before improving.

Deflationary policies

These may take the form of higher taxes and interest rates, tighter hire purchase regulations and constraints on lending, and reductions in government expenditure. The intention of all such policies is to reduce aggregate domestic demand, thereby reducing demand for imports as well. Further, as domestic demand is reduced, so will be the pressure on domestic prices, which may then fall; a lower rate of inflation will improve the competitiveness of exports and domestic import substitutes.

Direct control measures

These may involve import controls or export subsidies. However, direct measures run the risk of retaliation by trading partners, and may contravene the rules and regulations of trade associations of which the deficit country may be a member, e.g. the General Agreement on Tariffs and Trade (GATT), the EC, etc. The success of direct controls will largely depend upon the willing co-operation of trading partners.

Exchange controls

If stringently applied, these will place restrictions on the access to foreign currency by domestic residents. Buying foreign goods or foreign services has a negative effect on the current account; exchange controls may help reduce either or both, thereby reducing any current account deficit. However the effects of exchange controls on the currency flows are often more dramatic, and it is to the capital account that we now turn.

Adjustments on currency flows

A number of measures may be adopted:

(a) Higher interest rates encourage a greater inflow of currency; for example foreign short- and long-term investment may be attracted by higher returns. Higher interest rates may also discourage outflows of currency to other financial centres.
(b) Lower taxation on profits and an easier repatriation of capital and profits may attract even more foreign investment capital.

■ Financing a current account deficit

The deficit *must* be financed. The following methods may be used to obtain foreign currencies to finance the deficit:

(a) Attract overseas capital, by higher interest rates and good prospects of high profitability, into factories, equipment, etc. or indirect portfolio investment in purchasing stocks and shares.
(b) Draw on official currency reserves.
(c) Borrow from the IMF, other central banks and/or eurocurrency markets, without creating future repayment problems.

If the deficit is temporary and not unbearably large, then it need not be unfavourable to the country concerned. Since the economy is importing more than it is producing, there is some short-term gain in living standards. If the economy is coming out of recession it will need more imports than exports, i.e. a deliberate current account deficit in the short term in order to have a surplus in the long term.

■ Useful applied materials

The structure of the UK balance of payments accounts

There are three components of the UK balance of payments accounts:

(1) current account;
(2) external assets and liabilities (capital account);
(3) balancing item.

Current account

There are two sections in this account:

1. *The visible trade balance (or balance of trade)*. An excess of exports of *goods* over imports of *goods* results in a surplus balance of trade (+); an excess of imports of goods over exports of goods results in a deficit balance of trade (−). A surplus on visible trade means, other things being equal, an inflow of foreign currency; a deficit means an outflow of foreign currency.
2. *The invisible trade balance*. The *'invisible'* earnings of a country result from the sale of *services* (banking, shipping, tourism, insurance and other financial services); the receipt of transfer payments (e.g. receipts by residents of monies transferred by relatives abroad, and more recently payments to the EC and refunds from it); the receipt of interest (payments from abroad for investments held abroad); and the receipt of profits (from successful trading by overseas subsidiaries) and dividends and interest (from the ownership of the share capital of foreign firms and their subsidiaries), transport and travel, government services. The *'invisible' payments* are in respect of the above items, but in reverse.

A surplus (+) on the 'invisible' trade balance suggests an excess of 'invisible' receipts over 'invisible' payments, and a deficit (−) on the 'invisible' trade balance suggests an excess of 'invisible' payments over 'invisible' receipts. As with the visible trade balance, a ' + ' or a ' − ' on the invisible balance will, other things being equal, result in an inflow or outflow respectively of foreign currency.

The *current account* is the sum of the visible and invisible trade balances; it represents the UK's claims against or indebtedness to the rest of the world on the current basis.

External assets and liabilities

Capital transactions include *official* capital transactions (inter-government and inter-governmental agencies; e.g. loans, grants and subscriptions), and *private* capital transactions (long-term and short-term, direct and indirect, investment and speculative balances): purchases of and sales to overseas governments and public bodies' stocks, business company securities, etc.

Private long-term balances are attracted overseas by the prospect of greater profits on investments; private short-term funds (hot money) are attracted overseas by the prospect of short-term gains, either because of interest rate differentials, or because of the possibility of exchange rate movements in the leading international financial centres. In addition to the above capital transactions, there are borrowings and lendings by banks and other financial institutions, and import and export credits, i.e. importers delaying payments or exporters allowing delayed payments. The changes in external assets and liabilities are added to the current account balance and *in theory* the total of the two components should result in a zero balance.

Balancing item

In practice, the total of the current account and changes in external assets and liabilities does not result in zero; any unidentified items form the *balancing item*. The balancing item balances the difference between the *actual* amount of currency received by the monetary authorities of a country and the amount that they *should* have received as recorded in the current and capital accounts. The imbalance between what has been received, and what should have been received results from errors and omissions in the recording of payments. If the balancing item is positive (+), then *more* foreign currency has actually been received than the recorded items show; if it is negative (−), then less foreign money has actually been received than the recorded items show. Over a number of years, + and − values of errors and omissions largely tend to cancel each other out.

If there is no balancing item then the sum of the current account and external assets and liabilities *will* be zero because of an extension of double-entry bookkeeping, i.e. every debit must have a credit, which can either be a current account item or involve an external asset or liability. For example, exports for cash involve the current account (the receipts from the exports) and also an increase in an asset (cash). If the exports are financed by a loan then this loan is an asset. When interest is received on the loan then invisible exports (and cash) rise. When the loan is repaid then there is a switch on the composition of the assets from the loan to the cash received. All the debits should equal all the credits.

Table 8.1 shows the UK balance of payments accounts constructed according to the method described above.

After the abolition of exchange controls and the coming on stream of North Sea oil at the end of the 1970s, UK investment overseas has been increasing strongly. Foreign investment in the UK, however, did not really increase until after 1985, with the most marked increase being in direct investment by non-oil companies. The main reasons for this rise in inward investment are the UK's continuing high rate of economic growth (until 1989), the approach of the single European Community Market (in 1993), and relatively high interest rates, until the end of 1992 (see p. 139: Exchange controls).

In recent years the large positive balancing item, which can also be revised drastically, has caused the accuracy of the balance of payments data to be questioned. For example, it was published at £3.5 billion for 1987 in January 1988, but in March 1988 it was revised up to £12.4 billion for 1987. These uncertainties over the balancing item − the figure for unidentified items − which the then Chancellor of the Exchequer called 'another name for errors and omissions', led him to qualify the £14.6 billion current account deficit for 1988 with 'whatever the true figure is, it is undoubtedly large'.

The critical element in the UK balance of payments for 1988 was the £39 billion borrowed from overseas by the UK banks and non-bank private sector because it was this money which financed the 1988 current account deficit. If this kind of borrowed money begins to be withdrawn because the overseas investors lose confidence in the strength of the UK economy and the stability of sterling, then a 'hard landing' for sterling will be inevitable, involving depreciation, high inflation and more unemployment, causing recession in the UK economy.

Between mid-1980 and Easter 1984, the UK enjoyed fifteen successive quarters of current account surpluses, but now it is faced with an even longer succession of deficits. The main cause of this deterioration has been the substantial increase in the deficit on the *visible trade*.

The expected decline in North Sea oil production has begun but further cut-backs have resulted from the Piper Alpha disaster. Not only has output fallen but so has price. Export revenues from oil have fallen by about 36 per cent in 1988 compared with 1987. Between 1985 and 1988, the volume of non-oil exports rose by 14 per cent but the volume of imports rose by 29 per cent. The current account quarterly deficits have been as high as £3 or £4 billion during this period.

In the invisibles, under 'Services', only the 'financial and other services' sub-section is in substantial surplus, all other sub-sections are in deficit. 'Interest, Profits and Dividends' section is also in substantial credit, largely due to heavy investment overseas since the

Table 8.1 UK balance of payments accounts

	£ million			First two quarters of
	1986	1987	1988	1989

1. *Current account* (exports and imports of goods and services, investment income and transfers).

Visible trade

	1986	1987	1988	1989
(Credits) Exports of merchandise	72,656	79,421	80,602	44,336
(Debits) Imports of merchandise	82,020	90,350	101,428	56,147
(a) Visible trade balance =	− 9,364	− 10,929	− 20,826	− 11,811

Invisibles

	1986	1987	1988	1989
Services (insurance, banking, transport, travel)	6,247	5,682	4,165	2,171
Interest, profits and dividends (including overseas subsidiaries)	5,364	4,987	5,619	1,631
Transfers (including payments and receipts from EC budget)	− 2,181	− 3,411	− 3,575	− 1,632
(b) Invisible balance =	9,430	7,258	6,209	2,170
Current balance ((a) + (b)) =	66	− 3,671	− 14,617	− 9,641

2. *Transactions in UK external assets and liabilities (inward and outward investments).*

Assets (− = increase)

	1986	1987	1988	1989
UK direct investment overseas*	− 11,304	− 18,615	− 15,219	− 8,770
UK portfolio investment overseas**	− 23,068	+ 2,702 (fall)	− 9,718	− 14,783
Bank and other lending overseas	− 54,689	− 55,200	− 21,484	− 14,231
UK government external assets	− 509	− 796	− 891	− 356
UK governemt official reserves	− 2,891	− 12,012	− 2,761	+ 2,636 (fall)
Total transactions in assets =	− 92,461	− 83,921	− 50,073	− 35,504

Liabilities (+ = increase)

	1986	1987	1988	1989
Overseas direct investment in UK	+ 4,846	+ 8,108	+ 7,346	+ 9,233
Overseas portfolio investment in UK	+ 8,135	+ 10,440	+ 4,639	− 12 (fall)
UK bank and other borrowing from overseas	+ 68,210	+ 56,136	+ 39,522	+ 28,787
UK government borrowing from overseas	+ 178	+ 1,570	+ 902	+ 28
Total transaction in liabilities =	+ 81,369	+ 76,254	+ 52,409	+ 38,036

Summary

	1986	1987	1988	1989
Increase in assets	− 92,461	− 83,921	− 50,073	− 35,504
Increase in liabilities	+ 81,369	+ 76,254	+ 52,409	+ 38,036
Net change	− 11,092	− 7,667	+ 2,336	+ 2,532

	1986	1987	1988	1989
3. *Balancing item.*	+ 11,026	+ 11,338	− 12,281	+ 7,109
Balance on current account	+ 66	− 3,671	− 14,617	− 9,641
Difference	nil	nil	nil	nil

* Direct: Investment in houses, factories, warehouses, etc.
** Portfolio: Investment in stocks, shares and other financial securities.
Source: Press release for 1989 data.
Note: Another and, according to the CIB Chief Examiner, acceptable way of presenting the UK Balance of Payments Accounts, is shown in Table 8.2.

Table 8.2 UK balance of payments accounts (alternative)

1. *The current account:*
(a) Balance of trade
   Exports (visibles)   (+)
   Imports (visibles)   (−)
                                                              Visible trade balance (±)
(b) Invisibles
   Services (insurance, shipping, banking)   (±)
   Interest, profits, dividends   (±)
   Transfers (remittances to and from
      residents and governments including
      to and from EC budget)   (±)
   Transport and travel   (±)
   Government services (consular,
      diplomatic, troops)   (±)
                                                              Invisible trade balance (±)
                                                              Net current balance (±)

2. *Investment and other capital flows:*
         Inward flow (+)   Outward flow (−)
Overseas investment in the UK: Official long-term capital
   private sector   UK private investment overseas
   public sector   Import credits
Overseas currency borrowings by UK banks   Export credits
* Exchange reserves in sterling

* Other external and money market liabilities
   in sterling
Other transactions
                     (+)   (−)
                          Net investment and other capital flows balance (±)

3. *Total currency flow:*
Net current balance   (±)
Net investment and other capital flows
   balance   (±)
                                                              Net currency flow (±)

4. *The balancing item* (±)

5. *Official financing:*
Net currency flow   (±)
Balancing item   (±)
                                                              Balance for official financing (±)

Sources of official finance (a) (b)
   (i) Overseas monetary authorities:
       International Monetary Fund   (+) or (−)
       Central banks   (+) or (−)
       Others   (+) or (−)
   (ii) Foreign currency borrowings by:
       The UK government   (+) or (−)
       Public bodies   (+) or (−)
   (iii) The UK official reserves   (+) or (−)
               Total official financing   nil

Note:
(a) The balance of payments is an account, and like any other account it must balance: the function of official financing
   is to achieve that balance.
(b) In the context of official financing:
   a '−' sign is a favourable entry because it reflects a positive net currency flow; a '−' sign here means either an
   increase in assets or a reduction in liabilities. For instance a balance of payments surplus can be used to increase
   official reserves or to pay off previous borrowing.
   A '+' sign is an unfavourable entry because it reflects a negative net currency flow; a '+' sign here means either
   a decrease in assets or an increase in liabilities. For instance a balance of payments deficit can be financed by running
   down official reserves or by extra borrowing.
* These two entries, under the Capital Account, are called 'Sterling Balances', and are highly sensitive to interest rate
differentials and exchange rate movements. Holders of these balances are always seeking capital gains from such differentials
and movements.

beginning of the 1980s. The 'Transfers' section is in slight deficit in both the government and private sub-sections. The government's deficit is increased by net transfers to the EC.

By keeping the UK interest rates higher than the USA, Germany and Japan, the Chancellor had been able to attract sufficient short-term funds from overseas, so that *financing* the deficit had not proved a problem; much will depend upon overseas investors maintaining their confidence in the authorities' ability to manage the economy satisfactorily.

Correction of the huge deficit is being undertaken solely through the rate of interest, which is kept at a high enough level not only to finance the deficit but also to reduce domestic demand in order to lower inflation. However, the problem with the high interest rate policy is that it leads to high rates of exchange, which worsen the trade deficit by making exports more, and imports less, expensive.

Exchange controls

When, in the past, exchange controls operated in the UK all the private sector's foreign currency earnings had to be exchanged for sterling at the Bank of England, and only the Bank authorised withdrawals from the currency reserves to the UK importers, investors, banks and tourists. The objective of exchange controls was two-fold: to keep the balance of payments out of deficit and to ration currency reserves according to the national priorities. However, the major problems with exchange controls were the development of black markets in 'hard' currencies (i.e. the currencies which were hard to get because their countries of origin were running balance of payment surpluses), the frustration of firms who could not import the required raw materials to carry through their expansion projects and the inability of investors and banks to obtain the best returns from their activities in the international markets. In October 1979, the new government, because of their strong commitment to the free operation of market forces on the domestic and international levels, abolished exchange controls in the UK. The abolition of exchange controls has led to an increase in investment overseas as large institutions broadened their portfolios of asset holdings. This has resulted in increased receipts of interest, profit and dividend payments (IPD) in the UK balance of payments invisible account. By the end of 1988, the net external assets of the UK private sector were approximately six times higher than they were in 1979. The increase in UK capital outflow is now producing substantial IPD earnings, which will be a major support to the balance of payments as the North Sea oil production declines.

■ Recent examination questions

The questions on this topic tend to be repetitive. The following six questions from recent CIB exams are good examples of the types of question which are commonly asked. Try to spend ten minutes or so in preparing your own outline answers to each question before reading the outline answers provided.

Question 1

(a) Distinguish between the concepts of balance of (visible) trade and terms of trade.
(b) Analyse how changes in the terms of trade help to determine a country's balance of trade.

Question 2

Is a deficit on a country's visible trade account necessarily of concern to its government? Discuss the ways in which a deficit may be corrected.

Question 3

The media often talks of a balance of payments deficit. How can this occur if 'the balance of payments always balances'?

Question 4

Explain, with regard to a country's balance of payments:

(a) how overall balance is achieved if the current account is in surplus;
(b) why and how a country might seek to reduce its current account surplus.

Question 5

The figures below are taken from the annual balance of payments of Ruritania. Prepare:

(a) Ruritania's balance of visible trade;
(b) Ruritania's balance of payments on current account.

Do these figures support the contention that Ruritania is a developing economy, and not highly industrialised? Give reasons for your answer.

	Million Rurits
Banking earnings (net)	− 30
Capital movements (net flow)	+ 1,280
Insurance earnings (net)	− 20
Interest paid abroad	− 1,400
Interest received from abroad	+ 30
Manufactured goods:	
exports	+ 120
imports	− 2,000
Raw materials and fuel:	
exports	+ 3,000
imports	− 1,000
Shipping earnings (net)	− 80
Tourists earnings (net)	+ 100

Note: There were no changes in Ruritania's official reserves during the year.

Question 6

What do you understand by the 'invisibles' section of a country's balance of payments accounts? Assess the importance of and recent influences on the invisibles account of the UK.

∎ Outline answers

Answer 1

(a) Balance of visible trade: the value of exports *minus* the value of imports of goods for a given period. The balance can be in surplus or deficit.

   (i) Terms of trade. Changes in export prices expressed as a percentage of changes in import prices of a country during a given period; then expressed as an index, with some base year = 100.

   (ii) The concept of terms of trade measures the purchasing power of a fixed 'bundle' of goods exported in terms of goods imported. Terms of trade refer to multilateral, not bilateral trade.

(b) The effect of changes in terms of trade on the balance of trade:

   (i) Elasticities of demand for exports and imports are crucial:

     – If elastic, then total receipts will be greater at lower prices. This means that a *lower* price for exports will help raise export earnings and a *higher* price for imports will help cut import spending – i.e. unfavourable terms of trade will help the balance of payments.

     – If inelastic, then total receipts will be greater at higher prices. A higher export price/lower import price will help the balance of payments – i.e. favourable terms of trade.

Answer 2

A deficit on visible trade is not necessarily of concern to the government, provided it is not excessive or permanent. Note the following points:

(a) The position on the current (i.e. visibles + invisibles) and external assets and liabilities in the balance of payments.

(b) The sign and size of the *overall* balance for financing; only if this is negative will there be a need for running down reserves and/or borrowing overseas.

(c) Whether the deficit on visible trade is temporary or permanent.

(d) The stage of development for the national economy.

The main ways of correcting (not financing) a balance of trade deficit:

(a) By devaluation (fixed exchange rates) or depreciation (floating rates) of the exchange rate. Success depends on: adequate price elasticities of demand for exports and imports, no competitive devaluation or depreciation; no offsetting increase in wages, profit margins, or indirect taxes.

(b) By deflationary policies: higher taxes and interest rates, and less attractive hire purchase terms; more attractive saving schemes; a credit squeeze.

(c) By direct measures: import controls; export subsidies.
Success will depend upon no retaliatory measures by trading partners.

Answer 3

(a) Media talk of 'a deficit' normally relates to the 'current account', which is only one part of the total balance of payments. Sometimes it could even refer to the 'visible trade' deficit, which is only one part of the current account.

(b) Balance of payments *as a whole* must balance because it is an accounting identity: total debits must equal total credits.
(c) If one section of the balance of payments accounts is in deficit, the whole structure must balance in the following way:
  (i) Visible trade account + invisible account = current account.
  (ii) Current account + external assets and liabilities + balancing item = 0.
(d) A current account deficit must be balanced by capital inflows (including government borrowing).
(e) Balancing item is the *difference* between what is, and should have been, received; it is not introduced simply to make the balance of payments balance.

Answer 4

(a) Equilibrium is achieved by some or all of the following:
  (i) capital outflows (direct or portfolio);
  (ii) other external assets and liabilities transactions;
  (iii) reduction in reserve accumulation;
  (iv) balancing item.
(b) A country may seek to reduce a current account surplus because of:
  (i) pressure from trading partner countries with current account deficits;
  (ii) reduced ability to import by trading partners;
  (iii) foreign currency reserve accumulation generating inflation.
  The surplus can be reduced by:
  (i) revaluing the currency in order to raise export and lower import prices: success will depend upon the elasticities of demand for export and imports;
  (ii) boosting domestic demand in order to attract imports and divert potential exports to the home market; reducing interest rates and tax rates;
  (iii) removing any import restrictions or export encouragements in force;
  (iv) giving aid to less developed countries.

Answer 5

	Dr. (million Rurits)	Cr. (million Rurits)
(a) Balance of visible trade		
Exports of manufactures		120
Exports of raw materials/fuel		3,000
Imports of manufactures	2,000	
Imports of raw materials/fuel	1,000	
	3,000	3,120
Visible trade surplus		120
(b) Invisibles		
Banking	30	
Insurance	20	
Interest paid	1,400	
Interest received		30

Shipping	80	
Tourism		100
	1,530	130
Deficit on invisibles	1,400	

$$\text{Balance of payments on current account} = \text{visibles} + \text{invisibles}$$
$$= + 120 - 1,400$$
$$= - 1,280$$

Capital inflow was 1,280 million Rurits, because official reserves were unchanged.

Ruritania is a developing country because:

(a) of its greater reliance on exports of raw materials and less on exports of manufacturers;

(b) its low earnings from commercial services;

(c) its large interest payment on current account and heavy borrowings on capital account;

(c) its sizeable tourist earnings suggest unspoilt countryside, 'golden' beaches, lower price level, etc.

Answer 6

The 'invisibles' section of a country's balance of payments shows the following:

(a) The net receipts or payments in respect of commercial services, transport, interest, profit, dividends, and tourism in the private sector.

(b) Overseas grants and aid by the government.

(c) Transfer payments: private (to relatives abroad); government (e.g. the UK payments to the EC).

The importance of recent influences on the invisibles account of the UK:

(a) In the earlier 1980s, the relatively strong sterling exchange rate had a negative effect on inward travel and a positive effect on outward travel (i.e. deterioration of tourism section of the account).

(b) A major portion of investment in North Sea oil was by overseas oil companies, which led to large payments abroad of profits and dividends.

(c) The abolition of exchange control led to an increase in investments overseas as large institutions broadened their portfolio of asset holdings. This resulted in increased receipts in the UK of interest, profits and dividends. It is now rising only slowly, due partly to increases in interest earned on the government's official reserves.

(d) A sharp deterioration in the transfer account, despite rebates, because of payments by the UK to the EC. The deficit on transfers in 1988 exceeded the UK net earnings from services.

(e) The heavy fall in the exchange rate of sterling at the end of 1984 and in early 1985 has had a positive inward and negative outward travel effect.

▌ A tutor's answer

The following question has been chosen for the specimen answer because variants of this question are most frequently asked on the topic of the Balance of Payments. You will notice from the answer plan that it is essential that you avoid confusing the two elements of the question.

Question

In which ways can a deficit on the current account of a country's balance of payments be (a) financed and (b) rectified?

Answer plan:

(a) Definition of the 'current account' within the balance of payments (briefly).
(b) How does a deficit on current account occur (briefly)?
   (i) Deficit may be *financed* by:
       – private capital inflows;
       – sources of official finance.
   (ii) Deficit may be *corrected* by:
       – devaluation/depreciation;
       – deflation;
       – direct controls.

Specimen answer

The current account of a country's balance of payments consists of the following:

(a) *The balance of trade.* This is the difference between the value of goods exported and the value of goods imported; this balance may be positive $(+)$ or negative $(-)$.
(b) *The invisible balance.* This shows the net receipts $(+)$ and payments $(-)$ in respect of services, transfer payments, and interest, profit and dividends.

A deficit on the current account occurs when (a) + (b) is negative. It implies that the country is a debtor on its external current account transactions with its trading partners, and suggests a poor performance in buying and selling goods and services with the rest of the world.

A current account may be **financed** by the following:

(a) Private capital inflows. If the country in question offers good prospects for high profitability, then overseas private *long-term* investment in foreign currencies will be attracted into the country. The long-term overseas investment may be direct investment into factories, equipment, etc. or it could be indirect portfolio investment, in purchasing stocks and shares in the country. If the country offers opportunities of interest rate differential gains or capital gains due to exchange rate movements, it may attract *short-term* private capital (hot money). The net receipts of foreign currencies from long-term and short-term foreign capital will help balance the deficit on current account.
(b) If the current account deficit is not wholly financed by the inflow of private capital, then the government of the country will need to tap the three main sources of official finance:
   (i) transactions with overseas monetary authorities and the International Monetary Fund to obtain supplies of the currencies needed;
   (ii) borrowing, by the public sector, of foreign currency in the international financial market;
   (iii) drawing on official reserves of the country.

The country may take three main measures, singly or in a 'mix', to **rectify** the deficit on its current account.

1. By devaluation or depreciation of the exchange rate of its currency. This would make exports cheaper and imports more expensive. The effectiveness of this approach depends on:
   (a) the relative price elasticities for exports overseas and for imports at home; the greater than one the *sum* of these elasticities, the more favourable the impact of a fall in the exchange rate on the balance of payments (this is Marshall and Learner theory);
   (b) no competitive devaluation or depreciation by trading partners.
   There will tend to be a time lag of twelve months or so before the fall in the exchange rate has its full impact on export sales and import purchases ('J' curve effect). A depreciation/devaluation of a currency may initially lead to a an increase in the balance of payments deficit. Subsequently, however, the current account should, depending on elasticities, move into surplus, and hence the name 'J' curve: falling to begin with, then rising.
2. Using deflationary policies (increasing tax rates and interest rates, credit squeeze, etc.), will reduce aggregate domestic demand in general, thereby dampening the demand for imports. Furthermore, deflationary policies will tend to lower the domestic rate of inflation which, in turn, will improve the competitiveness of its exports and its production of import substitutes.
3. By using direct controls, involving either import tariffs and other controls, or export subsidies. However, direct measures run the risk of retaliation, and may prove to be self-defeating. The success of direct controls will depend upon the willing co-operation of the trading partner countries.

■ A step further

The topic of balance of payments is an important area, both for examination questions and also for practical bankers in the international arena, who may have to evaluate a country's economic performance for credit assessment purposes. You are expected to be able to appreciate *recent* influences on the constituent parts of the UK balance of payments accounts. You need to keep abreast of developments by reading the Central Statistical Office publications *Balance of Payments 'Pink Book'*, *Monthly Digest of Statistics*, *Press Releases*, current banking journals, financial reports, The Chartered Institute of Bankers *Examiners' Reports* and *Updating Notes*. The UK government releases a monthly balance of payments statement, which is the basis for comments by the quality press, television and radio programmes. Look out for this media coverage of the monthly balance of payments statement.

CHAPTER 9

Exchange Rates

Syllabus requirements

- Need for foreign exchange rates.
- Theories and determination of foreign exchange rates.
- Factors which cause changes in foreign exchange rates.
- Types of foreign exchange rate systems.
- European Monetary System.
- European Currency Unit.
- Relationship between foreign exchange rates and interest rates.

▌ Getting started

'Foreign exchange' generally means any currency other than your own. The 'foreign exchange rate' of a currency implies the exchange value of the currency (its price) in terms of other currencies and, like any other price, it is determined by the supply of and demand for the currency on the 'foreign exchange markets'. Foreign exchange (forex) markets provide an international system of buying and selling claims to currencies immediately (spot) and in the future (forward) involving a world-wide group of banks, brokers, commercial companies and other financial institutions.

The need for foreign exchange (i.e. foreign currencies) arises for many reasons. A country, its business companies and citizens may require foreign currencies to pay the purchase price for imported goods and services, to invest in other countries, to provide for its tourists going abroad and to sustain the sending of gifts and other payments overseas.

If the bilateral (between two currencies) and multilateral (among all currencies) exchange rates are absolutely fixed on the forex markets, then there will be certainty in receipts and payments; for instance, as regards imports, it will be clear how much the buyer in the domestic country needs to pay in terms of his currency, and how much the seller in the foreign country will receive in terms of his currency. However, the domestic purchasing power of the currencies does not remain static, mainly due to inflation rate and interest rate differentials and major changes in the supply and demand of currencies (e.g. via balance of payments deficits and surpluses and consequent changes in international indebtedness). These factors put too much pressure upon the central banks to hold the absolutely fixed exchange rate parities. Hence absolute certainty may have to be replaced by the compromise of relative certainty, i.e. the absolutely fixed exchange rate system is replaced by one in which there is some movement of the exchange rate between specified upper and lower limits. However, international circumstances may make it difficult even to uphold a system with this degree of flexibility in exchange rates. If so, then the monetary authorities of individual countries have no option but to allow the exchange value of their respective currencies to be determined by supply and demand on the forex markets, i.e. to accept a system of freely floating exchange rates. The authorities may still intervene in a free exchange rate system, buying or selling their own currencies to affect the exchange rate.

Such a 'managed' system can be compared with a 'pure' system in which no intervention takes place.

The international monetary system, whether of fixed, managed or pure floating exchange rates, exists to facilitate international trade and the settlement of debt; it is the international counterpart of the national monetary systems of the trading countries.

∎ Essential principles

The basis of bilateral and multilateral trade

The objective of *bilateral* trade is to regulate trade with each single country in such a way as to secure an exact balance of trade with it. The need for bilateral trade arises where one currency cannot be easily converted into other currencies, so that the earnings from trade with one country cannot be used to pay for goods and services imported from other countries; the only way to pay for imports is then by exports. Bilateral trade, therefore, is completely controlled by inter-governmental agreements.

Under *multilateral* trade, a country aims, not at exactly offsetting imports and exports with each single country, but at a general balance of trade. Multilateral trade is not possible without the 'convertibility' of one currency into other currencies. Only then can countries use their surplus earnings from one country to offset deficits with other countries, so that a multilateral trade system becomes possible. The basis of multilateral trade is the theory of *comparative cost advantage*. Under this theory countries specialise in those economic activities in which they have a relative advantage in terms of efficiency over other countries. Specialisation, based on comparative cost advantage, reduces costs of production, and international trade not only passes on this advantage to consumers in other countries, but also widens their choice of goods and services.

Multilateral trade makes possible international investment, so that investors in one country can take advantage of national differences in yields on investments and can reduce overall investment risk by diversifying their investment portfolios. Investment capital can then flow to countries with projects offering the highest projected returns; these may be low cost centres of production, which can then expand at the expense of other countries where costs are higher. Thus multilateral trade, unhindered by tariffs, exchange controls and other artificial barriers, can lead to an efficient, world-wide use of resources.

International trade and investment are therefore only possible if suitable means are available for international payments. Most international trade nowadays is settled by using national currencies, either the currency of the exporter, importer or one of a limited number of 'hard' currencies that command general confidence and are widely accepted in international payments.

∎ Operation of foreign exchange markets

Traders and investors must be able to buy and sell national currencies if they are to make international payments. The forex markets have developed to allow this. Trading in these markets determines the rates at which one currency can be exchanged for others. The forex markets play a central role in facilitating international trade, and their smooth functioning is essential for the expansion of trade and investment.

National currencies are bought and sold in major financial centres, e.g. New York, Singapore, Hong Kong, Tokyo, Frankfurt, Paris and London. Foreign exchange buying and selling, however, take place in all countries. London is one of the largest centres of activity with several hundred institutions, mainly banks, dealing in foreign exchange, and with more currencies actively traded than in any other major centre. Foreign exchange dealers in forex markets do not meet in a particular location but keep in touch via telephone, telex and other more sophisticated forms of electronic communication. Exchange rates adjust continually, depending on the balance between orders for buying and selling currencies, and instant communications, combined with extreme competitiveness, ensure that exchange rates in different financial centres keep closely in step.

The main brokers and dealers in these markets are as follows:

(a) *Commercial banks* who deal on behalf of their personal and corporate customers, and also on their own account to 'square' their positions daily in major currencies and to make arbitrage profits arising from exchange rate differentials on various centres.

(b) *Business companies* who make and receive currency payments for their international trade transactions, and for investments, particularly in buying overseas subsidiaries.

(c) *Central banks* who buy and sell their national currencies to assist their exchange rates to move up or down in accordance with their economic objectives.

Inconsistencies between exchange rates, if they appeared, would be quickly exploited by a process known as *arbitrage*. This involves buying currencies in the financial centres where they are quoted more cheaply and selling them on forex markets where they are quoted at a better rate. The overall result of arbitrage is that the exchange rates soon adjust and come into line in each centre until there is no incentive for arbitrage (see below).

There are two basic types of foreign exchange transactions: spot and forward. Currency is bought and sold for prompt delivery (i.e. two working days hence) in the *spot* market; currency is bought and sold for delivery at a specified future date in the *forward* market. Forward contracts can reduce or even eliminate the risk of adverse movements in exchange rates, which may upset the profitability of importers and exporters. The extent to which importers and exporters choose to avoid exchange risk by using the forward market depends partly on their expectations of future movements in spot rates compared to the cost of covering forward, and partly on their own attitude to risk.

Whereas arbitrage exploits the inconsistencies between exchange rates quoted on various centres, *speculation* aims at profit-making from the *expected* movements in exchange rates, e.g. by selling a currency on the spot market in the hope of buying it later at a lower rate of exchange, or by buying a currency on the spot market in the hope of selling it later at a higher rate. Like arbitrage, speculation on forex markets hastens the realignment in exchange rate differentials on different forex markets by anticipating changes; thus, in this sense, both arbitrage and speculation are market forces which help forex markets regain equilibrium quickly, so that it can be argued that these market forces serve an economic purpose. However, in recent years, the amount of speculative balances has increased substantially, both in volume and volatility. Movements of such balances in response to anticipated changes in exchange rates in the forex markets can *overcompensate* for any possible degree of non-alignment, thereby causing much greater short-term volatility in exchange rates. This will place intense pressures on the central banks of the countries whose currencies are the object of speculation, whether for appreciation or depreciation.

∎ The determination of exchange rates

Since the exchange rate of a currency is its price on the forex markets in terms of other currencies, it is determined by its demand and supply conditions on the forex markets:

instant communications and extreme competitiveness among the forex markets make them almost perfect markets. The demand for, and supply of, a country's currency are derived from the country's balance of payments position; if it is a surplus country, i.e. if the value of its exports of goods and services and capital inflows (demand for its currency) is greater than the value of its imports of goods and services and capital outflows (supply of its currency) then the demand for its currency will be rising relative to the supply. The forex markets will then quote the currency at a higher exchange rate. On the other hand, if it is a deficit country, the supply of its currency will be rising relative to the demand and the forex markets will quote a lower exchange value for it. There are two main theories which seek to explain the determination of exchange rates: one relates to the current account, and the other to the capital inflows and outflows.

The purchasing power parity (PPP) theory

In its original form the theory states that the equilibrium exchange rate between one currency and another is that rate which equalises the domestic purchasing powers of the two currencies. If, for example, £1 buys the same amount of goods and services in the UK as do 10 francs in France, then, according to PPP theory, the equilibrium exchange rate must be £1 = 10 francs. If this were not the case, there would be strong incentive to import goods from the 'cheaper' country, which would lead to a deficit on the current account for the 'expensive' country; as the supply of its currency increased in settling its current account deficit, the forex markets would mark down its exchange rate. The incentive for importing goods and services from the 'cheaper' country would only disappear when the sterling/franc exchange rate becomes equal to £1 = 10 francs.

The PPP theory was originally developed to explain the values of exchange rates in the long run. However, there are many problems associated with this theory in its original form. For instance, the theory ignores transport and insurance costs and import duties. More importantly, it depends on the extent to which the goods and services involved may enter into international trade; there are many goods and services which are traded internally, but which *cannot* be traded internationally, e.g. houses, haircuts. The theory has been refined to take account of differences in patterns of consumption and levels of income in different countries. Nevertheless, the problem of devising baskets of goods and services which reflect common consumption patterns in different countries, yet which only include goods which are traded internationally, has limited the usefulness of the theory in predicting exchange rates. Since the relative costs and prices of *non-traded* goods and services can vary between countries, a comparison of *general* price levels is not therefore a reliable way of determining the exchange rate equilibrium.

However, the theory has a broad relevance in times of *differing* inflation rates in the domestic economies of trading partners. If a country's inflation rate significantly exceeds that of its trading partners, then, generally speaking, its exports will become uncompetitive at any given exchange rate; as a result it may encounter balance of payment problems, and, under a floating exchange rate system, its exchange rate will fall.

The portfolio balance theory

This theory emphasises the importance of interest rate differentials on the financial centres, and their impact on international investment and speculative capital flows, as a major determinant of exchange rates. It is assumed that large sophisticated investors are aware of interest rate differentials and move funds to take advantage of higher yields; also that they seek to reduce overall investment risks by diversifying their investment portfolios. The inflow of these funds into financial centres offering higher yield increases the demand for the currencies of such centres, so that the exchange rates of these currencies rise on the forex markets.

▋ Different types of exchange rate systems

National monetary policies of the trading partners are to some extent interdependent, on account of the exchange rate links between their currencies. Therefore changes in national monetary policies, even if in pursuit of internal objectives, put pressure on the international exchange rate system in operation.

There are two main exchange rate systems, absolutely fixed and freely floating.

Absolutely fixed exchange rates

The central bank of each country is obliged to intervene to increase or decrease the supply of its currency by selling or buying it on the forex markets, using the national gold and foreign currency reserves, so that its exchange rate is maintained at a predetermined exchange parity with certain other currency or currencies.

Advantages of fixed exchange rates

(a) They largely eliminate, without costly hedging, uncertainty in international trade and investment, and therefore encourage both by ensuring that the exporters' profits, importers' payments and investors' income and capital remain stable.
(b) They impose discipline on governments to pursue sound monetary and fiscal policies.

Disadvantages of fixed exchange rates

(a) Unbearable pressures build up on the central banks of those countries whose inflation rates and economic performance drastically worsen relative to their trading partner countries, and this may lead to the stigma of 'devaluation', i.e. lowering the exchange parity of the national currency. Of course, before devaluation the governments concerned will employ monetary and fiscal measures to curb inflation and improve balance of payments in order to defend the predetermined exchange parity.
(b) Central banks need to hold or borrow large amounts of gold and foreign currency reserves to neutralise exchange rate fluctuations.
(c) If a currency is suspected to be weakening or strengthening, speculation may build up and may in fact cause its devaluation or 'revaluation', i.e. raising its exchange parity.

Freely floating exchange rates

The exchange value of each currency is determined not by the monetary authorities but by the market forces of supply and demand for each currency on the forex markets. In a 'pure' float, the central banks take no action, whatever the exchange values quoted for their respective currencies.

In between these two extremes, there are a number of compromise arrangements:

(a) *Fluctuation limits around parity values*. The international trading community agrees that exchange rates can vary within specific bands either side of an agreed central parity, the central banks only intervening on the forex markets to ensure that the foreign exchange value of their currencies remains within the agreed bands.

(b) *'Dirty' floating*. The monetary authorities profess to follow freely floating exchange rate policies, yet intervene, behind the scenes, to limit the fluctuations in the exchange rates of their currencies to such levels as are most beneficial for their own economies. This is sometimes called a 'managed' float.

(c) *Crawling peg*. The monetary authorities, instead of declaring and maintaining a fixed parity, allow the parities to adjust from time to time, i.e. a system of 'gliding' fixed parities.

(d) *Direct foreign exchange control*. Each central bank states the terms and conditions for the release of foreign exchange. An extreme type of direct control is 'counter trading', i.e. all foreign trade transactions are undertaken as purely bilateral barter arrangements.

Advantages of freely floating exchange rates

(a) Since there are no fixed exchange parities to defend, there is no need for large gold and foreign exchange reserves: *in theory*.

(b) Imbalances in balance of payments are *automatically* corrected by the movements in exchange rates: a deficit country's exchange rate will depreciate, making its exports more and its imports less attractive, and the reverse in the case of a surplus country.

(c) Countries with freely floating exchange rates can pursue unfettered national economic policies, because they have no exchange rates to defend.

Disadvantages of freely floating exchange rates

(a) For the automatic adjustment of balance of payments imbalances, it is essential that the price elasticities of demand for exports and imports are elastic, otherwise the imbalances will worsen and will put pressure on exchange rates.

(b) Unfettered national economic policy aimed at economic growth may lead to inflation which will cause the exchange rate to depreciate and import prices to rise, causing a further rise in inflation; such economic freedom may therefore be more illusory than real.

(c) Uncertainty caused by fluctuating exchange rates discourages international trade and investment.

(d) If 'free' floating becomes 'managed' floating, there will be need for substantial gold and foreign currency reserves.

▌ Fixed versus floating exchange rates

If the fixed exchange regime is to function satisfactorily, it is essential that all countries under this regime should ensure that they do not let their interest rates, inflation rates and monetary expansion rates move too far out of line with those prevailing elsewhere within the regime. Those countries which are unwilling or unable to abide by the strict discipline of fixed exchange rates will find their price levels rising above those of the countries which *are* adhering to such discipline; their exports will become less, and imports more, competitive, leading to rising balance of payments deficits year by year. In order to defend the fixed exchange rate parities, the central banks of these countries will have to continue buying their own currencies on an increasing scale, spending their foreign exchange reserves, until their reserves fall dangerously low, forcing them to borrow currencies. The monetary authorities may then be forced to devalue their currencies by declaring lower exchange parities, in order to avoid continuous intervention on the forex markets. There is a stigma of mismanagement of the economy attached to 'devaluing' under a fixed exchange rate regime, which countries under such a regime will try to avoid at almost any cost. The strongest argument in favour of fixed exchange rates is that, since currencies will be accepted at known and fixed exchange rates, there will be certainty in international payments and receipts. Fixed exchange rates will eliminate exchange risks and thereby promote international trade and investment.

With fixed exchange rates, however, inflation in the economies of some trading partners will be 'imported' into other, non-inflation, economies, unless the demand for imports is relatively price-elastic, and cheaper domestic import substitutes are preferred.

Fixed exchange rates also provide speculators with a one-way option. Currencies which are perceived to be potentially weak can safely be sold in the knowledge that the relevant national central bank will be a buyer in order to maintain the parity (or at least until there is devaluation). Conversely, strong currencies can be bought with confidence, because their central banks will sell the national currencies to keep the exchange rates down and maintain the parity.

In stark contrast to the fixed exchange rate regime, there is the freely floating system. With freely floating, market-determined, exchange rates, it is claimed that there will be less need for official reserves; this follows since (a) there will be no exchange parities to defend, and (b) balance of payments imbalances should be automatically corrected by movements in exchange rates. Furthermore, with no fixed regime rules to obey, national governments will be able to pursue independent domestic economic policies aimed at higher growth and employment. Individual economies will be insulated against 'imported' inflation. The economies with the higher inflation rates will tend to experience an automatic fall in their exchange rates. This will reduce their export prices, making imports into the non-inflation economies somewhat cheaper.

However, these theoretical advantages of floating exchange rates do not always fully materialise. For instance, if the adjustment of balance of payments imbalances is to be automatic, it is essential that the elasticities of demand for imports and exports are sufficiently high to support the automatic adjustment process. Again, even though there is no exchange rate parity to defend, countries are not always free to follow independent monetary policies. For example, rapid growth may bring about higher imports and a fall in the exchange rate; even if this raises import prices and curbs the growth in imports, it may stimulate domestic inflation so that the 'cost' of this policy is still too high, despite balance of payments equilibrium.

There will be less need for official reserves or international borrowing only if the exchange rates are *truly* floating. If floating is 'dirty', i.e. managed, there will still be a need for official reserves so that the authorities can intervene on forex markets.

The principal weakness of freely floating rates is that they might discourage international trade and investment. It is not so much the flexibility in current exchange rates that discourages trade and investment; rather it is the uncertainty about future exchange rate movements which might have this effect. If, however, movements in exchange rates were easily predicted, then traders and investors could take them into account when planning overseas business and investment.

■ Influences causing exchange rate movements

If a country's inflation rate significantly exceeds that of its trading partners, then, in due time, its exports will become uncompetitive and as a result it will face a balance of payments deficit, and in the long term its exchange rate will fall against the currencies of its trading partner countries. The *purchasing power parity* theory of exchange rates states that the equilibrium exchange rate between one currency and another is that rate which equalises the domestic purchasing powers of the two currencies.

Despite the purchasing power parity theory, which states that competition in trade will tend to compensate for *differences in national inflation rates*, i.e. that exchange rates will be constant in real terms, there is little evidence that the real exchange rates do in fact tend to be stable. Real exchange rates have varied markedly over both short and long periods. It may be that in the *very long term*, say fifteen to twenty years, the forces represented by the purchasing power parity theory may become dominant and create stability in real exchange rates, but it is a largely unproven hypothesis.

It is likely that some of the longer term movements in real exchange rates which occurred between 1972 and 1980 were partly due to a movement towards more diversified reserve currency portfolios, following the collapse of the US dollar-dominated Bretton Woods regime. It is also possible that the transfers of wealth towards OPEC (Organisation of Petroleum Exporting Countries), due largely to the huge oil price increases, had a significant impact on global currency preferences: a few major oil producers were then able to place, or withdraw, huge sums in financial centres and currencies of their choice. For the UK, the advent of North Sea oil certainly raised the demand for sterling from the early 1980s, hence the title, 'petro-sterling'.

The comparison of data on various countries' *balance of payments positions* indicates that changes in the current account balances have frequently influenced exchange rate movements in the short term. This would suggest that the current account does have an impact on the longer term value of a country's exchange rate.

Short-term movements in exchange rates appear to have been linked to *relative interest rates*, but this relationship has sometimes been positive and sometimes negative. A *positive* relationship has prevailed most frequently in recent years, as monetary authorities have followed an interest rate policy directed more towards domestic than external objectives. A high relative interest rate has tended to raise the exchange rate of the currency in question. Where there has been a *negative* relationship, e.g. where a high relative interest rate has been associated with the exchange rate remaining constant or falling (as happened in the UK in 1985), it has perhaps been due to *expectations* of a still greater rise (or fall) in interest rates.

In addition to the above influences on exchange rate movements, there are other influences, such as the stance of economic policy (expansionary or deflationary) and the level of economic activity. However, these influences will reflect themselves in both the balance of payments current accounts and in interest rates.

In *summary*, then, exchange rates may be influenced by relative inflation rates, by relative current account positions, by relative interest rates, by relative economic stances and by a range of other factors, such as the degree of official intervention on forex markets and political developments. In the forex markets, though, it is often merely 'expectations' as regards one of the above that causes movements. (See also 'A tutor's answer' at the end of this chapter.)

■ The European Monetary System and its origin

It became clear to the European countries that, despite the wider fluctuation bands around central rates introduced in 1971 under the Smithsonian agreement, the fixed exchange rate system could not be saved. In an attempt to keep the narrowest possible exchange rate fluctuation among themselves, ten European countries moved in the opposite direction in April 1972. They introduced narrower cross exchange rates against each other's currencies (1.12 per cent either way), while maintaining the wider band (2.25 per cent) against the US dollar. This arrangement was quickly nicknamed the 'Snake in the Tunnel.' The Snake aimed at reducing uncertainty as regards the exchange rates of the members by limiting the extent of fluctuations against each other. This took place at a time when most major currencies were beginning to show signs of abandoning the Bretton Woods/Smithsonian arrangements prior to floating against each other. However, balance of payments imbalances, largely due to the oil crisis in 1973, caused volatile exchange rate fluctuations, making it very difficult to maintain par values within the narrow bands of the Snake. Despite currencies entering and leaving the Snake at various times, it remained in existence until 1979, when the Snake was replaced by the European Monetary System (EMS).

The EMS

The EMS was established by the Brussels Resolution dated 5 December 1978, which was signed by all EEC countries and was implemented on 13 March 1979. The objectives of the EMS were to combat the international monetary instability caused by the weakness of the US dollar in the 1970s, to establish a zone of monetary stability in Europe, to assist in drawing together the monetary and economic policies of EEC countries, to promote inter-community trade by stabilising exchange rates and to achieve, in the long run, Economic Monetary Union (EMU).

The EMS has two major elements:

1. An exchange rate intervention system which attempts to preserve stability between the different currencies participating in it. It organises exchange rate relationships between the participants according to a system of stable parities, but ones which can be adjusted when necessary. It allows for periodic realignments and permits margins of fluctuation between currencies. Thus the EMS is a 'movable peg' exchange rate system for the participating currencies.

    The heart of the EMS is the *European Currency Unit* (ECU), which is a weighted 'basket' of twelve EC currencies, of which the Greek drachma is not a member of the exchange rate mechanism (ERM, see below) of the EMS; the weight of each currency is determined by the economic strength of the country concerned. The *units* of national currencies in the ECU basket remain fixed for five years, when they are recalculated; the last calculation was in 1989. However, the weights of national currencies change when they part from their central parities.

    With effect from 21 September 1989 the currency unit composition and weight percentage of each currency are shown in Table 9.1.

    Each currency participating in the exchange rate mechanism (ERM) of the EMS has an ECU-related central rate, and these values determine a grid of bilateral central rates between the members. Every country must maintain a margin of + or − 2.25 per cent on either side of its bilateral rate, with Spain, Portugal and Britain as exceptions, because of the weakness of the peseta, escudo and sterling; their intervention limits roughly

6 per cent on either side of their central rates (see p. 169). If a currency nears its upper or lower bilateral intervention point in relation to another currency, its central bank must intervene on the forex market to buy or sell its currency for ECUs, to raise or lower its exchange rate respectively. The EMS supplements the compulsory intervention rules with a 'divergence indicator', which is based on the ECU as the common numeraire, and which gives countries a forewarning that their currencies are getting out of line from the Community average. If a currency moves to 75 per cent of its maximum spread of divergence in relation to the Community average, then it is an 'early warning' to the country concerned to take corrective monetary and/or fiscal measures before the compulsory intervention points are reached. Therefore all participant currencies are pegged against the ECU directly and against each other indirectly. Clearly ERM is the cornerstone of the EMS, and is vital to the achievement of EMS objectives.

Table 9.1   Currency units and weights in ECU basket

Currency	Units	Weight (%)
Deutschemark	0.6242	30.10
French franc	1.332	19.00
UK sterling	0.08784	13.00
Italian lira	151.8	10.15
Netherlands guilder	0.2198	9.40
Belgian franc	3.301	7.60
Spanish peseta	6.885	5.30
Danish kroner	0.1976	2.45
Irish punt	0.008552	1.10
Greek drachma	1.44	0.80
Portuguese escudo	1.393	0.80
Luxembourg franc	0.13	0.30
		100.00

2. Each member country of the EEC (including the UK) makes 20 per cent of its gold and dollar reserves available to the European Monetary Co-operation Fund (EMCF) in return for ECUs. EMCF is empowered to lend to those member countries which are unable, by economic measures, to correct excessive divergences. The EMCF credit facilities available to such member states are as follows: unlimited amounts up to ten weeks; ECU 14 billion up to nine months; ECU 11 billion from two to five years. *Note*: While intervention is carried out through national currencies, debts are settled in ECUs. Thus EMS is an improvement on the old Snake arrangement which was simply an exchange rate agreement.

EMS failures

The staunch critics of the EMS point to its lack of success in achieving fully many of its objectives. For instance, critics question how the EMS can bring about a zone of exchange rate stability when there were so many realignments of exchange rate parities in its first 11 years of existence! There are still differences in inflation rates and in balance of payments performances among member countries; the fact that such differences continue to exist may suggest further realignments. The EMS has failed in leading the member states towards the objective of Economic Monetary Union (EMU), in which the economic policies of the members are fully harmonised. The ECU has not become a major 'reserve' asset for the EC countries, and the EMCF has not developed, as was expected, into a fully fledged European Monetary Fund (on the pattern of the International Monetary Fund).

EMS successes

The supporters of the EMS counter-argue, emphasising the degree of success the EMS has been able to achieve in moving towards its objectives. For instance, it has survived, despite many realignments, because it has an in-built flexibility the IMF did not possess and which caused its downfall. The member states are *beginning* to accept the need for convergence of their economic policies, e.g. French monetary policy is much closer to the monetary policies of Germany and the UK.

It is true that the EMCF has not developed in importance as was expected, and that the hopes of it becoming a fully fledged European Monetary Fund have been shelved indefinitely. However, the ECU has remained stable, due largely to the stabilising influence of the EMS, despite massive exchange rate swings and interest rate fluctuations. This is because stronger, more stable currencies comprise a greater proportion of the basket (see table above) than do the weaker, more volatile currencies. Thus the overall stability of the ECU is very marked, and its fluctuations are more muted because of the combination of weak and strong currencies. In addition, nine of the twelve constituent currencies are still members of the ERM of the EMS which maintains the parity of the member currencies within the agreed range. The combination of these two factors enhances the stability of the ECU. The ECU has gradually become a fully fledged financial instrument used by banks, businessmen and governments for accounting, investment, savings and payments purposes. The ECU is, for all intents and purposes, a reserve asset for the EC countries and is now a major currency for loans and bond issues. Companies, too, now often insist on paying or being paid in ECUs. This removes the risk of one currency fluctuating far from the other currencies — a weighted average of currencies is inherently more stable than just one currency (see below).

The EMS, unlike the IMF, is not an institution in its own right. It has no powers to force member states to pursue some prescribed monetary and fiscal policies. A basic precondition for the successful operation of the EMS is that there is convergence of economic policies and performance of member countries; *how* they achieve this convergence largely rests with their own respective governments.

Absolute rigidity in exchange rate commitments by member countries who are *not* at the same level of economic performance is a recipe for failure. The strength of the EMS lies in its pragmatic flexibility which allows for differences in the economic performances, inflation rates and balance of payments positions of member states by explicitly permitting currency realignments.

∎ European Currency Unit (ECU)

In 1987 the ECU Banking Association launched the ECU clearing system, to operate with a final complement of over thirty commercial banks. All clearing members have settlement accounts with the common clearing bank — the Bank for International Settlements in Basle.

The ECU has a powerful attraction for citizens of countries with weak currencies. These include currencies which have been devalued in the past, or are likely to be devalued in the future. By denominating deals in ECUs, buyers are increasingly availing themselves of the protection offered by an ECU against the down-grading of their own national currencies.

As a basket currency the ECU smooths out interest and exchange rate fluctuations of the currencies of which it is composed, thus offering some protection against those fluctuations. The relative stability is attractive to both borrowers and lenders. This is because the spread of the basket over a number of stronger currencies means that the dramatic changes which occasionally occur between two currencies are spread over all the currencies in the basket. This also means that those countries with strong currencies do not have any great incentive for going into ECU-denominated investments. On the other hand, countries with weak currencies greatly benefit from ECU linkage. For example, Italy has authorised the use of the ECU as an official foreign currency, and up to 20 per cent of Italian export invoicing is in ECUs.

The ECU has been one of the main beneficiaries of the massive exchange rate swings and interest rate fluctuations, in recent years. For instance, firms with subsidiaries in several EC countries can avoid the problem of dealing in several different currencies by using ECUs. Due to its relative stability against most EC currencies, it has been used increasingly by business companies as a hedging instrument against foreign exchange rate fluctuations. For example an exporter whose receivables are in EMS currencies in broad proportion to the ECU basket can clearly be seen to hedge the exchange risk by invoicing in ECUs. The ECU is gaining in importance and its use will continue to increase. Some knowledge of the ECU for those living in rural areas of the UK will be of particular relevance, since the EC support payments to farmers are made in the ECU.

In the autumn of 1988 the UK government issued ECU Treasury bills, which are similar to conventional Treasury bills but denominated and payable in ECUs. Arrangements have been made to ensure secondary market liquidity through the qualified intermediaries, e.g. commercial banks. According to the then Chancellor of the Exchequer, the ECU Treasury bill 'introduces a useful new facility. It widens the options for managing the UK's reserves and will establish London's position as the centre of the ECU market, which we wish to see develop further'. The amount of ECU Treasury bills outstanding in March 1991 was £3.6 billion.

ECU interest rates parallel those in the domestic market for the major currencies, reflecting the weights of these currencies in the ECU basket. ECU exchange rates, which are the same for official and private ECUs, are published in the financial press. By linking via a major currency, say, the US dollar, exchange rates can be calculated for most major currencies.

■ UK entry into the ERM of the EMS

The UK government joined the ERM on 8 October 1990 – over eleven years after it was set up. The following are the major considerations which convinced the authorities that the time was right to enter the exchange rate mechanism.

(a) The *prospective*, if not the actual, inflation rate of the UK had sufficiently converged towards the average inflation rate of the ERM member countries.
(b) The stability against the strong deutschemark (DM) would help contain domestic inflation and lower interest rates.
(c) Over 50 per cent of the UK's foreign trade was conducted with the EC member states, and exchange rate stability would benefit UK exporters and importers.

(d) The prospects of the UK becoming isolated, and therefore without influence, in European monetary developments would be avoided.

The operation of the system

The UK authorities, until they, along with Italy, left the ERM in 1992, had to keep the exchange rate of the pound to within 6 per cent either side of central parities with the other ten ERM currencies. This meant that the pound could not be more than 6 per cent above its central parity against the weakest currency or 6 per cent below the strongest currency in the ERM. Thus the 12 per cent total band was the maximum variation against another currency which the pound's exchange rate − or another currency's exchange rate against the pound − could show at different times. (The same is still the maximum variation between the exchange rate of pesetas and escudos and the other ERM currencies. Apart from the pound, escudos and pesetas all the other ERM currencies have the narrower band: 2.25 per cent either side of each other's central parities.) The pound, for instance, could rise to a 'ceiling' of DM3.13, i.e. 6 per cent above its central parity of DM2.95, and it could fall to a 'floor' of DM2.78, i.e. 6 per cent below its central parity against DM.

The pound (like other member currencies) was also restricted in the extent of its fluctuation against the ECU. If it rose to its ceiling of 6 per cent against the other currencies it rose less against the ECU because it is itself a part of the ECU. For example, suppose the weight of the pound was one-eighth of the ECU basket, a 6 per cent rise against all other currencies would be reduced by one-eighth against the ECU, i.e. to 5.25 per cent.

In the ERM, the ECU is used to measure which currency is diverging most from the average, so that its central bank should take the corrective action it is expected to take when a currency reaches 75 per cent of its ECU divergence limit − the so-called 'early warning'. All the ERM central banks are required to intervene when any currency reaches the edge of its parity bands. In practice, however, central banks intervene soon after a currency moves any distance from its central parity to prevent speculation on its being devalued/revalued.

If the pound moved significantly below, say, its DM central rate, then the intervention by the Bank of England involved it using the UK foreign currency or credit facilities available from the European Monetary Co-operation Fund (EMCF) to buy sterling to strengthen (raise) its central rate against the DM, and, when the pound was strengthening, to sell it and use the DM receipts to repay credit facilities from the EMCF, and build up the UK foreign currency reserves. The same activity would be involved in managing the pound's exchange rate within the bands of its central rates against all other ERM currencies.

The UK sacrificed a good deal of its monetary independence. The UK authorities had to manage short-term interest rates, not to control demand in the domestic economy but to stabilise the pound's exchange rate. On the other hand, locking into a fixed exchange rate system did prove to be a more effective way of controlling the domestic economy, provided the ERM discipline was adhered to by the UK authorities. If the pound was growing too weak, because the UK economy was growing too slowly, the authorities had to lower taxes and/or raise government expenditure; and, of course, the reverse fiscal measures if the pound was growing too strong. If wage claims were in excess of the economic growth rate, higher unemployment had to be accepted.

The UK could still revalue or devalue (re-align, as it is termed) within the ERM, as other countries did during early stages of their ERM membership, but subject to the agreement of the ERM member states. The UK authorities, however, decided firmly against the realignments, especially devaluation, in order to retain the credibility of the rate to which they committed themselves on 8 October 1990 (for update, *see p. 169*).

▮ Economic Monetary Union (EMU)

There are *three stages* towards full monetary union. Stage 1 will be completed when all twelve member currencies are participating in the ERM. The UK is already in Stage 1. Stage 2 will see the setting up of a European Monetary Institute (EMI). The EMI should strengthen co-operation between national central banks and co-ordination of monetary policies; monitor the ERM; facilitate the use of the ECU, including functioning of the ECU clearing system; and prepare for Stage 3.

Before the beginning of Stage 3, the European System of Central Banks (ESCB), comprising the independent European Central Bank (ECB) and the independent national central banks, will be set up, and it will replace the EMI. The basic tasks of the ESCB will be to define and implement Community monetary policy; to conduct foreign exchange operations; to hold and manage official foreign reserves of member states (member states could still hold foreign exchange working balances); and to promote smooth operation of payment systems.

There is growing consensus amongst EC member states that full monetary union is not desirable until there is a high degree of *economic convergence* (see box below). The key indicators of whether a member state is ready to participate in monetary union will be its ability to adhere to the narrow 2.25 per cent *exchange rate* limits; and these limits are expected to narrow further.

Apart from the exchange rate stability, together with *inflation and interest rate* convergence, the other key pre-requisite for participating in full monetary union concerns the level of *government debt* and the *size of budget deficits*. The former should be no higher than 60 per cent of GDP while budget deficits should be contained to 3 per cent of GDP. This particular restriction is intended to ensure that individual countries are unable to raise European interest rates by 'excessive' borrowing, and to avoid the risk that heavily indebted countries might need to be bailed out by other member states.

Convergence criteria

(a) *Exchange rates.* The currency staying within the normal (2.25±per cent, or narrower) fluctuation margins in the ERM for *at least two years*.

(b) *Price stability.* The rate of inflation should be no more than 1.5 per cent above the average of the three best performing member states.

(c) *Interest rates.* These should not rise more than 2 per cent above the three best-performing states over the previous *twelve months*.

(d) *Government deficit and public debt.* The deficit should not exceed 3 per cent, and the public debt should not exceed 60 per cent of the GDP.

The European Monetary Institute will monitor the progress of member states towards convergence.

At the time of writing (August 1993), only two of the nine ERM states are sufficiently close to satisfying the exchange and inflation rate criteria to move speedily towards monetary union. They are Germany and the Netherlands; all the other ERM member states, viz. France, Belgium, Luxembourg, Denmark, Ireland, Spain and Portugal are on 15 per cent ± fluctuation bands (see p. 169). Even Germany, under the burden of unification costs, has had to keep its interest rates high.

The above convergence criteria do not include other important indicators, e.g. unemployment and living standards, because these, arguably, are not considered critical criteria for monetary union. Rather, the establishing of a stable internal and external environment is seen as the background against which 'real' economic convergence can be nurtured.

The final decision to be taken during Stage 2 on full monetary union will involve the following principles. No country can be compelled to join; no country can be excluded, provided that it has met the convergence criteria and wants to join. Provided a minimum number of countries (seven of twelve or one less if the UK does not intend to join Stage 3 [see below]) meet the convergence criteria, and wish to establish a monetary union, Stage 3 could commence.

When Stage 3 begins, all the participating member states will agree the conversion rates at which their currencies will be irrevocably fixed and will be exchanged for ECUs. The ECU will then become a currency in its own right. The ECB will have the exclusive right to authorise issue of ECU bank notes in the Community.

The UK can 'opt out' from joining Stage 3. If it does *not* join Stage 3 it will retain sovereignty over its monetary and exchange rate policy, not subject to EC disciplines; it will not be able to vote on EMU decisions; will not be eligible to participate in the appointment of the executive board of the ECB, and ECB statutes will not apply to the UK; it will be able to join Stage 3 at a later date by notifying its willingness to do so and satisfying the necessary conditions of convergence.

Maastricht Treaty

On 11 December 1991, EC leaders meeting in Maastricht agreed on a Treaty of European Monetary Union that 'marked a new stage in the process of creating an even closer Union among the peoples of the Community'.

The timetable agreed in Maastricht is as follows:

1 Jan. 1996 Stage 2 to begin with establishment of European Monetary Institute.

31 Dec. 1996 UK to notify the Council whether it intends to move to Stage 3; or by 1 January 1998 if no decision has yet been taken by the Council.
Deadline for decision by qualified majority to launch Stage 3, Economic and Monetary Union, if a 'critical mass' of member states (a majority would currently mean seven out of twelve member states, or six if the UK were not taking part in Stage 3) meet the convergence criteria.

1 July 1998 European Central Bank (ECB) and European System of Central Banks (ESCB) to be set up if this has not already happened.
Deadline for member states to make the national central banks independent (if ECB and ESCB are only now being set up).

1 Jan. 1999 EMU to begin 'irrevocably' if this has not yet happened.

■ The relationship between interest rates and exchange rates

Earlier in this chapter, under the portfolio balance theory, it was stated that high interest rates will attract inflows of capital from lower interest rate economies, which in turn will raise the exchange rate of the former. Note that it is changes in the interest rates in a country *relative* to interest rates in other countries that is the key factor in determining exchange rates.

Interest rates may be raised to reduce outward capital movements and/or to attract capital back. However, the relationship between interest rates and exchange rates extends further. The interest rate is the price of *borrowing* currency, whereas the exchange rate is the price of *buying* currency. The relationship between interest rate and exchange rate, although indirect, is nonetheless significant in equalising interest differentials between major international financial centres.

The interest rate and exchange rate link may be shown by the following example. Suppose that DM interest rate is 5 per cent per annum, and £ interest rate is 10 per cent p.a., then by switching funds from DM to £ an interest gain of 5 per cent can be made, *but* there is an exchange risk of DM appreciating and causing a capital loss in the converted DM receipts. This risk can be eliminated by paired forward transactions: (a) sell DM and buy £ *spot*, and invest at 10 per cent per annum; (b) buy DM and sell £ twelve months *forward*. Transaction (a) is at spot exchange rate. Transaction (b) is at spot exchange rate *plus/minus* forward discount/premium margin. Thus the difference between the two is the forward margin. If the forward margin is not equal to the difference in DM and £ interest rates, an arbitrage exists, which will be exploited until the difference between transactions (a) and (b) equal forward margin.

Arbitrage in the forex markets involves buying and selling currencies to take advantage of exchange rate differentials between currencies.

Suppose a London exchange dealer notices that in New York the dollar/sterling rate is being quoted at £1 : $1.55, whereas in London the dollar/sterling rate is £1 : $1.44. He will at once realise that he will make a quick profit by buying 'cheaper' dollars with pounds in New York and by selling 'dearer' dollars for sterling in London. Thus arbitrage will drive up the dollar/sterling exchange rate quoted in New York and push down the dollar/sterling rate quoted in London; once the exchange rates in the two financial centres equalise, there will be no incentive for arbitrage. The London dealer will, of course, take into account the *cost* of his buying and selling dollars to decide whether arbitrage is worthwhile. On account of arbitrage opportunities, rates quoted in different financial centres are generally only *slightly* different, but not by enough to trigger arbitrage.

The movement of *long-term* funds between countries will largely depend upon factors such as political stability and the long-term profitability potential of the project which is being financed. Therefore, movements in exchange rate play a less important part in long-term overseas investment decisions.

The relationship between interest rates and exchange rates means that governments can intervene in two ways:

1. By directly buying and selling their currency in the markets.
2. By raising or lowering interest rates.

It may be the latter which has the major impact on their exchange rate (see p. 74).

Investment portfolio approach, as seen in the US economy

Suppose there are two alternative investment possibilities, say, either in dollars or DM deposits. The expected relative return will be influenced by the *known* interest rates differential plus the *expected change* in the exchange rate of the DM against the dollar. These are of course connected. An increase in US interest rates will, other things being equal, raise the dollar's exchange rate against the DM, due to increased demand for the dollar and increased supply of the DM.

Thus the *appreciation* of the dollar, despite the huge US federal budget deficit and its higher inflation rates than those of Germany and Japan, its main trading partners, can best be explained in terms of the higher levels of US interest rates in recent years.

The relatively high US short-term interest rates were due to two factors: (1) a tight domestic monetary policy to contain inflationary pressures; and (2) the need for a substantial inflow of foreign capital to finance the budget deficits. Therefore, according to the investment portfolio theory, higher interest rates have led to the high exchange rate of the dollar (itself a factor in the high US current account deficits), and, by causing large inflows of overseas capital, to the huge surplus in the US *capital* account.

In addition to high interest rates there have been other factors which have led to the movement of overseas capital into the USA: the purchase of dollar assets by Japanese investors after the liberalisation of Japanese exchange controls; the rapid growth in the US economy in 1983–4; and the slowing down of US bank lending overseas following the international debt problem.

However, in explaining exchange rate behaviour, the investment portfolio approach cannot be considered in *isolation* from other economic fundamentals, such as the current account position, inflation rate differentials and the level of economic activity.

▮ Sterling trade weighted exchange rate index (SERI)

In times of floating and rapidly moving exchange rates, it can be misleading to focus on the rate of exchange for sterling against any *one* currency. For example, the strength of the US dollar in the early months of 1985 had tended to obscure sterling's relative stability against other currencies. The SERI measures the overall change in the value of sterling against other currencies *as a whole*. SERI therefore is a better indicator of the average exchange rate of sterling, and of the impact of exchange rate movements on UK trade competitiveness or inflation, than is any individual rate such as the dollar/sterling rate. SERI is calculated by taking a *weighted* average of the sterling exchange rate against 16 other currencies, including the dollar. The weighting reflects the importance of the individual currencies to UK trade. To make it easier to monitor sterling's overall movements, the SERI is calculated and published every hour by the Bank of England, with 1985 as its base date. The trade-weighted index takes into account the importance of each country's trade with the other countries in the basket by utilising a weighting system (see pp. 163, 166–7).

▮ Recent examination questions

The following seven examination questions should give you a good idea of the breadth and depth of knowledge required to answer questions on this topic satisfactorily. After you have read this chapter carefully, spend ten minutes or so making answer plans for each question. Only then turn to the outline answers given below.

Question 1

(a) To what extent does the theory of purchasing power parity explain a change in a country's exchange rate?
(b) Examine the consequences of a depreciating exchange rate on a country's:
  (i) current account of the balance of payments;
  (ii) inflation rate.

Question 2

Discuss both the desirability and the feasibility of a return to world-wide fixed-exchange rates such as operated under the so-called Bretton Woods system.

Question 3

(a) What are the fundamental economic factors affecting exchange rate movements?
(b) Explain the relevance of these factors to the ability of a system such as the Exchange Rate Mechanism (ERM) to operate successfully.
(c) What are the advantages of keeping exchange rates in close relationship?

Question 4

(a) Outline the reasons which might lead a central bank to intervene on foreign exchange markets.
(b) Apart from imposing exchange controls, how might a central bank intervene to influence the exchange rates?
(c) Can central bank intervention succeed in stabilising a country's exchange rate in the long term? Give reasons for your answer.

Question 5

Following the breakdown of the so-called Bretton Woods system in the 1970s most major currencies were allowed to float. To what extent have the theoretical advantages of floating exchange rates been borne out in practice?

Question 6

Discuss the factors which determine changes in the foreign exchange rate of a country's currency.

Question 7

(a) What is meant by measuring changes in a country's exchange rate on a 'trade-weighted' basis?
(b) What are the fundamental factor's underlying currency performance?
(c) Between late 1980 and early 1985, the index of the US dollar's trade-weighted exchange rate rose by almost 70 per cent. To what extent did this appreciation, and subsequent developments, reflect the fundamental factors underlying currency performance?

▮ Outline answers

Answer 1

(a) *PPP theory*: exchange rates are determined by the *relative* domestic purchasing power of each currency. It attempts to explain a depreciation of a currency *simply* in terms of different rates of inflation for traded goods, i.e. its weakness.

   In the short term, this would not be an adequate explanation since interest rate differentials, balance of payments performances, government intervention, and relative costs and prices of non-traded goods included in the domestic price level would need to be considered.

(b) (i) – A depreciating exchange rate tends to increase a current account surplus or decrease a deficit, after the 'J-curve' effect.
   – Home-produced goods become cheaper in international markets, while imports become dearer.
   – The extent of improvement in trade performance depends on the elasticity of demand for traded goods.
   – The invisible account in the current account may also improve from increase in, say, tourism.

   (ii) Since the price of imported goods and raw materials has increased due to the depreciation, inflation will increase; the extent will depend on second-round effects and the domestic monetary and fiscal policies.

Answer 2

Arguments for fixed exchange rates:

(a) They provide a measure of certainty and are favourable to the growth of world trade.
(b) Individual countries are prevented from pursuing inflationary policies by the need to avoid excessive upward pressure on their exchange rates.

   Arguments against fixed exchange rates:

(a) They preclude independent domestic policies, requiring deflation rather than devaluation to correct balance of payment deficits.
(b) Large holdings/borrowings of official reserves are essential to defend the fixed rate.

   Feasibility of a return to fixed exchange rate system: Bretton Woods system of fixed exchange rates broke down because of:

(a) differences in inflation rates; and
(b) large imbalances in the balance of payments.

   These two factors have increased since the breakdown of Bretton Woods.
   Bretton Woods-type exchange rate system is unlikely to be durable.
   Frequent realignments, even in the 'fixed' exchange rate parities in the EMS, cast doubt on the durability of a fixed exchange rate system.

Answer 3

(a) *Fundamental factors:*
   (i) Inflation differences.

(ii) Interest rate differentials.

(iii) Relative balance of payments (especially current account) performance.

(b) *Relevance of fundamental factors to the ERM:*

    (i) Divergence in these factors will result in a fixed rate system, in pressures for realignment; the success of fixed rate system requires their *convergence.*

    (ii) According to PPP theory, different inflation rates between trading partners are incompatible with fixed exchange rates; exports of a country with the higher inflation rate become uncompetitive, and its exchange rate must fall to counter this.

    (iii) A persistent current account imbalance (surplus or deficit) for a participating country will affect its currency's performance within the exchange rate system.

    (iv) According to portfolio balance theory, interest rate differentials cause exchange rate movements; higher interest rates can be used to raise exchange rate.

(c) *Advantages of ERM (fixed exchange rate system):*

    (i) Reduces uncertainty in trade with participating members.

    (ii) Revenues and costs of trade and investment with participating members are easier to calculate on long-term basis.

    (iii) Imposes discipline on all participating governments to pursue sound economic policies to keep inflation and total spending in check.

    (iv) Linking to a strong currency (such as DM) helps to control inflation.

    (v) Lays the foundation for greater economic and monetary union.

Answer 4

(a) Reasons for intervention:

    (i) To defend a parity within a 'fixed' exchange rate system, the authorities must intervene.

    (ii) To avert sharp fluctuations in exchange rates.

    (iii) To achieve a desirable depreciation to improve export competitiveness and/or curb imports.

    (iv) To revalue currency to reduce import costs and the domestic inflation rate.

(b) (i) By direct intervention – buying/selling domestic currency.

    (ii) By raising/lowering interest rates.

(c) Intervention would not succeed if:

    (i) other fundamental factors, notably inflation and balance of payments performance were markedly adverse.

    (ii) By keeping domestic interest rates relatively high, could succeed for several years in preventing the adverse effects of inflation and balance of payments performance being reflected in a falling exchange rate.

Answer 5

(a) Advantages claimed from floating exchange rates:

    (i) A continuous and automatic adjustment of the balance of payments.

    (ii) Independent domestic economic policies can be pursued; no exchange rate target to defend.

    (iii) To insulate internal economy from 'imported' inflation; exchange rate moving in line with relative inflation rates. If low relative inflation, balance of payments improves, exchange rate rises and price of imports falls.

    (iv) A reduced need for official reserves.

(b) How far have the theoretical advantages of floating rates actually been achieved?
   (i) Automatic adjustment of the balance of payments, especially on current accounts, not a notable success; partly because exchange rates did not move in line with relative inflation rates (purchasing power parity theory), and partly because of low elasticities, at least in the short run. Adjustment of current and capital accounts was not really automatic, but was rather via highly volatile short-term capital flows.
   (ii) Although there were no specific exchange rate targets to defend, yet the strength of the US dollar (due to higher interest rates) has constrained the domestic economic policies of other countries.
   (iii) Insulation against 'imported' inflation has not been achieved because relative exchange rates have not moved in line with relative inflation rates: low inflation countries (e.g. Germany and Japan) have been most vulnerable to 'imported' inflation.
   (iv) 'Free floating' has in fact been 'managed' floating; therefore official interventions have been almost as expensive as under fixed exchange rates, and there is still the need for more official reserves.
   (v) The fixed or semi-fixed exchange rate under the EMS means that eleven European currencies have *not* been 'floating'. Since August 1993, all but two are floating – see p. 169.

Answer 6

Any factors which affect the supply and demand for a currency will affect its exchange rate.
(a) Factors affecting supply and demand for a currency:
   (i) The balance of payments position on current account; a deficit implies less demand and more supply of the currency and therefore lower exchange rates.
   (ii) Interest rate differentials: these will affect the level and direction of capital transactions (including dividends, profits, interest).
   (iii) Inflation rate differentials: these will influence relative cost structures, activate purchasing power parity theory and thus affect current accounts.
   (iv) Political stability affects long-term capital flows.
   (v) Possession of natural resources, e.g. oil, for which there is, in the short term, inelastic demand overseas.
   (vi) Official intervention via exchange controls or intervention on the foreign exchange markets.
   (vii) Changes in expectations; 'leads and lags' – traders advance payments in a currency which they expect to appreciate (to avoid capital loss) and delay payments in currencies they expect to depreciate (to make capital gain).

Answer 7

(a) (i) Under floating rates there is no one simple yardstick for measuring currency performances.
   (ii) Therefore a basket of the currencies of the major trading partners of the country whose currency's performance is to be measured, is constructed.
   (iii) The importance, or weight, given to each currency in the basket depends upon the volume of trade conducted by the UK with each country in the basket.
   (iv) A currency's performance is then measured on an index basis against the basket.

(b) (i) The fundamental factors affecting a currency's performance are:
  - interest rate differentials between countries;
  - relative national inflation rates;
  - relative current account performances.

(c) (i) Factors responsible for the *appreciation* of the dollar:
  - Higher short-term interest rates to finance huge budget deficits and to contain inflationary pressures.
  - Purchase of dollar assets by the Japanese after the relaxation of their exchange controls.

  (ii) Factors responsible for the *depreciation* of the dollar:
  - US economy became less attractive to overseas investors (balance of payments deficits, slowing down of economic growth).
  - Short-term interest rates have begun to fall.
  - It is US official policy to reduce the value of the dollar to repair the damage done to the economy and industrial growth.

▌A tutor's answer

Make an answer plan for the following question, which is related to the outline answer 6 above, before looking at the answer plan and specimen answer below.

Question

In the absence of official intervention in the foreign exchange market, what factors are likely to influence changes in a country's exchange rate?

Answer plan

Factors affecting the supply and demand for a currency:
(a) The balance of payments position.
(b) Relative inflation rates.
(c) Relative interest rates.
(d) Expectations.
(e) The stance of fiscal and monetary policies.
(f) Political stability.

Specimen answer

Any factor that can influence the supply of, and demand for, a currency can effect changes in the foreign exchange rate of that currency. The major factors, apart from official intervention, are outlined below, although the strength of each factor varies both between countries and over time.

The balance of payments position

A country experiencing a balance of payments surplus on current account will on this count alone experience upward pressure on the exchange rate of its currency; similarly, countries with a current account deficit will tend to experience 'weak' currencies, i.e. a downward pressure on their currencies' exchange rates. Although relative current account performance is widely seen as a key factor in influencing exchange rate movements, the significance of capital fund movements should not be overlooked. If, for example, overseas investors have confidence that a country has a considerable development potential and political stability, then they may initiate large-scale capital inflows. These may be sufficient to offset the otherwise downward pressure on its currency of a current account deficit.

Relative inflation rates

A country with a high inflation rate relative to its major trading partners will tend to lose competitiveness. This would signal, other things being equal, a deterioration in its balance of payments, which, in turn, will normally cause a fall in the exchange rate of its currency, and vice versa.

Relative interest rates

In order to maximise the aggregate returns from his investment portfolio, an investor with a spread of investments in different currencies will seek to ensure that the returns he expects on the marginal investment in different currencies will be approximately equal. By definition, the expected return will be equal to the interest differentials plus the expected change in the exchange rate. Higher interest rates will raise the expected rate of return and lead to a higher demand to invest in the currency offering higher interest rates; this will lead to upward pressure on its exchange rate.

Expectations and speculative activity

Foreign exchange markets generally seek to anticipate changes in key economic variables, such as in a country's economic performance and in its level of interest rates. For example, if the markets expect a country's balance of payments to deteriorate, then the exchange rate of its currency may well move downward in anticipation. An expectation of a rise in interest rates for a currency may well move its exchange rate upward. The influence of expectations and speculation are of central importance.

The stance of fiscal and monetary policy

A government's fiscal and monetary policy stance is seen by the foreign exchange market as a yardstick against which to judge exchange rate behaviour. For example, an increase in money supply, on account of an expansionary economic policy, will be seen by many, especially the monetarists, as inevitably leading to a fall in its exchange rate: high money supply growth leads to a high inflation rate and a weak balance of payments position, and hence a weak currency.

Political stability

Political stability, or instability, has a very important influence on long-term capital inflows, which will significantly influence the overall balance of payments position, and therefore the exchange rate.

■ A step further

The factors likely to influence exchange rate movements, under a floating exchange rate system, are assuming ever-increasing importance. Sharp changes in exchange rates are of particular concern to many bank customers and to banks themselves, especially their foreign exchange dealers. Although there is no definitive answer to the problems to which foreign exchange rates – whether fixed, floating or permutations in between – give rise, yet as a prospective banker you are expected to speak intelligently on the broad topic of foreign exchange rates. Try to keep abreast of changes in foreign exchange rates and their effects on the national and international economic scene. You can do this by reading the quality press, *Banking World*, the *BEQB* and the Chartered Institute of Bankers' *Examiners' Reports* and *Updating Notes*. Pay especial attention to the developments in the EMS; the UK joined and the ERM of the EMS. Keep abreast of the implications of this for the UK economy, and of the move towards a single currency operated by a European central bank in the Economic Monetary Union. Read the article 'EMU – where are we now?', *Banking World*, January 1991.

Note: During the week beginning Monday 14 September 1992, the pound and the lira came under massive speculative attack on the foreign exchange markets. The Italian Government eventually devalued the lira, and then withdrew it, temporarily, from the ERM. At first, the UK government boldly defended the pound by raising interest rates to 15 per cent on 16 September. On the same day, the Bank of England spent between 10 and 15 billion US dollars of the UK foreign currency reserves in buying back the pound. Unfortunately, both measures failed so the UK authorities then withdrew the pound from the ERM, and it floated down against the DM to around DM 2.50. It is not certain if and when the pound will re-enter the ERM. At the time of writing, the UK authorities have suspended their progress on the road to EMU. (See note below.)

At the end of July 1993, the speculative pressure against the *perceived* weaker ERM currencies, particularly against the French franc, became unbearable. Consequently the governments of these currencies decided to adopt much wider fluctuation bands of 15 per cent; with the exception of DM and Dutch guilders, which remained on the narrow 2.25 per cent fluctuation band. None of the currencies, however, left the ERM, and none has allowed its currency, as yet, to move away from the previously agreed narrow and broad fluctuation margin. The new 15 per cent bands will be reviewed on 1 January 1994, with a view to narrowing them. The ERM has *not* been abandoned – not yet!

The main reason for this latest ERM crisis is that France, Spain, Portugal and Belgium are in recession of varying degrees but are unable to cut their interest rates until the German interest rates come down. The Bundesbank cannot cut its discount rate appreciably because inflation in Germany is, by German standards, very high at 4.3 per cent.

Note: Britain's foreign currency reserves amount to approximately $40 billion. The principal source of the reserves is *borrowing* by the government in foreign currency. The other main source is *intervention*. When the Bank of England intervenes to buy foreign currency (and sells sterling), the proceeds are added to the reserves. On the other hand, sales of foreign currencies (and purchase of sterling), to protect the exchange value of sterling, reduce the reserves. However, that does not mean that the reserves have been spent: the foreign exchange reserve 'asset' has merely been converted into a sterling 'asset'.

CHAPTER 10

Supervision and Regulation

Syllabus requirements
- Supervision by the Bank of England under the Banking Act 1987.
- Supervision and regulation by the international institutions.
- Prudential controls.
- Third World debt problem and banks' capital positions.
- Regulation of the investment industry under the Financial Services Act 1986.
- Regulation and supervision of the building societies and insurance companies.

▌ Getting started

This is a descriptive chapter setting out the provisions of the relevant acts and describing the legal powers and duties of the supervising and regulating institutions. The contents of this chapter provide a hinterland of useful knowledge relating to the supervision of the operations of the main types of financial institution in the UK. You are *not* expected to memorise the legal provisions of the enactments discussed for the MFS exams.

The Banking Act 1987 gives the Bank of England legal supervisory powers to ensure that only fit and proper institutions take deposits. The chief objective of the Act is to protect depositors and potential depositors in banks. The Financial Services Act 1986 has as its main objective the protection of investors. To achieve this it has established the Securities Investment Board (SIB) and Self-Regulating Organisations (SROs).

The directives of the European Community give guidance and freedom to the financial institutions of member states in order to harmonise the 'rules of play' and the 'playing fields'.

Since the building societies and insurance companies are outside the supervisory jurisdiction of the Bank of England, they are supervised by the Building Societies Commission and the Department of Trade and Industry (DTI) under the Building Society Act 1986, and the Insurance Companies Act 1982. The contents of this chapter have practical relevance to the UK's financial system, and you should keep that point in mind as you read and learn the information contained in it. Due to the nature of the content, the sections 'Essential Principles' and 'Useful Applied Material' have been combined.

▌ Essential principles and useful applied material

Banking Act 1987

Origin and aims

The 1984 Johnson Matthey Bankers (JMB) crisis pointed to the weaknesses of the 1979 Banking Act supervision regulations, under which the Bank of England oversaw the management of UK banks. These weaknesses were principally the ease with which JMB could lend the equivalent of their entire capital to a single, doubtful borrower, the failure of JMB auditors to spot the trouble, and the slowness with which the Bank responded to JMB's imprudence. The failure of the Bank of Credit and Commerce International (BCCI) in 1991, the failure of the Bank of England in detecting the fraudulent state of affairs in the BCCI operations, and the consequent suffering of BCCI depositors demonstrate that the supervisory strings provided under the 1987 Banking Act are still not sufficiently tightly drawn. It also points to the need for a serious look at how banking should be supervised *globally*. Supervision is a complex and detailed business, and recent events have made it more so. These include the growing internationalisation of banking and capital markets, and the increased involvement of banks, either directly or through subsidiaries, in securities and other investment business.

One of the central aims of the 1987 Act is to establish the Bank of England as the *legal* supervisory authority (something which was never fully formalised in statute before) and to strengthen its statutory powers to prevent financial institutions taking in illegal deposits. The basic concern of the Act is the protection of banks' *depositors*; the protection of *investors* is the province of the 1986 Financial Services Act.

This Act brought about the following major amendments to 1979 legislation:

(a) A *Board of Banking Supervisors* consisting of Bank of England officials and outside experts has been established to advise the Bank on supervisory matters. The purpose of the Board, which will report separately to the Treasury, is to make the Bank more accountable for the way it carries out its supervisory responsibilities. The Board has the right to approach the Chancellor of the Exchequer directly if it feels that its advice to the Bank is being ignored.

(b) The two-tier system of authorisation under the 1979 Act ('recognised' and 'licensed' institutions) is replaced by a unified system with a single category of '*authorised*' institutions.

(c) All authorised institutions have to meet *statutory prudential requirements*, which, in brief, are that:
   (i) an institution's directors, controllers and managers are '*fit and proper*' persons to hold their positions;
   (ii) the business is conducted properly, which covers, among other things, *adequate capital and liquidity provisions* (see below) for bad and doubtful debts, accounting and other records, and internal controls;
   (iii) when authorisation is granted, the institution has net *assets of not less than £1 million*.

(d) A UK authorised institution will be permitted to use the title 'bank' provided it has at least £5 million paid-up share capital and/or undistributable reserves (or is incorporated abroad).

(e) For *continuing supervision*, an independent firm of accountants will make available to the Bank of England three separate annual reports for each authorised institution: on its internal control system; on its accounting and other records; and on its prudential statistical returns.

(f) The Bank of England is empowered to *intervene in the merger or acquisition* of a bank on prudential grounds.

(g) Authorised institutions are required to report to the Bank of England *loan exposures* of over 10 per cent of capital and to give *prior notice* of proposed transactions exposing them to the risk of losing over 25 per cent of capital.

(h) The *Deposit Protection Scheme* is extended to cover all authorised institutions: 75 per cent of the first £20,000 of sterling deposits made with an authorised institution is protected.

(j) The *'exempt' institutions* (i.e. building societies, the National Savings Bank, the Banking Department of the Bank of England, insurance companies and pension funds) are excluded from the jurisdiction of the Act because they are already satisfactorily regulated and supervised under separate legislation.

(k) The Treasury can *amend the definition* of 'deposit' and 'deposit taker' to help it keep up with changes in the financial markets/services industry.

(l) The Bank of England has been granted *greater information gathering powers*. In particular, the auditors of banks can inform on them without being in breach of their duties.

Thus the 1987 Banking Act provides a more elaborate supervision system backed by stronger statutory powers, including supervision at international level in order to achieve common standards for the UK and overseas banks on capital and liquidity adequacy. (See pp. 187–88 below.)

Capital measurement: Risk Asset Ratio

Like any other company, a bank needs permanent capital as a stable resource to absorb any losses arising. A bank's lending will typically be financed mainly by deposits; but losses, e.g. when a loan has to be written off, ought to be borne by the shareholders, not the depositors. For the protection of depositors, each bank must have adequate shareholders' capital and other capital.

For many years the Bank's capital requirements for commercial banks has been based on the *Risk Asset Ratio* (RAR). A bank's assets are broken down into broad categories according to their riskiness; and similar calculations are made for off balance sheet risks, such as guarantees. The capital base is then measured as a *percentage* of the weighted portfolio of risk. This percentage is the RAR; and for some banks it will be higher, e.g. for a bank with inexperienced management or high concentration of risk, and for some lower. There is however an *absolute minimum* of 8 per cent, set by an international agreement (see below).

International agreement on capital measurement and adequacy

In July 1988, the central banks of the ten leading countries (the Group of Ten) agreed on a set of rules for how much capital banks must have in relation to the size and riskiness of their assets and off balance sheet exposure. The key features of the agreed set of rules (known as the *Basle Agreement*, because the Committee on Banking Regulations and Supervisory Practices of the Group of Ten meets at the Bank for International Settlements in Basle, Switzerland) are as follows:

(a) By the end of 1992, banks with significant international business must maintain capital equivalent to at least 8 per cent of assets weighted according to risk.

(b) At least half of the banks' capital base must consist of 'Tier 1 capital' (equity, disclosed reserves and non-cumulative participating preference shares). The other half should consist of 'Tier 2 capital' (which may be revaluation of reserves; some unrealised capital gains on securities; general provisions; hidden reserves; subordinated fixed term debts, subject to certain limits).

(c) In calculating the capital requirements, off balance sheet items will be taken into account by using credit conversion factors to establish their credit risk equivalent (see below).

(d) Assets and off balance sheet exposure must be given weightings of 0, 10, 20, 50 or 100 per cent which reflect their risk. For example, in the 100 per cent weighting category are all loans to the private sector, premises, fixed assets and investments. In the 0 per cent category are cash and claims on the central government and central banks of other countries, if they are funded and denominated in the currency of the country concerned.

Claims on non-OECD governments which are not in national currency are weighted 100 per cent. Claims incorporated in the twenty-four member countries of the Organisation for Economic Co-operation and Development (OECD) are weighted 20 per cent, as are claims on non-OECD banks with less than one year to maturity; longer term claims are weighted 100 per cent. Loans fully secured by mortgages on residential property for owner occupation or rental are weighted 50 per cent.

The countries in the Basle Agreement are Belgium, Canada, France, Italy, Japan, Luxembourg, the Netherlands, Sweden, Switzerland, West Germany, the UK and the USA.

The following table is an example of capital adequacy ratio calculations, in a supervised bank's balance sheet, according to the Basle Agreement.

Table 10.1

	£m	Weight	£m weighted
Assets			
Cash	25	–	–
Treasury bills	5	10	0.5
Other eligible bills	70	10	7.0
Secured loan to discount houses	100	10	10.0
UK government stocks	50	20	10.0
Other instruments			
government	25	20	5.0
company	25	100	25.0
Currency loan – Hungarian government	20	100	20.0
Commercial loans	380	100	380.0
Personal loans	200	100	200.0
Mortgage (secured) loans	100	50	50.0
Total	1,000		707.5
Off balance sheet risks			
Guarantees of commercial loans	20	100	20.0
Standby letters of credit	50	50	25.0
Total risk-weighted assets			752.5
Capital adequacy ratio 8 per cent			60.2*

* At least £30.1 million (50 per cent) must be in Tier 1 assets, and the rest in Tier 2 assets.

Source: Bank of England (Banking Supervision) Fact Sheet, August 1990 (modified).

Note: The Bank can require a supervised bank to hold an RAR *in excess* of 8 per cent (required under Basle Accord) if it feels that the bank has a high concentration of risk.

One effect of the new capital adequacy standards, which include off balance sheet items, might be to encourage the *securitisation* process, which involves the sale of risk assets and a move from lending business to acting as a broker or guarantor between suppliers and users of capital. In the securitisation process the bank earns fee income without increasing its balance sheet exposure. The Bank views securitisation with caution, since some residual liability may rest with the banks involved, and has therefore advised them to allow for any such residual risk in their capital adequacy ratios.

Since all the twelve countries will be implementing the same rules, foreign banks in London will have no advantage or disadvantage (except that the risk asset ratios may be above the 8 per cent minimum) by operating in London. The additional cost due to higher ratios in London may be offset by increased cost of doing business in other financial centres with hitherto more liberal regimes, once they come into line with the supervised banks.

Liquidity adequacy

Cash flows

Banks have to be capable of meeting their obligations as and when they fall due. The Bank of England believes that in order that a bank should be able to meet its obligations, it should have sufficient cash and liquid assets, and also a future cash flow showing its position in the months ahead.

Banks have obligations to their depositors, whose money may be repayable at sight or at short notice. The banks must ensure that they hold cash and liquifiable assets to meet these demands. For each particular institution, the mix of maturing assets and cash will be different. Two points are important:

1. The sole responsibility for a bank's liquidity rests with its management. For this reason the Bank of England does not seek to impose all-embracing liquidity ratios. The Bank will need to be satisfied, however, that banks have given adequate attention to liquidity and that their policies are prudent in this area. The Bank realises that every institution is different and it takes this into consideration when deciding what is prudent.
2. The Bank of England discusses with each bank the adequacy of its stock of liquidity and also conducts a regular analysis, on the basis of statistical returns, of the cash flow profile of each bank. A cash flow profile may be in the following format:

Table 10.2 *Cash flow format*

	Sight−8 days	8 days−1 month	1−3 months	3−6 months	6−12 months
Liabilities					
Deposits					
Commitments					
Less Assets					
Marketable					
Non-marketable					
Standby facilities available	_____	_____	_____	_____	_____
Net position c/f	_____	_____	_____	_____	_____
Net cumulative position	_____	_____	_____	_____	_____

Weights are given to assets depending on how 'safe' they are. For example:

Nil discount – Treasury bills, eligible local authority bills, and eligible bank bills. Government and government-guaranteed marketable securities with less than 12 months to maturity.

5% discount – Other bills and CDs with less than six months to maturity. Other government, government-guaranteed and local authority marketable securities with less than five years to maturity or at variable rates.

10% discount   –   Other bills and CDs and Floating Rate Notes with less than five years to maturity. Government, government-guaranteed and local authority marketable debt with more than five years to maturity.

Source: BEQB, July 1982.

Primary liquid asset requirement

After 1985, the Bank issued a number of liquidity proposals. These proposals, among other things, incorporated a 'primary liquid asset requirement' for banks, comprising cash, bank balances at the Bank, Treasury bills, gilts *less than* one year to maturity, eligible bills *up to* ninety-one days, and money placed on a secured or unsecured basis *up to* one month with bill and gilt market-makers. The Bank applies a liquidity formula based on the level of primary liquid assets held, measured as a proportion of total sterling liabilities with a maturity of sight to eight days.

The level of primary liquidity has been set at approximately 12 per cent. The Bank requires liquidity returns to be made quarterly, although banks are expected to maintain the liquidity requirement on a day-to-day basis.

▮ Prudential controls and banks' balance sheets

Liquidity adequacy of a bank shows the extent to which its liquid assets are sufficient to meet its obligations as they fall due, e.g. withdrawal from sight and time deposits, commitment to lend at a specific date, unforeseen demand for financing, unused overdraft facilities, daily interbank settlements. The components of a bank's balance sheet relevant to its liquidity adequacy (as under the liquidity adequacy requirement by the Bank of England) are notes and coins, operational deposits with the Bank of England, Treasury and eligible bills, secured on-call and short-notice lending to discount houses and GEMMS, short maturity government stocks (and the ability to borrow on the CDs and interbank markets). However, the bank has to be mindful that the 'quality' of its marketable assets can vary due to asset price fluctuations and changes in interest rates. It should also so manage its assets portfolio as to ensure appropriate cash flows from maturing assets, keeping in mind that defaults can occur. It must maintain a diversified deposit base and high standing in the markets so that it is able to attract new deposits without undue costs.

Although the Bank of England, in its supervisory role aims to ensure that individual banks follow prudent liquidity management policies, it leaves banks' managements free to choose what they consider to be the optimal combination of liquid assets vis-à-vis the liability structure in their balance sheets, their financial objectives, and the prevailing economic and financial circumstances.

Capital adequacy means the extent to which a bank's capital covers the risks inherent in its operations, as seen from its balance sheet. Clearly the risks of each bank will differ from the risks of other banks. Capital adequacy and liquidity are required under the 1987 Banking Act, but the banks under their own prudential practices need capital adequacy to withstand possible losses on operations, notably bad advances. A bank's capital adequacy ratio can be gauged from the ratio between its total assets or deposits and its capital in its balance sheet. If its capital adequacy ratio becomes unacceptable, it must either raise more capital (e.g. by rights issues) or reduce its operations.

▍ Supervision/regulation under EC Directives

By the end of 1992, the remaining physical, technical and fiscal barriers to free movement of goods, services, capital and people have been removed among the twelve member states of the European Community (EC), and a single market will be created. The single market will cater for over 320 million people — over 7 per cent of the world's population — with high disposable income. A number of directives are already in force (and are reflected in the Bank of England's supervision); others are planned as part of the EC's internal market programme.

The First Banking Directive in the EC (1977) achieved three things: the freedom of establishing banks and other credit institutions anywhere in the EC: the acceptance of common standards for granting banking licences, and the introduction of the basic principle of home country control of the financial institutions established abroad in the EC.

The Second Banking Directive (1988) has established two new principles: that the home country of an institution will be responsible for regulation and supervision: and a mutual recognition by all member governments of each others' regulatory arrangements. Thus, the Second Directive has removed all remaining obstacles to freedom of establishment in the EC banking sector.

The implications of the Second Directive for UK banks are:

(a) easier cross-border banking business;
(b) international expansion via location in member states;
(c) cheaper location, because committed capital will not be required for foreign branches;
(d) no specific solvency ratios or large exposure limits on foreign branches;
(e) the opportunity for a bank to undertake in other states whatever it is able to undertake in the home country.

The central issue for competing banks is *access* to potential customers and the creation of effective *delivery* systems for financial services. Access to customers in the EC states would be possible in the following ways:

(a) By establishing a network of branches.
(b) By mergers with institutions in other states.
(c) By acquiring subsidiaries in other EC countries.
(d) By developing cross-border business links with other institutions in the community.
(e) By successful marketing of banking services in other states.

With regard to delivery in the single market, a distinction needs to made between retail and wholesale banking, because the competitive conditions in these two types of banking business vary both within and between member states. The wholesale banking business tends to be large scale, with comparatively few, but large, customers. Therefore, delivery can be made without a network of branches. Retail banking, on the other hand, involves a large number of small accounts, and access *and* delivery are, usually, through a network of branches. Therefore, the future European integration is more likely to be strongly felt in the retail banking sector.

However, the impact within the UK retail banking sector may not be substantial, because in the UK deregulation (*see* pp. 60–65) of the financial industry and the presence of so many foreign banks in the City — banks of over 73 countries are operating in London — mean that competitive conditions are already demanding for the UK retail banks. Furthermore, in the UK there is no exchange control; all major EC banks already have a presence in London; there are no restrictions on the range of business activities; and branches of retail banks are not required to have committed capital.

The unique strength of the UK banks, arising from their long experience and expertise in innovatory skills and financial strengths and acumen, will give them the opportunity both to compete with the EC banks with advantage and to shape banking in the European single market.

The EC's Investment Services Directive (ISD), December 1988, proposes that by 1 January 1993, *inter alia*, financial services (including banking, insurance, investment and pensions) will flow freely across EC member states borders. Except for a certain code of business conduct rules, the ISD does *not* apply to banking and credit institutions that already comply with the Second Banking Directive (see above), and therefore such institutions need not seek authorisation under the ISD to provide their *investment* services. This would give banks an advantage over securities and investment houses.

■ Banks and the Third World debt problem

In March 1990, the UK clearing banks announced the huge £4.6 billion of Third World debt provisions in their 1989 accounts. (Two banks had the unusual situation of having more in provisions than they did in shareholders' funds.) However, these colossal figures are really of historical interest because the clearers are now in a position to write most of the Third World debts off if they want to.

Individual banks have been, understandably, reluctant to give new loans, unless persuaded by the IMF or the US Treasury, and they have been content with debt *rescheduling*. So, the most striking feature of any table showing sources of finance for the less developed countries (LDCs) during the 1980s has been a decline in private lending to LDCs. From a peak of $83 billion in 1982, this fell to $18 billion in 1987. The counterpart has been an increase in official lending – from 33 per cent of the total in 1982 to 43 per cent in 1987. Within this, the decline in IMF credits has partially reversed the increase in IBRD (International Bank for Reconstruction and Development) funding.

The banks' attitude towards the international financial market has changed from a philosophy of asset growth towards improving profitability, in particular by improving the quality of assets, or by increasing fee earning off balance sheet business. Deregulation, the creation of new financial instruments (FRNs – Floating Rate Notes and NIFs – Note Issue Facilities), and the process of *securitisation* and disintermediation (avoiding the bank as intermediary) have required banks to turn their attention away from trade and project lending and sovereign loans towards preserving their share of business with corporate customers and high-quality institutional borrowers in OECD countries. Hence, funds are recycled more between surplus and deficit OECD countries than between OPEC and LDCs. Indeed, OPEC's surplus has diminished during the 1980s as a result of the fall in real price of oil, and this process looks likely to continue for some time to come. The new surpluses are from Japan, Germany and the Asian newly-industrialised economies.

There has, nevertheless, been a flood of innovations in financing instruments which bankers have invented to help with the problem of LDC debt. Financing in 1984–5 saw the use of certain financial instruments, interest retiming, trade facilities, debt conversions. More recent schemes have included securitisation (bundling together a series of doubtful debts and selling the bundle to outside investors as a new asset in the secondary market at much less than their nominal value), debt buy-backs (as in the case of Bolivia), and *Debt Equity Swaps* (DESs).

In 1987, some $15 billion in DESs was traded, and this amount was expected to double. DESs have certain advantages for banks and debtors: a country can turn a debt with a fixed stream of payments due into equity, the dividends of which will depend on the profitability of the particular investment: the banks can use DESs as a way of tidying up their books, or for the smaller banks to leave the debt crisis altogether − removing these assets from their books and passing them to another bank or an industrialist who wishes to keep up long-term links with that country. There is also the advantage of opening up access to foreign investment, and thus to management skills and technology. DESs can mobilise for domestic investment those assets held by residents overseas, i.e. reversing the capital flight problem.

For example, a company wishing to set up, say, a $10 million tyre factory in Mexico could buy $10 million of Mexican debt at the market price, around 33 cents in the dollar, in April 1989. The company would then sell the debt to the Mexican authorities for close to its face value and receive payment in pesos. In theory, everyone benefits from this transaction: banks − typically, small-and medium-sized regional banks − are able to unload their bad loans on the *secondary-debt market* (see below); Mexico reduces its debt and gains a tyre factory; and the traders make a profit on the difference between the buy and sell price of the loan.

The problem with swaps is that the debtor countries are encouraged to *print more money* to purchase debt, thereby worsening the already horrendous inflation problems in LDCs. Instead of printing more local currency, the debtor government may sell domestic debt instruments. The public sector deficit may, thus, be higher if the cost to the government of this new debt is higher than the cost of servicing the old debt. Some LDCs have been more worried than others by these problems and they have wrapped their debt equity swap schemes in layers of restrictions which have limited their effectiveness. Others have acted as did Chile, which swapped $4 billion since 1985 and had swapped another $4 billion by 1990. A good DES is a useful tool but it will only make a marginal − if useful − contribution to easing the debt crisis of a debtor country.

Few of the *cut-price investments* (as in the example of the tyre factory, above) can be proved to be genuinely additional investments. Most would have been made anyway, bringing desperately needed hard currency into the developing country.

There is a flourishing re-sale, or secondary, market in Third World debt, which grew from zero to over $30 billion per annum in the five years to 1980. Chile, with the help of the secondary market, reduced its debt by 36 per cent in a few years (1984−88).

The secondary debt market, now a profitable sideline for at least a dozen international banks, is based on the willingness of some LDCs to *buy back* their debt in local currency or in company shares.

International banks with big debt portfolios also do direct *debt-for-equity swaps*, exchanging debts at favourable rates for shares, or full ownership, of companies in LDCs. The UK's Midland Bank, saddled with over $4 billion of debt, has been specially active in this way.

The *secondary debt market* has developed a dynamic of its own, at one stage removed from real supply and demand. The IBRD estimates that about $10 billion of debt was traded back to the Third World countries in 1988. However, the volume of trading on the secondary debt market was over $30 billion. The debt claims, once sold by the original creditor, may be sold over and over again between traders profiting from the market fluctuations. The US government would like to see more such activity as part of its voluntary debt-reduction plan. So would the banks: but the debtor countries themselves are less enthusiastic. Countries of the secondary debt market say that this market preys on the suffering of the Third World.

Bankers and traders say that it rationalises the chaotic portfolios of smaller banks and that it has helped to convert debt into productive investment in some LDCs.

Supervision and regulation of investment business

Financial Services Act 1986 (FSA)

You will recall reading in Chapter 4, under the section, 'Big Bang' (pp. 60–2), the reasons for the above enactment, and the supervisory and regulatory bodies set up under it.

Until the passing of the FSA, financial services in the UK were regulated either by a number of government acts or by codes of practice set by such bodies as the Stock Exchange. It became clear that the measures then in place to protect investors needed reform and, additionally, with 'Big Bang' and internationalisation of markets, some restructuring. After due consideration, the FSA was passed.

The Act has empowered the Department of Trade and Industry (DTI) to 'authorise' and 'regulate' the carrying on of investment business. The DTI has transferred the majority of its operational powers to the Securities and Investment Board (SIB), set up under the Act, and armed with a formidable armoury of regulatory sanctions. The SIB is not a government department, and is financed by the financial markets.

The SIB recognised five self-regulating organisations (SROs) to assist in the supervision and regulation of investment firms according to the requirements of the FSA: Association of Futures Brokers and Dealers (AFBD); Financial Intermediaries, Managers and Brokers Regulatory Association (FIMBRA); Investment Management Regulatory Organisation (IMRO); Life Assurance and Unit Trust Regulatory Organisation (LAUTRO); and The Securities Association (TSA). The AFBD and TSA have now merged to form the *Securities and Futures Authority* (SFA).

The SIB is responsible for the protection of investors, and it aims to achieve this via 'authorisation' of only 'fit and proper' firms and individuals to carry on investment business, i.e. they must have capital adequacy, a good business record and compliance with supervisory requirements.

Major aspects of the regulatory regime under the FSA

To remain authorised the investment firms must comply with the following codes of conduct laid down by the SIB and SROs.

(a) Investment firms are required to have proper regard for a client's best interests in any advice given, and therefore should do their best to ensure that they are aware of the client's circumstances.

(b) A firm must subordinate its own interests to that of the client when acting on his behalf, and act fairly towards the client whether it is dealing as a principal or agent.

(c) The contents of investment advertisements must give clear warnings about such matters as the volatility or the marketability of the product advertised.

(d) A firm must disclose information about charges, fees, commission and other remuneration which it would receive after doing business with a client, and where it manages an investment portfolio on a client's behalf it must also periodically send to the client details of its investment performance.

(e) A customer must be made aware of the status of insurance sales people so that he knows whether he is dealing with a company representative tied to one range of products, or a fully indepencent intermediary acting as the agent of the customer.

(f) Firms must set out the basis of their relationship with private clients in customer agreement letters which set out the functions or services the firms are to provide and their total charges.

(g) Firms must make proper arrangements for keeping clients' funds separate from those of the business.

(h) Unsolicited visits or telephone calls to sell investments should not be made, except for calls to sell life assurance and unit trusts. Where cold calls result in a sale the customer must have a fourteen-day cooling-off period during which he may withdraw from the transaction.

(i) Firms are required to adhere to a proper complaints procedure, fully investigating and dealing with client complaints and keeping records of the complaints and subsequent inquiries for production to the SRO or SIB if necessary. If a client remains unsatisfied, he must have access to a complaints procedure approved by the SRO or SIB.

(j) All published recommendations must be fair and not misleading, must state foreseeable risks, and must be reasonably justified in any predictions or forecasts.

(k) The FSA has established an *Investors' Compensation Scheme*, funded by the authorised investment firm, including building societies and insurance companies, from which compensation must be paid to private investors of up to £48,000, if an authorised firm goes into default and cannot meet its obligations to its customers.

Under the FSA it is a criminal offence to carry on investment business without authorisation or exemption, and is punishable by fines and/or imprisonment.

Note: All investment carries some degree of risk, whether relating to business or general economic conditions. The existence of the regulatory system under the FSA does *not* remove the need for investors to pay attention to where they place their money, just as the existence of the Highway Code does not remove the need for people to look before crossing the road.

∎ Regulation of building societies, unit and investment trusts

Building Societies Act 1986

This Act came into effect on 1 January 1987 and it provides a further spur to competition between banks and building societies. The implementation of the Act will be through the Building Societies Commission (BSC), which was set up, as a legal entity, under the Act. The Commission is responsible for the prudential supervision of the activities of the societies. For its operations, which are financed by the societies, it is accountable to the Treasury. The Act requires the Commission to perform the following functions:

(a) To 'authorise' the societies to take deposits, provided they abide by the liquidity and capital adequacy criteria, possess suitable accounting records and internal control systems, and have directors who are 'fit and proper' persons to hold their posts.

(b) To ensure the societies' financial stability, by closely regulating the size of their liquid funds and the manner in which these funds are invested. For example, about 80 per cent of their commercial assets (total assets *less* liquid and fixed assets) are in the form of loans for house purchase to individuals which are secured by first mortgage and that they do not lend more than 100 per cent of the valuation of property. Broadly speaking, the societies can invest their liquid funds only in authorised banks and government and government-guaranteed securities. A proportion of their liquid funds must be in short-term securities; in practice, most of their investments are held on a fairly short-term basis.

(c) To promote the aims of the societies, i.e. enable them to raise funds from deposits and from wholesale deposit markets in order to make loans for house purchases on competitive terms.

(d) To promote the protection of depositors/shareholders funds (see below).

(e) To monitor advertising by the societies, and to amend or withdraw inappropriate advertising.

(f) To monitor closely the activities of the societies, who are required to submit to the Commission detailed, monthly, quarterly and annually returns on their activites, and to identify any potential difficulties at an early stage.

(g) To restrict the activities of any society which is failing to exercise prudently the powers granted under the Act.

(h) To advise the government on the operations of the societies.

The statutory investor protection scheme

The Building Societies Act 1986 provides a new legislative framework for building societies and includes provision for a statutory *Investor Protection Scheme*. This replaces the voluntary scheme set up by the Building Societies Association in April 1982 and covers all 'authorised' building societies. The statutory scheme is along similar lines to that which exists for the banks, with two important differences:

1. Unlike the banks' scheme, the building society scheme does not have a permanent fund of money. The reason given by the Treasury for this is that 'experience suggests that calls on the scheme are likely to be much less frequent than those on behalf of depositors with small authorised deposit takers under the Banking Act Scheme'.

2. The level of protection is 90 per cent of amounts up to £20,000. Hence an individual investor would be guaranteed a maximum of 90 per cent of £20,000 regardless of how many accounts are held in the society. (Depositors of larger amounts than £20,000 can of course split their funds between two or more societies, but then they will lose out on the increasingly popular high interest accounts with a £25,000 minimum.)

When the investor/depositor protection provisions under the Banking Act 1987 and the Building Societies Act 1986 are compared, building societies appear to provide greater protection: e.g. the maximum fund which could be raised under the Banking Act would not be nearly sufficient to repay the depositors of any one of the big four clearing banks, in the unlikely event of a bank losing all its funds.

The Financial Services Act 1986 and building societies

The FSA will create a number of challenges for the societies, because the prime objective of the FSA is to regulate any person who conducts investment business. As many building societies and their subsidiaries may carry out ancillary services of an investment nature for their customers they too fall under FSA jurisdiction.

The main investment activities of the societies which will come under the requirements of the FSA include:

(a) Arranging for the provison of, and advising on, life insurance, including endowment policies linked to mortgages.
(b) Establishing and managing of unit trusts.
(c) Providing of personal pensions.
(d) Establishing and managing of personal equity plans.
(e) Arranging for the provision of services in connection with stocks and shares.

It will be a criminal offence to engage in investment activities of this nature without authorisation. Societies can obtain authorisation from either the SIB or from one or more of the SROs, depending upon the breadth and mix of investment business activities undertaken.

Whether or not a society requires authorisation depends on its activities and the manner in which they are undertaken. Each society therefore will need to do the following:

(a) Determine whether any of its current or proposed activities constitute investment business; if not, it does not require authorisation.
(b) Decide its policy on whether it will be an introducer or a representative; introducers (who restrict their investment service to introducing customers to authorised independent intermediaries on a commission basis), and representatives (who represent a single authorised life office or unit trust operator for a fee), do not require authorisation.
(c) Choose to become an independent investment intermediary or manager, in which case it will need authorisation from appropriate SRO(s) or the SIB.

■ Regulating the insurance industry

The group banking structure often includes insurance business. Therefore it is relevant for you to know the main provisions of the enactments under which the insurance industry in the UK is regulated and supervised.

Insurance Companies Act 1982

This Act is now the definitive legislation on the subject of the regulation of the insurance industry, because it has consolidated and extended the previous insurance legislation, such as the Insurance Companies Act 1974, Policyholders Protection Act 1975 and Insurance Brokers (Registration) Act 1977. It has also taken account of the *EC Directive on Insurance* business so that laws governing insurance business in member states could be harmonised, enabling insurance companies based in one state to operate in other states of the EC, and for the policy holder resident in one state to be protected when the insurance company that sold the policy is resident in another state. It has two main aims: to protect policy holders from the failure of the insurance company which sold insurance cover to them; and to protect purchasers of insurance cover being sold policies unsuited to their requirements.

Its main provisons are as follows:

(a) Before a company can write insurance business, it must be authorised by the DTI. To obtain DTI authorisation, it must:
  (i) comply with the solvency (capital adequacy) regulations;
  (ii) possess sufficient financial resources to meet its needs;
  (iii) have controllers, directors, managers and underwriting agents who are 'fit and proper persons';

(iv) submit to the DTI a detailed plan of its business projections for some years (normally five) hence, setting out the type of business that it proposes to underwrite, the premium rates to be charged, the reinsurance arrangements and so on.

Authorisation is granted for specific classes of business. The Act breaks down the classes of business into long-term (e.g. life business), of which there are seven classes, and general (e.g. non-life business), which comprises seventeen classes.

(b) No new authorisations will be given for companies to write both general and long-term business, other than on a reinsurance basis, although existing composite companies may continue writing both classes of business.

(c) Insurance companies are prohibited from carrying out non-insurance business anywhere in the world — although they can establish subsidiaries to transact other types of business.

(d) In terms of requirements for trading, the Act defines, at present, three categories of insurance company.

  (i) *External companies*. These have their head offices outside the EC, and are subject to extremely stringent controls. They must appoint a person, or a company, resident in the UK to act on their behalf and this representative, and its relevant executives and main underwriting agents, must be 'fit and proper persons'; additionally they must keep assets of a prescribed value within the UK, as well as placing a deposit with the High Court.

  (ii) *Community companies*. These have head offices in EC countries, other than the UK. They have to satisfy the authorisation requirements of the member country in which they have their head offices, and they are governed by what are called matching and localisation provisions of the Act.

  (iii) *United Kingdom companies*. These are indigenous UK companies, with UK head offices, formed under various Companies Acts, Royal Charter, Acts of Parliament, or are registered friendly societies. They will be subject to the full weight of the 1982 regulations.

(e) As the codifying Act, the 1982 Act also covers matters provided for in earlier legislation (see above). For example, it covers matters relating to the conduct of business within the insurance industry, for the protection and benefit of the insuring public, and relates to such things as advertising, misleading statements, connected intermediaries and the issue of 'cooling-off' notices which allow a proposer to withdraw from a long-term contract of life assurance.

(f) The Act lays down restrictions on companies transferring business to other insurers, including Lloyds. If it is the general business which is to be transferred then the approval of the Secretary of State (DTI) is required, and details must be sent to the affected policy holders, whilst with long-term business the sanction of the High Court, or the Court of Session in Scotland, is required.

DTI, the major watchdog

The DTI keeps a very tight control over insurance companies' activities. It checks on their solvency and management generally, as per the 1982 Act, which requires that all companies must deposit detailed accounts with the DTI each year, together with other information relating to premiums, claims analyses and reinsurance arrangements. Companies transacting long-term business are also required to carry out an annual valuation of the assets and liability of their life fund, or funds, details of which must be submitted to the DTI for checking.

Should an insurer fail to comply with the requirements of the 1982 Act, the Secretary of State may intervene; should there be any concern over an insurance company's activities, the DTI can invoke its powers of intervention: these powers would be used in the following main areas:

(a) To protect existing or potential policy holders against the risk of the company becoming insolvent, or unable to meet the expectations of its long-term policy holders.

(b) If the company, or its parent or subsidiary, fails to meet any of the obligations of the 1982 Act, submits misleading information, or if any grounds exist that would prevent the Secretary of State from granting authorisation, or its authorisation has been withdrawn in another EC member state, the DTI will intervene.

(c) There seems to be an open power of intervention by the DTI within five years of an authorisation to trade being given, or a person who is unapproved becoming a controller of a company.

The Secretary of State can, in such circumstances, take whatever action he considers necessary, by specifically ordering the company:

(a) not to make or realise investments of a specified class;
(b) to maintain adequate assets in the UK to cover liabilities;
(c) to deposit such assets with an approved person;
(d) to limit premium income to a specific amount;
(e) to carry out a special valuation of its long-term business;
(f) to liquidate certain investments;
(g) to stop the office taking new business or even renewals;
(h) to produce its accounting returns more speedily;
(i) to produce specified information, books, documents;
(j) to prohibit the appointment of certain persons as directors or senior controllers of the company;
(k) to instruct an insurance company to reduce its bonus rate applicable to with-profit life contracts.

An insurance company can be wound up under the normal Companies Acts rules, but also by the DTI if the company cannot comply with the provisions of the 1982 Act, or if it is felt that to wind it up would be in the public interest.

∎ Examination questions

The contents of this and of the next chapter are new, post-Wilkinson additions, therefore there are, as yet, few exam questions and answers which cover these topics. The following *specimen* questions and answers are intended to pinpoint specific information from a long chapter.

Question 1

(a) Outline the areas of responsibility of the main bodies involved in supervising and regulating investment business in the UK.

(b) What protection do these bodies offer investors against losses on their investments?

Question 2

What are the requirements of the Insurance Companies Act 1982, of which a banking group, with an insurance subsidiary company, should be aware?

Question 3

What is the 'Basle Agreement', and what are its provisions?

Question 4

What are the implications of the Second Banking Directive of the European Community (1988) for UK banks?

Question 5

(a) (i) For what reasons does a commercial bank need liquidity?
     (ii) How may liquidity be provided?
(b) How does the Bank of England currently exercise its supervisory role with regard to commercial banks' liquidity?

∎ Outline answers

Answer 1

(a) (i) *Regulation* is covered by the Financial Services Act (FSA) 1986. Under the Act the *DTI* is responsible for overall regulation of the investment industry, with *operational* powers delegated to the *SIB*. (Soon these responsibilites will pass on to the Treasury and the Bank of England.)
     (ii) The *SIB* (the Bank of England in due course) is responsible for *supervision* of the four SROs:
          – *The Securities and Futures Authority* (SFA), responsible for supervising the activities of the members of the London Stock Exchange and the financial and commodities futures and options.
          – *Life Assurance and Unit Trust Regulatory Organisation* (LAUTRO), responsible for the life assurance and unit trust industry.
          – *Investment Management Regulatory Organisation* (IMRO), responsible for independent investment managers.
          – *Financial Intermediaries, Managers and Brokers Regulatory Association* (FIMBRA), responsible for independent intermediaries dealing with the public's investments such as unit trusts and life assurance.
     (iii) Other bodies:
          – *Bank of England*, for regulation of the gilt-edged securities market.
          – *DTI*, for regulation of unit trusts and insurance companies and insider trading and takeovers.
          – *Recognised Professional Bodies* (RPBs).
          – *Recognised Investment Exchanges* (RIES).
          – *Recognised Clearing Houses* (RCHs).

(b) Only 'Fit and proper' firms can carry out investment business. If investors lose money, only some investors are protected and only in some circumstances:
  (i) Only private investors covered.
  (ii) Only covered if the loss is due to insolvency of an authorised firm or because of fraud involving such a firm.
  (iii) Compensation limited to the first £30,000 *plus* 90 per cent cover for the next £20,000.

Answer 2

(a) Before the company can write insurance business, it must be authorised by the DTI; authorisation is given only after the company has met strict conditions.
(b) No new authorisation to write both 'general' and 'long-term' business, other than reinsurance business.
(c) The company cannot do non-insurance business itself, but can do it via a subsidiary.
(d) The Act recognises three categories of insurance company:
  (i) External companies (head offices outside EC states, subject to stringent controls).
  (ii) Community companies (head offices in EC states, must satisfy the authorisation requirements of the state in which head office is located).
  (iii) UK companies (indigenous UK companies, subject to the 1982 Act).
(e) Matters such as conduct of business rules, protection of policy holders, misleading advertising and oral statements, cooling-off period, are covered.
(f) Restrictions on transferring business to other insurers.

Answer 3

In July 1988, the twelve most developed countries agreed on a set of rules on capital adequacy for banks in each country. The key features of the agreed rules are known as the Basle Agreement, because it was agreed at the Bank for International Settlements in Basle, Switzerland. The agreed set of rules are as follows:

(a) By the end of 1992, banks with significant international exposure must maintain capital equivalent to at least 8 per cent assets, weighted according to risk.
(b) At least half of the bank's capital must consist of 'Tier 1 capital', and the other half 'Tier 2 capital' (*see* p. 187).
(c) In calculating capital adequacy, off balance sheet items will be taken into account, according to specified weightings.

Answer 4

(a) Easier cross-border banking.
(b) International expansion via location in EC member states.
(c) Cheaper location because no committed capital is required for foreign branches.
(d) No specific solvency ratios or large exposure limits on foreign branches.
(e) Opportunity for a bank to undertake in other states whatever it is able to undertake in the UK.
(f) Central issue for UK competing banks:
  (i) access to potential customers;
  (ii) efficient delivery systems for financial services.

Answer 5

(a) (i) A bank needs liquidity to:
- meet withdrawals of deposits (including the daily inter-bank settlement);
- meet unforeseen demand for finance;
- provide for any interruptions in cash flow;
- maintain confidence of depositors and shareholders.

(ii) Liquidity may be provided by:
- maintaining a certain percentage of assets in highly liquid forms: cash; operational deposits with the Bank; Treasury bills; short gilts; call money; commercial bills;
- holding a proportion of loans in short maturites to ensure cash flow;
- having access to the inter-bank and CDs markets (provided the system as a whole is not short of funds);
- seeking liquidity provision from the Bank.

(b) (i) The Bank does not impose across-the-board liquidity ratios – it discusses the position with individual bank managements to ensure that a prudential liquidity position is maintained.

(ii) Institutions are expected to:
- hold sufficient cash or liquid assets;
- secure an appropriately matching future profile of cash flows from maturing assets;
- maintain an adequately diversified deposit base.

▋ A tutor's answer

The following question, which seeks to examine your understanding of banking supervision issues discussed in this chapter, was asked recently in the CIB exams. Try to answer it from the knowledge you have obtained from the study of this chapter, before looking at the outline answer provided below.

Question

Outline the ways in which the Bank of England:

(a) supervises and regulates the activities of banks in the UK;
(b) ensures that there is always adequate liquidity in the banking system.

Specimen answer

(a) The 1987 Banking Act makes the Bank of England responsible for the supervision and regulation of the UK banking system. This role involves the Bank's regulation of the following main areas:

(i) *Capital adequacy.* The Bank has largely adopted the criteria for capital adequacy established under the Basle Accord: banks must hold a minimum of 8 per cent of assets (weighted for risk); at least 4 per cent in the form of Tier 1 capital (equity and disclosed reserves); and the remainder in Tier 2 capital (undisclosed reserves, revaluation of property, debt capital and general provisions).

(ii) *Liquidity.* The liquidity adequacy is agreed with each bank individually in discussion with the Bank. Commercial banks must hold suffcient cash or liquid assets to meet obligations, ensure adequate cash flow from maturing assets and maintain an adequately diversified deposit base.

(iii) *Foreign currency exposure.* The Bank sets guidelines for and monitors foreign currency positions.

(iv) *Risk supervision.* The Bank monitors large exposures. Banks are required to advise the Bank of individual customer large exposure (over 10 per cent of capital).

(v) *Authorisation.* Institutions must be authorised and must maintain suitable accounting and other records and internal control systems, all of which are monitored by the Bank.

(b) If liquidity shortage is likely to develop, the Bank injects liquidity by buying eligible bills (mainly commercial bills) from the discount houses; normally maturity bands 1 and 2.

The Bank will accept offers of bills from the house at a discount rate of its own choosing, i.e. within the undisclosed interest rate band.

Sale and repurchase agreements of gilts directly with commercial banks are also undertaken from time to time, especially during the tax gathering season.

Late assistance through unsecured direct loans to the market is provided when the Bank wishes to give the market a firm indication about short-term interest rate levels.

∎ A step further

Your best sources of keeping up-to-date with the requirements of this topic are the quality financial press and articles in *Banking World*; especially watch out for updating articles by the Chief Examiner. The *BEQB* and *Fact Sheets* must remain your most authoritative source for guidance on relevant legislation on the regulation and supervision of commercial banks.

CHAPTER 11

Corporate Finance and Risk Management

Syllabus requirements
- Reasons for hedging.
- Hedging instruments.
- Corporate short-term finance.
- Corporate long-term finance.
- Role of equities in corporate finance.

▌ Getting started

Hedging reduces exchange rate and interest rate risks. In the context of this chapter, hedging means using the financial machinery, via hedging instruments, to gain protection against loss arising through fluctuations in the exchange rates and interest rates. A financial intermediary, say, a bank, can do the matching of two or more offsetting transactions entered into by hedgers.

The growth in the use of hedging instruments is generally thought to have been caused by the volatility which followed the collapse of the Bretton Woods fixed exchange rate agreements. It is also attributed to the widespread exploitation of arbitrage opportunities between different financial markets, where the interest rates and exchange rates had gone out of alignment. However, the financial (hedging) instrument market has now grown to such an extent that it is probably capable of generating its own volatility, which in turn requires further use of more and varied instruments. These factors have resulted in the development of many ways of risk management by which risks may be transferred between different participants in the financial markets.

The corporate finance part of this chapter deals with the financial instruments which are used in obtaining short- and long-term finance by the companies, including venture capital providing new equity funds for them.

Short-term finance means making available funds for short periods of time; money borrowed for periods up to one year may be termed short-term finance. There are no definite dividing lines between short-term, medium-term, and long-term finance, but one-year to five-year borrowing may be termed medium-term, and borrowing over five years may be called long-term.

▌ Essential principles

The following are the main hedging and corporate financing instruments.

▌ Hedging instruments

Exchange rate risks protection

(a) *Foreign currency options (FCOs)*. An FCO is a contract between a buyer and a seller of a foreign currency which gives the option buyer (say, a bank's customer) the right, but not the obligation, to buy (a call FCO) or to sell (a put FCO) a specific amount of one currency for another currency at a predetermined price (the exercise or strike price) on or until a certain future date (the exercise period or date). An FCO has a predetermined maturity date; and if it can be exercised at any time between the date that it was written and the date of its maturity it is called an American option; if it can be exercised only at maturity date it is known as a European option.

   The customer, on purchasing an FCO on payment of a premium, obtains complete hedge against adverse exchange rate movements, but is still able to benefit from favourable movements. Taking out an FCO is therefore not just a hedging operation.

(b) *Forward foreign exchange contract (forward cover)*. A forward cover is a *binding* deal between two parties (say, a bank and its customer) to buy or sell a fixed amount of one currency for a fixed amount of another currency either on a specific future date (fixed forward cover) or on any day during the specific period (option forward cover). The rate at which the exchange is agreed between the two currencies by the parties to the forward deal is called the forward exchange rate. Like the FCO, a forward cover is a hedging operation, and the main difference between the two is that whereas with a forward cover the exchange rate is always quoted from the bank's own point of view − the bank buys and the bank sells − with an FCO it is the customer who buys the *right* to buy or sell, from or to, the bank an underlying foreign currency at a specified rate of exchange; with an FCO a customer can 'walk away' if the actual rate of exchange on the day the currency is to be bought or sold becomes unfavourable, losing only the premium. With a forward cover he cannot 'walk away' even if he is unable to comply with the terms of the binding contract.

(c) *Currency swap*. At the start of a currency swap two companies exchange the principal amount of a currency for the currency equivalent of the other currency, calculated at the spot exchange rate. At maturity, the *exact* amounts exchanged at the outset are re-exchanged, even though the spot value of the two currencies may have changed. It is this *re-exchange* of the principal that provides the swap's currency hedging element.

(d) *Currency loans and deposits*. These may be used as alternatives to forward cover, in the following ways. Take a *currency loan* equal in amount to the anticipated receipts in that currency, sell the currency borrowed immediately for sterling and deposit the sterling received. Interest will be payable on the currency loan, but will be received on the sterling deposited. Purchase at spot rate a currency amount equal to an anticipated payment in that currency and deposit the *currency purchased*. Interest will be received on the currency deposited but will be lost on the sterling amount utilised to purchase the currency. In both cases interest paid or received must be compared with the alternative cost of covering forward.

Interest rate risk protection

(a) *Yield curve*. It shows the spread of fixed rates payable on a particular type of asset (e.g. a loan or deposit) with different terms to maturity. By taking out a fixed interest term loan, the borrower is acquiring a hedge against increases in interest rates. Likewise, by making a fixed interest term deposit, a lender is locking on the fixed interest certainty even though the yield may become 'perverse' (see pp. 97–100). In hedging operations *certainty* is the main objective.

(b) *Interest rate cap.* This agreement places an upper limit on the rate of interest payable on a variable rate borrowing linked to the base rate or LIBOR. Interest rate caps can be traded quite separately from the borrowing to which they relate.

(c) *Interest rate floors.* A floor is structured in a similar way to a cap, but has the *reverse* effect. In fact, it achieves for the investor/lender who is receiving floating rate interest what a cap does for a borrower who pays it: while protecting the investor/lender from a fall in interest rates below a floor, it allows him to benefit from any rise.

(d) *Interest rate collars.* A collar is a cap and a floor *combined*. It gives a company protection against rates rising above a certain level (the cap), and the ability to take advantage of a fall in rates, but only down to a certain level (the floor). So a company buying a collar will have a band of tolerance across a minimum and maximum cost of borrowing. If rates rise above the cap rate, it is compensated by the writer of the collar. If rates fall through the floor, it will compensate the other party.

(e) *Forward rate agreement.* This is a contract between, say, a bank and a customer under which each party agrees to compensate the other party for the effect of movements in LIBOR upon a notional borrowing over a predetermined contract period (settlement date). The seller agrees to compensate the purchaser for any increase that occurs in the intervening period, and the purchaser in turn agrees to pay over to the seller the difference between the agreed and the prevailing rate if the rate falls.

(f) *Interest rate swap.* This involves a swapping of interest rate payments, and normally involves one company raising fixed rate borrowing and another raising floating rate borrowing. This arrangement enables both companies to achieve the type of interest rate each desires at a cheaper rate than is otherwise possible.

(g) *Interest rate option.* This contract is basically similar to a foreign currency option contract except that instead of a currency, a specified financial arrangement is bought (call option) or sold (put option) at a predetermined price (exercise or strike price) on or until a future date (exercise period or date). The buyer of the option will exercise his right only if he sees an interest rate advantage over the current interest rates.

Euro Currency Unit (ECU)

This unit provides a hedge against both exchange rate and interest rate risks. Therefore business companies trading in Europe and seeking protection against these risks should consider using ECU-denominated arrangements.

Although the ECU was created to facilitate payment of debts between member states of the EC, it is being used increasingly by the private sector throughout Europe. For business companies it provides two distinct advantages:

1. Interest and exchange rates fluctuations of its twelve component currencies are smoothed out, thus providing relative stability, even when, for example, the pound sterling is moving quite sharply against certain other EC currencies.
2. It provides protection or hedging opportunities for exporters and importers. The ECU enables businesses to take out protection against exchange risk in a *single* transaction rather than a range of separate transactions, which means it is both simpler and cheaper.

Transaction and translation risks

(a) *Transaction* exposure is the effect on *future identified* cash flows of exchange rate movements. This is the most obvious type of exchange risk, and the most likely to affect businesses. However, it is also the most usually and easily hedged of all exposures.

(b) *Translation* exposure is the effect on *assets and liabilities* of future exchange rate movements. This exposure affects the balance sheet of a business − for instance, investment in an overseas subsidiary whose assets and liabilities are denominated in a foreign currency.

■ Corporate financing instruments

Corporate finance involves provision of funds to incorporated bodies, e.g. business companies and other businesses, for varying periods of time, i.e. short term, medium term and long term.

Short-term financing techniques

(a) *LIBOR-linked (money market) lending.* The London Inter-Bank Offered Rate (LIBOR) is a true reflection of the cost of funds to the banks, and it is logical to use it as a true base rate when lending to other banks and to sophisticated non-bank businesses. A LIBOR-linked loan is a facility by the bank, whereby the customer borrows wholesale funds at market rates for periods between one and twelve months, usually at lower rates than the overdraft rate, which is linked to the bank's base rate.

(b) *Base rate-linked advances (overdraft).* The base rate is the basic lending rate of a bank or financial institution, on which its lending (and deposit) rates are founded. Base rate-linked advances may be fixed rate or floating rate lending. The advance period is usually up to one year. With the volatility of interest rates, some banks split their base rate-linked advances into two, one advance with a fixed rate of interest, the other with a floating rate. If the base rate goes down, the customer gains on floating rate − and if the base rate goes up, the customer is protected on the fixed half.

(c) *Acceptance credit.* This is a facility whereby the customer (usually larger businesses) draws a bill of exchange on the bank, up to an agreed limit, payable at a stipulated future date. The bank accepts the bill and arranges for it to be discounted. Acceptance credit can be arranged from a period of one week to over six months. This facility is not as flexible as an overdraft, but it offers the advantage of cheaper borrowing; a reputable bank's acceptance attracts the lowest discounts from the discounter, and certainty of cost; the customer is informed by the bank of the exact cost of his borrowing, i.e. acceptance commission and the discount he can obtain.

(d) *Sterling commercial paper (SCP).* SCP comprises sterling promissory notes of maturity periods between seven and 364 days issued by corporate borrowers direct to investors, thereby by-passing traditional bank lending (this process is known as 'dis-intermediation'). This source of finance is available to company customers with a listing on the International Stock Exchange and with minimum surplus resources of £25 million, and borrowing a minimum of £100,000. (*See* pp. 54–55.)

Medium-term finance

All major banks provide variations of the following loans to businesses:

(a) *Business loans.* The customer borrows at a fixed rate of interest and repays, in monthly instalments, the loan over a number of years, or early, at any time, with no penalty. In many cases the loan can be unsecured. The fixed interest means that the customer knows in advance exactly what his monthly commitment is, which assists him to forecast his cash flow more accurately. The period of business loans is usually between one and five years.

(b) *Flexible business loans.* For borrowing larger amounts than under business loans, say, for purchasing an expensive asset, a business, or for providing working capital. A company may seek a flexible business loan, borrowing a single lump sum or borrowing sums in stages as needed, paying interest only on what has been borrowed. Borrowers can choose either a fixed or a floating rate at the start and can switch between them during the loan period, which may be up to five years, but can be up to twenty years. Repayments can be monthly or quarterly spread over the full term. If the borrower chooses, he can enjoy no capital repayment for up to two years, but repaying only interest, thus reducing pressures on his cash flow early on. Flexible business loans can be tailored to borrowers' needs.

Long-term finance

(a) *Debenture stock.* A company may issue debenture bonds to borrow long-term funds. A debenture bond is an acknowledgement by the issuing company of its debt to the debenture bondholders. Debenture stock (the total of issued debentures) may be secured by a *fixed charge* over a fixed asset, e.g. land, premises, machinery of the issuing company, and the company must keep the mortgaged asset intact, i.e. it must not be sold, exchanged or other charge created against it. The secured charge may be a *floating charge*, applying to all assets, not already mortgaged, which normally can be traded. Therefore, debentures with a fixed charge are more secure than those with a floating charge.

Debenture stock carries a fixed rate of interest and normally a guarantee of repayment in full by a specified date. Payments of debenture interest rank ahead of dividend payments to preference and ordinary shareholders. If the issuing company is being wound up, debenture-holders rank before preferential creditors (e.g. unpaid wages, taxes, etc.) and before preference and ordinary shareholders, for repayment of capital from the sale proceeds of its assets. Not all indebtedness of a company can be described as debenture stock; the loan must have some permanence, say ten years or more, to be classed as debenture stock.

Banks lending via purchases of debenture stock of a company pay particular attention to the following aspects of the company:

  (i) Interest cover – the extent by which its gross profits exceed its interest obligations.
 (ii) Liquidity – the extent by which its cash inflow exceeds its cash outflow.
(iii) Debt redemption provision, if any.
(iv) Marketability of debentures – marketing will be restricted if the issuing company is not a 'blue chip' company.

(b) *Fixed and variable rate loans.* Flexible business loans, discussed under 'medium-term finance', can be geared to provide long-term finance, of up to twenty years.

(c) *Equity finance.* The larger commercial banks provide finance to businesses to buy-in the shares of retiring directors (management buy-outs), or other shareholders who wish to realise their holdings (another form of management buy-out). They also provide development capital where a business expansion may be limited by the fact that it is nearing the limit of what it can raise by other conventional means. The bank makes available the necessary finance (normally upwards of £150,000) to the business in return for minority shareholding in the business. Thus by providing a percentage of equity capital, the bank is injecting long-term funding and an equity subscription, in return for a proportion of the ordinary equity, usually 15–40 per cent. The bank will normally seek to appoint a member of its staff as a non-executive director. This means that although a shareholder the bank does not expect the board of directors of the business to alter their on-going successful business strategy, nor does it expect to interfere with the day-to-day management of the business. The role of the bank's non-executive director is to assist in an advisory capacity in the development of future business plans and to give financial guidance. For smaller amounts of capital injection (£100,000 or more), the bank may seek a mix of preference share capital and ordinary equity; the proportion of equity is normally 10–20 per cent. The bank will not expect board representation in such a mix but will expect a guaranteed preference dividend.

(d) *Venture capital.* A larger private company or a smaller public company may wish to raise new capital for investment in a specific project or for expansion, in which there is a risk. Fixed interest capital, even if available, is not suitable. The capital required is called 'venture capital'; the provider of this capital is being asked to share in the risks. The critical stage which determines whether a company will succeed in growing into a large company is rather like the chrysalis stage when a caterpillar turns into a beautiful butterfly; there is apparently not much happening on the outside, but inside a major transformation may be under way. Companies in the chrysalis stage need help. Venture capitalists can provide help. Control often needs to move from the entrepreneur who *started* the business to a management team who will help it *grow*. The high street banks usually provide the venture capital by lending up to about £100,000.

(e) *Invoice discounting (factoring).* The bank purchases a business's book debts on a continuous (therefore, long-term) basis, and provides the business customer with an immediate cash advance of up to 80 per cent of the value of invoices. This prepayment of invoices assists customers to sustain their cash flows, and to cut their overdrafts.

(f) *Eurobonds.* Eurobonds are an extension of eurocurrency markets' short-term lending and borrowing. They are sold in more than one country simultaneously, usually through an international syndicate of bankers, who may also agree to underwrite the issue. They are issued at fixed rates, as well as variable rates (then they are known as floating rate notes); the interest rate is fixed usually every six months in line with the changes in six-month eurodollar interest rate. Thus the interest rate on medium- and long-term bonds – average maturities are between ten and fifteen years – can be brought into line with the short-term interest rates. The currencies of issue are usually dollar, deutschemark, Swiss franc, and also sometimes pound sterling and ECU. Most bonds are payable to bearers and all are paid without deduction of tax. The amounts involved are large and therefore eurobonds are suitable for the needs of multinationals.

(g) *Rights issue.* A company may offer *new* shares direct to its existing shareholders. The price is usually set below the market price of the existing shares, in order to make the offer attractive. This is a method of raising long-term equity capital from within the company, and avoids the cost of raising funds from the outsiders.

■ Useful applied material

In this section we shall look at the practical aspects of hedging instruments and corporate finance techniques.

Hedging techniques

Forward exchange contract (forward cover)

These contracts provide a cheap and simple means of reducing businesses' exposure to exchange rate changes, because a forward cover is a contract between the customer and the bank to exchange a specified amount of a currency for another at a *future* date but at the rate of exchange between the two currencies set *now*. Thus a forward cover provides businessmen with *certainty* about the exchange rate at which the future transaction will take place. The future date may be as far away as five years, and even longer in some cases, and the currencies in which forward cover contracts are available may be as many as forty. Forward covers are available in large and small amounts, and therefore are particularly suitable for smaller businesses seeking exchange rate cover.

Suppose a company signs a contract to supply goods for $100,000 when the dollar/sterling exchange rate is $1.70, but on supply of goods and on receipt of payment the pound has risen to $2. The amount the exporting company would receive drops from nearly £59,000 to £50,000 – which could wipe out most or all of its profit on the transaction. However, this would not happen if the company had taken out a forward cover contract with a bank: its profit margin in sterling will remain unaffected by exchange rate movements during the *lifetime* of the contract.

Foreign currency options (FCOs)

FCOs allow bank customers to take advantage of favourable exchange rate movements while protecting them against adverse changes.

Suppose X plc invoiced their American customers for $5.1 million, for payment in ninety days. X plc estimated that at the existing rate of $1.70 there was a 20 per cent profit on the deal, and if the pound fell the profit would be even more. Nevertheless, X plc, in order to protect their profit margin to at least 15 per cent, took out an FCO to convert their dollar proceeds back into sterling at $1.78 in three months' time. As it turned out, the pound rose and the exchange rate moved to $1.85! X plc were glad to exercise their option at $1.78 and protect their profit margin. The premium paid in advance, of around 0.65 per cent, was well worth it to X plc.

Interest rate swaps

Company X is a capital-intensive company. Its treasurer, W, is worried about the possibility of interest rates rising because he has funded a large expensive project (£3 million) by a *floating* rate loan (say, 9.45%): six-month LIBOR *plus* margin from Bank Y. W wants to *fix* the interest rate on the loan. However, Bank Y is unwilling to do this. W finds Bank Z, who is willing to solve the problem by arranging an *interest rate swap*, as follows.

The swap, based on a notional principal of £3 million for a four-year term, involves W paying Z a fixed rate of 9.45 per cent, while receiving from Z six-month LIBOR. These payments enable W to service the floating rate obligations to Y under the loan, while at the same time fixing the interest costs for company X. The payments take place every six months as follows:

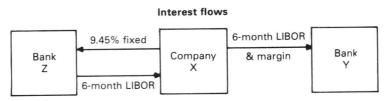

Interest flows

Fig. 11.1

Currency swaps

Suppose G, a Germany company, and A, an American company both wish to provide an inter-company loan for a five-year term to their respective subsidiaries: GA in America, and AG in Germany. G's loan to GA is to be in US$, and A's loan to AG in German marks (DM). Both A and G can eliminate currency exposure risk by entering into a five-year currency swap via a bank, as follows. G gives its DM principal amount to the bank, which passes it to A in return for A's US$ principal amount, which is paid to G. The exchange takes place at a spot rate of, say, DM2 = US$1. G on-lends US$ to GA, and A on-lends DM to AG. During the period of the swap, G and A will make periodic interest payments via the bank to each other for the currency amount they received. The funds for interest payments will come from GA and AG on inter-company loans. After five years, G and A re-exchange currencies at the spot rate of exchange at the outset (DM2 = US$1), regardless of the prevailing exchange rate. Thus unlike an interest rate swap, a currency swap gives G and A a currency and interest rate hedge.

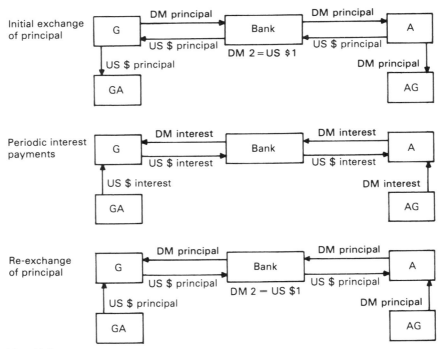

Fig. 11.2

Interest rate caps

These caps, on base rates or LIBOR, limit borrowers' interest rate costs to a specified level for a specified period of time. But, at the same time, they enable borrowers to benefit from a fall in rates.

Suppose LIBOR/base interest rate = 11 per cent. The bank is willing to lend to the customer at 2 per cent over LIBOR/base rate. The customer does not wish to pay more than 13 per cent (including the 2 per cent margin), i.e. he wishes to cap the LIBOR/base rate at 11 per cent. If interest rates rise to a figure in excess of 11 per cent, the bank will reimburse the difference to the customer.

Suppose the underlying cap ceiling is £1 million, and that the interest rates rose immediately after the interest rate cap agreement to 12 per cent for the year, the customer would be paid 1 per cent (difference between cap rate at 11 per cent and interest rate at 12 per cent) on £1 million for 1 year = £10,000.

The minimum and maximum limits usually for LIBOR caps are £5 million and £100 million, and for the base rate caps £250,000 to £10 million. The LIBOR cap term tends to be up to five years, and for the base rate cap, one or two years.

A cap is essentially an insurance policy for a company wishing to protect itself against a *rise* in short-term interest rates (e.g. six-month LIBOR) *above* a certain capped level, but at the same time hoping to take advantage of any future drop in interest rates.

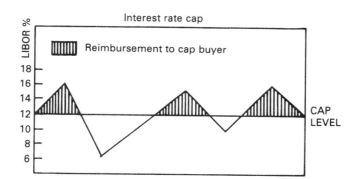

Fig. 11.3

Interest rate floors

A floor is also an insurance policy for an investor/lender who is receiving floating rate interest: it *protects* him *against a fall* in interest rates below the floor, but to benefit from a rise in rates.

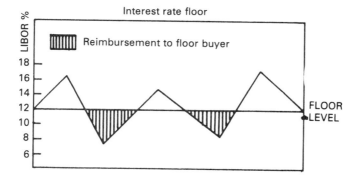

Fig. 11.4

Interest rate collars

A collar protects a company, *both* as a cap and a floor do: a collar is a cap and floor combined.

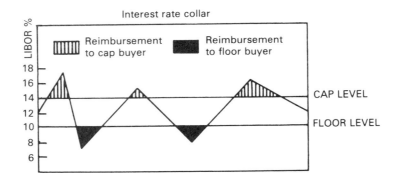

Fig. 11.5

Caps, floors and collars are usually not written for much beyond five years. Caps and floors become more expensive the *nearer* their terms are to the real level of interest rates (usually short-term LIBOR rates) at the time they are witten. Collars, however, become cheaper the narrower their spread.

Interest rate options

These are similar in character and purpose to FCOs (see above), in that a customer, having paid a single premium in advance, has the right to fix the rate on a future notional loan, deposit or investment for a specified period, but he is under no obligation to take up that right. Suppose he fixes a future loan rate at 15 per cent for a period up to two years, and afterwards interest rates fall sharply to say 11 per cent. He can simply walk away from the option and borrow instead cheaply at the lower prevailing market rate. If, on the other hand, interest rates rose sharply to, say, 18 per cent, he will be glad of being able to borrow at 15 per cent. These options are of particular interest to those businesses whose large customers do not pay on time!

Forward rate agreements (FRAs)

These agreements between corporate customers and their banks enable customers to borrow or lend a specified notional amount in the future at a fixed rate, fixed at the time of the agreement.

Suppose Company A has a seasonal borrowing requirement at £1 million for a three-month period commencing 5 January. In September LIBOR rate is 10 per cent, and the company purchases an FRA in September for January–March at 10½ per cent. LIBOR on 5 January is 11 per cent. Bank pays ½ per cent on the underlying contract of £1 million for contract period of three months, i.e. £1,250.

Company borrows at 11 per cent in the market, but with receipt of £1,250 the interest costs net 10½ per cent. However, if on 5 January the LIBOR had been 10 per cent the Company would pay to the Bank £1,250.

The amount of FRAs ranges between £1 million and £50 million, and the term ranges between one month and six months.

Corporate financing techniques

Short-term LIBOR-linked (money market) loans

These loans are normally available to companies needing working capital facilities or short-term finance for specific projects. The main advantages to borrowers include a loan facility 'committed' as to availability of funds at money market related interest rates which are usually cheaper than overdraft rates, and the borrowing costs are constant for the loan period. The actual interest rates charged will reflect the financial standing of the customer. Fixture periods (terms) range from one month to twelve months, although banks prefer fixture periods of three months or more. A fee may be charged from borrowers for early repayments or for the non-utilisation of the loan facility. All drawings are repayable on demand because it is a loan facility 'committed' as to availability of funds. Nevertheless, it gives companies another funding option with a minimum limit of £250,000, and with no upper limit.

Sterling commercial paper (SCP)

These are unsecured sterling bearer promissory notes issued direct to the investor through a 'dealer' and administered by an 'issuing and paying agent'. The dealer is responsible for quoting rates to authorised issuers, i.e. corporate customers with a full listing on the International Stock Exchange and with minimum surplus resources of £25 million. The dealer is also responsible for finding investors for the SCP issue. Normally the issuers announce a programme indicating the maximum volume of SCP that could be outstanding at any one time. Minimum issue is £100,000. The issuing and paying agent arranges for the initial payment to the issuer and on maturity repays investors. Interest rates will reflect the financial standing of the issuer, and will normally be linked to LIBOR/LIBID (London Inter-bank Bid Rate). The benefits of SCP to the issuer include a cheap source of short-term (up to 364 days) funds, costs are fixed for the period of the paper, flexibility of maturity, the ability to tap a wider investor market and advantages of comparative rates.

Acceptance credits

This is a short-term credit facility made available by banks to corporate trading customers. Banks accept bills of exchange drawn upon them by customers who can then get these acceptances discounted by the issuing bank or in the London Discount Market at very low rates of discount. At maturity the customers provide the banks with sufficient funds to pay the bills on presentation – these funds can be provided by drawing a new bill of exchange. Banks charge from the customers the accepting commission, which is the fee for accepting the bill and lending their name to its strength.

Acceptance credit is usually cheaper than overdraft borrowing, and the finance costs are fixed at the outset of each transaction. The minimum facility is for £100,000, there is no maximum. Each individual bill should have a minimum value of £50,000 and a maximum value of £1 million. For individual bills the minimum term is thirty days and the maximum is 180 days. The main purpose for acceptance credits is to obtain short-term financing for corporate trading.

The following example shows that although the customer would receive £97,250 immediately, he will need to repay £100,000 in three months' time. Thus the cost of his finance has been paid in *advance* rather than, as is usual on overdraft, in arrears. The true rate of interest is therefore higher than the quoted discount rate.

Suppose:

Face value of the bill	£100,000
Tenor	90 days
Acceptance commission	1% p.a.
Discount rate	10% p.a.

Therefore:

Face value of the bill		£100,000
Less commission (1% p.a. $\times \frac{3}{12}$)	£250	
Less discount (10% p.a. $\times \frac{3}{12}$)	£2,500	£2,750
Borrower receives		£97,250

Debenture loan stock

A company has benefit and drawback in raising the required finance via the issue of debentures instead of issuing more ordinary shares (equity capital) via a rights issue to existing ordinary shareholders.

(a) *Benefit.* Corporation tax on a company's profits is charged *after* interest on loan stock, but *before* dividends to any class of shareholder: preference or ordinary.

	£
Suppose Company Z has:	
(a) Profits before tax	1,000,000
less interest on loan stock (assumed)	100,000
	900,000
less corporation tax at, say, 35%	315,000
Profits available for ordinary shareholders	585,000
(b) Profits before tax	1,000,000
less corporation tax at 35%	350,000
	650,000
less preference share dividend (assumed)	100,000
Profits available for ordinary shareholders	550,000

Thus under (a) there is a tax saving to the company of £35,000 (£585,000 − £550,000), and the true cost of the interest to the company is £65,000 (£100,000 − £35,000). A 10 per cent loan stock, say, in debentures would cost the company only £6.5 per cent $\left(10 \times \dfrac{100 - 35}{100}\right)$.

Company Z can raise loan stock in the capital market when it is short of funds, and it can buy its own stock back when it has surplus funds. This provides the company with flexible means to adjust its liquidity.

The higher the loan capital, the higher the proportion of trading income allotted to meet the loan interest charge. But however much it may be it is a *fixed* sum, and therefore any increase in trading income has a more than proportionate effect (gearing) on the surplus available for net profit.

(b) *Drawback.* The drawback arises out of the fixed and committed claim of loan stock interest against a company's trading profits, which is also backed by a fixed (or floating) charge against its assets. Should there be a serious drop in the company's trading income, it must pay in full the loan interest, or risk losing its charged or mortgaged assets.

■ Specimen questions

There are not many exam questions on this topic as yet because it is a new, post-Wilkinson addition. The following specimen questions and their outline answers are intended to assist you in picking out required information from the contents of the chapter.

Question 1

(a) What is meant by 'hedging' operations?
(b) What are the particulars of interest rate hedging instruments?

Question 2

(a) 'Acceptance credits are a way for larger businesses to raise sums over £500,000, more cheaply than by overdraft'. Explain.
(b) Are acceptance credits always less costly than overdrafts?

Question 3

What are the advantages and disadvantages of debenture bonds to:

(a) the issuing company;
(b) the purchasers of debenture bonds;
(c) the company's ordinary shareholders?

Question 4

(a) Define interest rate swaps and currency swaps.
(b) Explain how each of these would be of benefit to a company in risk management.

Question 5

(a) Distinguish between interest rate caps and forward rate agreements.
(b) Describe how each of these operates.

■ Outline answers

Answer 1

(a) *Hedging operation.* Using the financial machinery to gain reduction in loss arising through fluctuations in the exchange and interest rates.
(b) (i) *Interest rate swaps.* Two parties agree to pay each other interest on a notional amount over a defined period but calculated according to different interest bases. At no time is the notional amount actually exchanged. Customers can fix interest

rate exposure from two- to ten-year terms, for a minimum of £1 million but with no maximum limit.

(ii) *Interest rate caps.* This agreement limits a borrower's interest rate costs to a specified level for a specified period of time. It allows borrowers not only to limit interest costs but also to benefit from a fall in interest rates. The term is from one year up to five years, and the minimum and maximum amounts for rate caps are £250,000 to £100 million.

(iii) *Interest rate options.* A contract which gives the borrower a guarantee against the unexpected, i.e. interest rates actually rising when the borrower expected them to fall but without eliminating his chance to borrow should the rates fall.

(iv) *Forward rate agreement.* A contract to borrow or lend an agreed notional amount in the future at a fixed rate which is agreed at the time of the agreement. Terms range from one month to six months, for amounts between £1 million and £50 million.

Answer 2

(a) (i) Acceptance credits are easy to arrange and simple to operate.
   (ii) Minimum for each individual bill of exchange is £50,000.
   (iii) While not as flexible as overdrafts, they offer cheaper borrowing, certainty of cost, a continuous source of funds, and funds in a wide variety of foreign currencies.

(b) (i) The customer receives the *discounted* amount immediately.
   (ii) The cost of his finance has therefore been paid in *advance* rather than, as is usual on overdraft, in arrears.
   (iii) The true rate of interest is therefore higher than the quoted discount rate.

Answer 3

(a) (i) Advantages to the *issuing company:*
     – saving on corporation tax;
     – ability to adjust liquidity conveniently.
   (ii) Disadvantages:
     – interest costs are fixed and must be paid annually;
     – assets charged can be sold if the interest is not paid.

(b) (i) Advantages to *purchasers* of debentures:
     – fixed rate of return guaranteed for the whole term;
     – repayment of the principal normally in full at maturity;
     – security of charged assets.
   (ii) Disadvantages:
     – interest rates may rise after the debenture stock has been subscribed;
     – market value of charged assets may fall.

(c) (i) Advantages to *ordinary shareholders:*
     – advantages of gearing;
     – higher dividends due to savings in corporation tax.
   (ii) Disadvantages:
     – if interest not paid regularly, their company's assets may be sold;
     – disadvantages of over-gearing.

Answer 4

(a) (i) *Interest rate swaps*. See Answer 1(a) above.

    (ii) *Currency swaps*. An agreement between two parties to exchange one currency for another now and to re-exchange the same currencies sometime in the future and in the intervening period each party agrees to pay the interest costs to the other. Unlike with interest rate swaps, with a currency swap the exchange of the principal as well as of the interest takes place.

(b) (i) *Interest rate swaps* enable customers to fix interest exposure, and enables customers to achieve the type of interest rate they desire at a cheaper rate.

    (ii) *Currency swaps* enable customers to borrow the currency they desire at a cheaper rate, and at the same time to cover a future currency exchange risk.

Answer 5

(a) (i) With *interest rate caps*, borrowers limit interest rate costs to a specified level. If interest rates rise above that level, the bank will reimburse them with the difference.

    (ii) *Forward rate agreements* enable customers to borrow or lend a specified *notional* amount in the future at a fixed rate, fixed at the time of agreement.

(b) (i) *Interest rate cap operation*. Suppose:
- base rate is at 11 per cent;
- bank is willing to lend at 2 per cent above the base rate;
- customer agrees, but does not wish to pay more than 13 per cent, i.e. wishes to cap the base rate at 11 per cent;
- if interest rate rises above 11 per cent bank reimburses customer.

    (ii) *Forward rate agreement operation*:
- the amount to be borrowed or lent in the future at the agreed interest rate, is notional;
- the bank reimburses customer if the rate on the contract commencing day is higher than agreed;
- customer borrows at higher rate in the market but is cushioned by the reimbursement amount;
- if on the agreed day, interest rate is below the agreed rate, the customer reimburses the bank with the difference.

∎ A tutor's answer

The following questions — one on risk management and the other on corporate finance — were asked in the 1991 MFS exams. Tutor's answers to both questions in point form are given below. Can you answer these questions without looking at the specimen answers? If yes, well done!

Question 1

The finance director of a small manufacturing company is concerned about the financial risks the company faces as it expands its business at home and abroad. He approaches you for advice. Explain to him:

(a) the main interest and exchange rate risks facing a company;

(b) how a company can protect itself against the risks you have discussed in (a).

Tutor's answer

(a) (i) *Interest rate risks*. When borrowing, the company has a choice of borrowing at fixed or floating rates of interest. Subsequent adverse interest rate movements will cause loss or reduce potential gain.

   (ii) *Exchange risk*. The company faces exchange risks when it has to make and receive payments in currencies of other countries. Adverse exchange rate movements may result in lower profits or even loss on transactions.

  (iii) *Translation exposure*. If the company has assets or liabilities in currencies different from its domestic balance sheet currency, it is vulnerable to exchange rate movements which might increase the value of liabilities and/or reduce asset value when expressed in domestic currency.

(b) (i) *Protection against interest rate movements:*
   - *Borrowing at fixed rates*. This will establish costs with certainty (but the company will lose if rates fall).
   - *Interest rate swaps*. The company can exchange floating interest rate commitments for fixed commitments (and vice versa).
   - *Forward rate agreements (FRAs)*. These provide a mechanism for a company to fix the interest rate for a specific forward period where borrowing is undertaken at floating rates. If rates rise above the agreed fixed rate, the bank selling the FRA will pay the company buying the FRA the difference. If rates fall below the fixed rate, the company pays the bank, foregoing the benefit of falling rates.
   - *Interest rate caps*. These allow the company to establish the worst case, but also to benefit from a favourable movement in rates; but it has to pay an up-front premium.

  (ii) *Protection against exchange risks:*
   - *Forward exchange contracts*. These will enable the company to hedge against transaction exposure. The exchange rate is fixed at the time of contract.
   - *Foreign currency options*. These allow the company to establish the worst case but also to benefit from a favourable movement in rates, the cost being the premium payable.
   - *Currency accounts*. These accounts will allow the company to hold or borrow foreign currency in anticipation of future currency flows.

Question 2

The finance director of a large manufacturing business informs you that his company is likely to require short-term finance.

(a) Outline the main methods available to the company to meet its short-term financing requirements.

(b) Discuss the advantages to the company of any *three* of the methods you have identified in (a).

Tutor's answer

(a) *Main methods available for meeting short-term financing requirements:*
   (i) *Bank overdrafts*. With arrangement with its bank, the company is allowed to overdraw its current account up to an agreed limit. Interest payable will be linked to the base rate.

(ii) *Money market loans.* The company will be allowed to draw under this arrangement in tranches up to an agreed limit. The interest rate on the loan will be linked to LIBOR.

(iii) *Acceptance credits.* Under this method the company will draw a bill of exchange which will be 'accepted' (payment guaranteed) by a bank. The acceptance (the accepted bill) can then be readily discounted at very low rate of discount (because the acceptor is a bank), and provide the company finance for the term of the bill.

(iv) *Commercial paper.* This financing facility is available to large public limited companies of good credit standing. The company can sell its commercial paper (its promissory note) directly, or via a bank, to investors. Commercial paper is a form of disintermediation because it enables borrowing directly from investors, by-passing financial intermediaries.

(b) *Advantages to the company:*

(i) *Overdraft.* Easy to arrange. Flexible interest, charged only on daily overdrawn balance. No need for the loan to be linked to a specific transaction.

(ii) *Money market loans.* Cheaper than overdraft, often at a very low margin over LIBOR.

(iii) *Acceptance credits.* Cheaper than overdraft. Self-liquidating – the company will reimburse the accepting bank at maturity of the bill.

(iv) *Commercial paper.* Cheaper than other forms of short-term borrowing for large public companies of highest credit standing. The borrowed funds are not committed to any specific transactions.

▌ A step further

Remember that risks are not necesarily something to be avoided. Risks are bad when things go wrong, but when all goes well they produce handsome profits. Therefore sometimes businessmen may want to increase the risk and sometimes reduce the risk via risk hedging instruments. The point to remember is this: not risk avoidance, but risk management, which both reduces, or even eliminates, risks and increases profits.

The most appropriate source for updating your knowledge of the contents of this chapter are the publications of your bank dealing with financial risk management and corporate finance. Study these publications carefully and you will get to understand the strategy of your bank in this profitable area of its activity. I am indebted to the risk management and corporate finance literature issued by Barclays Bank in writing this chapter.

There is an article on foreign exchange risk management in the June 1993 issue of *Banking World*. No doubt other *Signpost* articles will appear in *Banking World*, giving guidance on the parts of the syllabus covered in this and the previous chapters; you must of course look out for these articles.

CHAPTER 12

The Housing Market

Syllabus requirements

- Determinants of housing supply and demand.
- Interventionary forces.
- Regional policy.
- Role of personal sector.
- Effect of monetary policy on building societies and insurance companies.

▌ Getting started

Consequent upon the merger between the Chartered Institute of Bankers (CIB) and the Chartered Building Societies Institute (CBSI) in 1993, this chapter has been added to cover such topics as are specifically relevant to the operations of the building societies. You should also read the relevant sections in chapters three and ten in conjunction with this chapter.

Housing is an important social commodity and is therefore subject to both economic and political forces: there is nowhere a truly 'free' market in housing. Even after the passing of the 1986 Building Societies Act, the main purpose of the building societies' operations is to provide housing finance to the personal sector. Naturally the building societies are keenly interested in the forces that cause changes in the demand for and the supply of houses: for example, changes in housing legislation and policy, house prices, cost of mortgage finance, level of unemployment and demographic changes.

The role of the building societies, as financial intermediaries, is to provide for the housing finance needs of the personal sector by tapping the surplus funds of the surplus units at home and overseas, by developing facilities and financial instruments which make lending and borrowing possible.

The UK authorities implement their monetary policy via the banking system, using either restrictions on transactions, though mainly via transactions, since the 1980s. The money supply control and the interest rate policy affect the lending and borrowing operations of the banks, insurance companies, building societies and other financial intermediaries.

▌ Essential principles

Background

There has been an almost continuous decline in the private sector rented accommodation owing to many factors. Increased prosperity is one factor, but the advent of secured tenancies in the late 1960s accelerated an already irreversible trend. In direct contrast, the demand for owner-occupation has increased steadily throughout the twentieth century. Over 60 per cent of the dwellings in the UK are now owner-occupied, compared to only 10 per cent in 1914. The UK is the second largest home-owning democracy in the European community: Ireland has 76 per cent owner-occupation. Within the high level of home ownership in the UK, there are notable disparities in certain regions: for example Scotland lags behind the national average.

House prices have moved in a cyclical pattern since the 1970s, with relatively long periods of stability interspersed with short-term price booms. The so-called 'Barber boom' in 1971–72 saw prices rise by 40 per cent (48 per cent in London) in one year: the same period saw the first serious entry of the clearing banks into the field of mortgage finance. After a period of relative stability another boom followed in the late 1970s, and again another during 1986–88.

The period between 1986 and 1988 saw a period of phenomenal growth in house prices. This was due to the continued recovery of the UK economy from the 1983 economic recession, with gradually falling unemployment leading to greater demand for houses, and particularly demand for better houses by existing owner-occupiers 'trading up'. The rate of increase of house prices in 1987 and 1988 exceeded both the Retail Price Index and the Average Earnings Index. Within the national picture there were considerable regional differences in house price changes: for example, according to figures produced by the Anglia Building Society, some of the annual percentage changes for 1988 were: East Anglia +37; Outer South-East +28; South West +27; Greater London +20; Yorkshire/Humberside +9; Wales +8; Northern +3; Scotland −1; Northern Ireland −4. The main reasons for the regional disparities were: overall level of economic activity, particularly unemployment; commutable distance from major employment centres; and social status of the area, and therefore the investment value of houses in a particular area, which supported the argument about the 'North–South' divide.

The very rapid rise in house prices of 1988 was in marked contrast to what followed. In 1989, with the onset of the economic recession, house prices levelled as demand slumped, a trend that continued up until 1992. The slump in the housing market again showed significant regional disparities; this time, however, there is real evidence that the 'boom' in the South-East and the creation of a 'North–South' divide is reversing itself. The overall trend, however, was unambiguous: the housing market had become stagnant, due to the following possible causes. (a) After the credit boom of the mid 1980s, the UK was entering a period of slow economic growth, a prelude to the economic recession. (b) The government, committed to removing inflation, pursued a high interest policy, which directly suppressed the demand for owner-occupier houses. (c) Some of the tax incentives of owner-occupation were removed. (d) The ready availability of mortgage funds in the mid 1980s created problems for the marginal borrowers, who could only just afford to enter the mortgage market. Sustained high interest rates caused genuine problems for such borrowers. (e) Welfare benefits, such as the payment of mortgage interest by the Department of Social Security, were reduced. (f) It is feasible that the sharp downturn in the housing market is a direct and opposite reaction to the boom in the previous years, i.e. the market is adjusting itself.

The cyclical trends in the housing market have created new challenges for mortgage lenders on both the upswing and the downswing of the cycle. On the upswing, as the housing market expanded new lenders were lured into the market. What was once the sole domain of building societies became occupied by clearing banks, subsidiaries of overseas banks and insurance companies. The liberalisation of the financial services market by the Financial Services Act 1986, opened the door to mortgage lending by all-comers. The competition in the mortgage market led to greater level of innovation, with new types of mortgage instruments being developed in order to secure competitive advantage. Many lenders diversified. In particular, several building societies, banks and insurance companies bought estate agency claims and created vertical diversification, i.e. supplying services at different stages of house ownership. The downswing saw the reverse of the above happening. The contraction in mortgage demand created less business to go around for the now large number of mortgage lenders. For some lenders, mortgage lending became a merchandising activity, with 'special offers', such as huge income multiples and 100 per cent advances readily available. Some lenders experienced serious margin difficulties, as the competition of mortgage funds drove them downmarket. There is no doubt that some merger decisions were accelerated by this pressure.

There has been a growing concern in recent years as to the continuing deterioration of the existing housing stock in the UK. Despite some adventurous initiatives by private developers, local authorities, housing associations and building societies, there is a continuing problem of decline which inevitably results in some regional housing shortages. The current housing policies have many long-term implications for future generations. Sales of council houses has been a huge success: the 1980 legislation had the desired effect, particularly on the cash-starved local authorities. But what of their lower level of rental income from council houses in the future? The one-off sale of council houses will clearly have some important ramifications for local authority finances in years to come.

Current state of the market

In the post-recession mortgage market, home owners have been helped by the reversal of the upward trend in unemployment, lower interest rates and the direct payment of income support for mortgage interest. According to the Council of Mortgage Lenders, the worst of the arrears and repossession problem appears to be over. In the first half of 1993, mortgage lenders repossessed 31,780 homes, compared to 35,750 repossessions in the first half of 1992. At the end of June 1993, there were 191,560 loans between six and 12 months in arrears compared with 205,010 in the second half of 1992.

The popularity of *fixed-rate mortgages* recently suggests that the public do not believe that interest rates will stay low. Fixed-rate mortgages may be a sensible solution for borrowers but there are potential dangers for lenders. Fixed rates have given the societies an opportunity to offer mortgages at substantially cheaper levels, and at levels that also guarantee a satisfactory margin. This has been possible, firstly, due to the *steeply negative yield curve*: the long-term rates being lower than short-term rates. Secondly, the societies have entered into *interest rate swaps* to launch fixed-rate mortgages. It is not swaps which create fixed-rate mortgages; swaps are merely one method of achieving fixed-rate funding. Interest rate swaps enable a society to offer a fixed-rate mortgage by utilising existing liquidity. Instead of actually borrowing a three- or six-month wholesale time-deposit to match the variable-rate legs of the swap, liquid funds which would otherwise be invested for a three- or six-month period are used to provide actual funding. Thus, the fixed-rate product not only achieves increased mortgage demand, but also utilises excess liquidity. However fixed-rate mortgages pose many *problems* for the societies. (i) Interest rates may move once the product is launched. An *increase* in interest rates can create demand in excess of the swap arranged. Once interest rates have risen, the swap will no longer be available at the same price; this will swallow up any margin. Should the interest rates *fall* after the product launch, it will mean that the product is over-priced, and the demand for mortgages will fall, leaving the society with a very expensive swap and no underlying mortgages. (ii) Once the underlying finance has been arranged, societies cannot afford to be exposed to an early redemption, perhaps through moving house or a big fall in interest rates making other mortgages more attractive. The societies can protect themselves by charging severe penalties on early redemption, but the penalties must be stated clearly and up front. A society can also protect its fixed-rate mortgages, and increase its profitability, by purchasing a cap to protect against a very damaging rise in the interest rates, and by selling an interest rate floor to offset the cost of the cap.

By the second half of 1993, average house prices were around four per cent up on a year ago. According to the reports of Halifax and Nationwide building societies, there were 287,000 completed housing transactions in the April–June quarter, up from 271,000 in the first quarter of the year. Mortgages approved by building societies and banks rose to a two-year high of 274,000 in the second quarter, suggesting that housing turnover will continue to rise in the second half of the year.

The house-builders, according to the House Builders' Federation, are also planning for an upturn in the business. New housing starts by private builders totalled 70,000 in the first half of the year, a near 30 per cent increase on the 55,000 total of the first half of 1992. The latest figure represents around 60 per cent of the number of new housing starts in 1988, when the market was at the height of its boom.

However, this upturn is unlikely to give way to a 1988-style boom, when prices in some areas were rising by 10 to 15 per cent each quarter, for two main reasons. Firstly, unlike cars, houses have always been regarded as part-functional and part-investment; because houses have tended to appreciate in value from the day they are bought, new cars depreciate in value within a few days out of the showroom. For this reason, investing in bricks and mortar has been a powerful force driving the housing market over the past 25 years. Housing booms are driven by greed and fear: greed drove homeowners to seek ever-rising prices, and fear of missing out on the biggest and easiest capital gain available drove the buyers. The functional aspect of buying and selling houses thus gave way to an outright investment motive. People moved house, not because there was anything wrong with the property, but to maximise the potential for capital gains. A rising market was propelled ever upwards by the expectation that it would carry on rising. But the bubble burst, and it is unlikely for such attitudes to return for at least a generation, if then. Memories of the great housing collapse of the early 1990s, with house prices in parts of the south-east of England and East Anglia still down by a third on their peak at the end of the 1980s, will continue to influence home-buyers. Housing has returned to its first, and basic, purpose.

Secondly, the situation in the late 1980s was unusual. For the first time, with competition between mortgage lenders intense, there were virtually no constraints on borrowers. 100 per cent mortgages were commonplace and the lenders accepted generous house valuations. However having their fingers burned with repossessions and mortgage arrears, lenders are adopting a much more cautious attitude, generally not lending more than 90 per cent of the value of the property, and pegging back house valuations below levels buyers and sellers have accepted. A mortgage free-for-all has given way to a mood of caution and restraint.

Housing is unlike other goods because its supply is more limited. Most of the supply of housing comes from the existing stock of properties. New houses represent only a tiny annual addition to that stock. Thus, when there is a surge of demand from first-time buyers, properties are in short supply, and prices rise. Today there are many people who would like to sell, but are holding back until prices recover. For those who are caught in the so-called *negative equity trap* (where the value of their house is less than their mortgage), there is no alternative. This means that each rise in house prices will bring forth a new supply of houses coming onto the market, helping to keep that rise in prices in check.

The negative equity has been a prime factor holding back the housing market. However, a recent estimate by the Bank of England suggests that the number of households with negative equity peaked at 1.8 million in the first qurter of 1993 but dropped by 400,000 in the second quarter. The size of the negative-equity problem, measured in cash terms, fell from £12 billion to £9 billion.

▍Useful applied material

Housing market forces

In the UK housing market there is interaction between the *supply* of living accommodation and the *demand* of the public for such accommodation. House prices are subject to the forces of supply and demand. The housing market is not a 'free' market. Although many distortions have disappeared, social and political influences will continue to be exerted. Supply and demand in the housing market are reflections of economic activity and political intervention.

Before and since the passing of the Building Societies Act 1986, housing finance has been the main purpose of building society lending, and hence, for the building societies, the forces of supply and demand in the housing market, and the factors which cause changes in these forces, are of paramount importance.

Housing demand determinants

1. House prices

With housing, as with most other commodities, there is an *inverse* relationship between price and quantity demanded; there will of course be variations in demand according to the nature of housing concerned.

2. Cost of mortgage finance

The factors affecting the general level of interest rates are also the most important determinants of mortgage rates. A change in short-term rates, engineered by the Bank of England via its open market operations, gets translated into movements along the entire interest rate spectrum. In practice, a significant change in the Bank's dealing rate will be quickly reflected in the same direction of the mortage rates. Thus a significant increase in the Bank's dealing rate will increase the cost of mortgage finance, which, in turn, will tend to depress the demand for house buying.

3. Mortgage interest relief

At present, interest paid on the first £30,000 borrowed to buy a house is eligible for tax relief. Interest payments on qualifying loans within the mortgage interest relief at source (MIRAS) are made net of basic-rate tax, thus benefiting both taxpayers and non-taxpayers. An increase or decrease in the MIRAS ceiling will inversely affect the demand for house buying.

4. Level of incomes

As prosperity increases, not only does the level of unemployment fall but also the majority of the population enjoys higher incomes and increased living standards, and then the demand for owner-occupation increases. The post-war period has seen a strong increase in the demand for private housing for this reason. If incomes are falling, existing owner-occupiers are reluctant to leave the market for many reasons, although falling living standards deter new purchasers, as was evident during the recession.

5. Demographic trends

Population increases will increase the demand for housing, but a far more important factor is the structure of population. A large proportion of people in the 20 to 25 year-old age group, for example, will lead to higher demand for homes. An ageing population will alter the pattern of demand within the housing market. The end of the century will see a marked increase in the proportion of elderly people in the UK population, with an anticipated change in the type of accommodation demanded.

6. Availability of mortgage finance

For many years, the UK housing market suffered mortgage queues as the building societies often found difficulty in attracting sufficient inflows of savings to meet buoyant demand for loans. The breakdown of the 'cartel' amongst the societies in the early 1980s, the increased competition arising from other institutions, especially the clearing banks, entering the housing market, the ability of the societies to borrow limited funds in the wholesale market and to issue Permanent Interest Bearing Shares (PIBS) have wiped out mortgage queues permanently. Indeed, the proliferation of new entrants to the UK home loan market seems to have attracted more buyers into the market place through branding and 'special offers'.

7. Tastes and preferences

Research has identified taste for home ownership as a major deep-seated aspiration amongst young people in the UK. As the level of owner-occupation increases, this factor is likely to become even more important.

8. Price of alternatives to home ownership

In the UK there are several possibilities available: private rented accommodation and local authority houses are the main examples. Private rented accommodation has declined almost continually this century. The stock of private rented accommodation has fallen sharply from about 50 per cent of the homes market in the 1950s to 7 per cent in the 1990s due mainly to tenancy protection laws (Rent Acts of 1969 and 1974). Recent legislation, notably the Housing Act 1980, has provided greater encouragement to households to buy their own homes. In the same period rent on council houses increased substantially, helping to boost the demand for owner-occupation still further.

Housing supply determinants

1. Government housing policy

In the immediate post-war period all major political parties in the UK were committed to a housing drive led by building of council houses. Both the Conservative and Labour

Governments adopted aggressive policies towards increasing the housing stock, although much of this drive was aimed at public sector housing. The public and private sector competed for resources and a system of licensing was necessary to control resources in the construction sector. Since 1979, the Conservative Governments have been strongly committed to increasing the level of owner-occupation. Even fairly regressive forms of subsidy, such as the mortgage interest tax relief, have been retained with this aim in mind. Housing policies are a function of the times: a significant change has occurred in opposition political parties, with most influential politicians committed to retaining the 'right to buy' provisions of the 1980s legislation.

2. New housing

Construction of new dwellings is a very important factor. However the construction industry in the UK has been through a severe depression. The Labour party leaders are vigorously campaigning for the release of the large sums received by the local authorities from the sale of council houses as a result of the 'right to buy' drive, for the construction of new council houses. Sales of houses in the second-hand market also have an impact, but are usually matched by corresponding purchases. Since 1979, there has been a significant decrease in the provision of the public sector rented housing, creating additional pressure on the private housing stock.

3. Household breakup

This factor is mainly affected by the rate of death of owner-occupiers, which in turn is determined by the age structure of the population. The UK divorce and separation rates are increasing − one in four marriages is likely to end in a divorce − which is leading to household dissolutions, and it may be argued that when two persons in the same house separate, a demand for two houses may be created; hence the need to increase the housing stock.

4. Building technology

Building technology has improved by leaps and bounds this century, reducing the time required for housing completions and thereby increasing the potential supply of dwellings. Improvements in technology, however, have been tempered by a growing disillusion with system building and other techniques of construction diverging from the traditional. Timber frame housing has been particularly affected by adverse television publicity and subsequent debates. Other factors affecting the housing stock to be considered are: environmental requirements, development of prefabricated supplies, changes in raw materials.

The nature of UK housing market

The UK housing market is not perfect, and therefore house prices are not determined solely by the forces of supply and demand. Many interventions in the market are based on non-economic factors such as social considerations and value judgements. The following are the main official, non-economic market interventions.

- *Owner-occupier tenure* − It is now politically widely accepted that the owner-occupier is the tenure to which most households aspire, even though for a minority it will not become a reality.

- *Determination of council house rents* — In recent times these have converged on what are believed to be true market levels. There is, however, an element of political judgement in that the 'right to buy' measures contained in the Housing Act 1980 'coincided' with widespread rent increases.
- *Council Tax* — Its levels, like that of its predecessor, the Community Charge (poll tax), vary from area to area, but the consumption of some services in each local authority catchment is generalised. Some benefits will never be apportioned totally efficiently according to contribution, e.g. street lighting, resulting in externalities.
- *Mortgage interest tax relief* — National taxation measures affect the housing market; mortgage interest tax relief is a prime example. This is a regressive subsidy in that it is advantageous to those with higher interest charges. Some restrictions on the availability of this relief have been introduced in recent years. There is a possibility of its total abolition in an effort to reduce the government borrowing requirement. Until 1984, premiums paid on life assurance companies on certain policies were tax deductible, thus benefiting holders of endowment mortgages.
- *Housing legislation and local authority interventions* — The Rent Acts of 1969 and 1974 imposed significant controls on private landlords renting out furnished and unfurnished accommodation respectively. In practice this almost wiped out the already fast-declining private rented market, pricing such accommodation out of the reach of many, even those requiring the mobility enjoyed by tenants. The Housing Act 1980 introduced significant direct subsidies to those buying council houses, with discounts up to 60 per cent. The availability of such dwellings was subsequently restricted, preventing further sales for fixed periods. For social reasons, local authorities deliberately control certain rents such as those imposed on sheltered accommodation. Though decreasing in importance, some grants and subsidies are available to homeowners for repair and/or improvement of their properties. Housing does not represent a truly homogeneous commodity. In practice there are many sub-markets, segmented by various criteria. Some housing is extremely adaptable to need whilst some is subject to constraint such as local authority planning restrictions.
- *Imprecise information* — The UK housing market is distorted by the way in which information is presented. For example, a would-be seller is told what price his house should command, even though he may settle eventually for substantially less; the observer sees no evidence of what actually happened. If decisions were based on more precise information then prices would react accordingly.

▌ Regional policy

Regional policy may be *defined* as a set of measures which seek to increase employment and growth in the economy and to remove regional disparities between prosperous and less prosperous areas.

The first applications of regional policy, comprising mainly welfare measures, can be traced to the beginning of the twentieth century. Regionally the UK has constantly displayed sharp disparities in economic well-being. For example, during the depression of the 1930s, the national unemployment level in 1932 was 22 per cent, but the unemployment rate in London at the same time was 13.5 per cent. When unemployment was nearly eliminated in the early 1950s, areas such as Merseyside and Northern Ireland continued to experience higher levels than other more prosperous regions.

These differing levels of prosperity are due to many factors. In some areas, once great industries have suffered *structural* decline, i.e. substantial and long-term fall in demand of their products (e.g. coal, shipbuilding and textile industries in recent years), creating large pools of structural unemployment. Other areas are simply better endowed with natural resources. Demographic factors also play a part — for example, some towns have a large percentage of older, wealthier inhabitants.

Implementation and instruments of regional policy

Regional policy may be applied as:

- National UK policy;
- European Community policy.

National UK regional policy

National UK regional policy may be implemented in two main ways.

1. By taking workers to the work

This means encouraging unemployed workers to move to places where there is work, and involves the authorities in attempts to redress regional disparities by improving the *geographical and occupational mobility* of labour. Economists tend to agree with Adam Smith that 'a man is of all sorts of luggage the most difficult to be transported'; besides, direction of labour is incompatible with democratic government. However, the instruments which have been successful in encouraging geographical mobility, by overcoming the personal, social and occupational barriers inherent in workers moving house from one geographical area to another, are adequate financial incentives, appropriate housing: to buy or to rent, and efficient information service.

The forerunner of schemes to achieve movement of labour from one occupation to another, i.e. occupational mobility, was the Industrial Training Act 1964 which established Industrial Training Boards to provide training courses for certain industries. More recently schemes such as Youth Training Scheme and Training and Enterprise Councils have been introduced to train young persons for jobs in up-and-coming industries.

2. By taking work to the workers

This option involves the government relocating their own offices to depressed areas and placing contracts with firms that operate there, and giving to such areas the 'Assisted Area' status: special financial packages are available to both domestic and overseas firms (and their workers) who are willing to move to Assisted Areas. One recent initiative is the creation of Enterprise Zones where financial benefits and lenient planning regimes operate.

European Community policy

At EC level there is a European Regional Development Fund, which funds poorer areas of the EC. There are also two institutions, the European Investment Bank (EIB) and the European Coal and Steel Community (ECSC), which lend at low interest rates to aid development in Europe. The EIB makes long-term, fixed interest loans to help finance industrial (or infrastructure) projects which aid regional development in the EC states. The ECSC makes medium-term loans for employment-creating projects in areas where coal or steel closures or run-downs have taken place. Interest rate charged depends upon the number of jobs created.

Advantages and disadvantages of regional policy

Advantages

- It attempts to reduce unemployment, create economic growth and remove regional disparities in economic well-being.
- It improves geographical and occupational mobility and creates a more skilful and more flexible labour force. It has been estimated that up to 25 per cent of male workers move from one area of the country to another over a ten-year period.
- Training initiatives often include off-the-job general educational modules, which improve the quality of the labour force.
- Dependence of many in depressed areas on welfare payments is reduced.
- Localised social problems and 'housing stress' are reduced.
- Whilst its effectiveness may sometimes be doubted, it almost certainly prevents the economic circumstances in certain areas from getting any worse.

Disadvantages

- It has to be on-going and cannot be imposed as a short-term measure: it takes time to become effective.
- It can be *too* effective: too many workers migrate, creating labour shortages in those areas which previously had a surplus labour — the 'backwash' effect.
- It may be that it only re-distributes income, rather than creates any increase in prosperity.
- All regional policies involve some financial burden on the government.
- The level of prosperity experienced in different regions is constantly changing. How can the government ensure that the current package is appropriate?

▌Role of personal sector

In an open economy, such as that of the UK, there are four main sectors:

1. The *Personal Sector*, made up of individuals and households;
2. The *Industrial, Commercial and Financial Sector*, consisting of industrial, commercial and financial companies and institutions;
3. The *Public Sector*, comprising central government, local authorities and public corporations; and
4. The *Overseas Sector*, comprising firms, governments and individuals abroad who export and import goods, services and investment funds.

There is a *circular flow* of money amongst these four sectors, because of exchange of goods, services and investment funds.

The personal sector — individuals and households obtain money as wages or salaries from their employers, or as interest and dividend from deposits with financial institutions, investments in businesses (stocks and shares) and in public sector securities. Alternatively, they pay money to obtain goods and services, invest savings (directly or indirectly) in the industrial, commercial and financial sector in the economy, and pay taxes, fees and charges to the public sector, and some in the personal sector receive income from the public sector in the form of state pensions, social security, grants and interest payments.

The industrial, commercial and financial sector — firms pay wages, interest and dividends to individuals in the personal sector, and also receive income from the personal sector for sale of goods and services, and in the form of personal savings. They receive income from public sector spending and exports to the overseas sector, and pay money to the public sector in the form of taxes and other charges, and to the overseas sector for imports.

The public sector — central and local governments receive, in addition to taxes and other charges, the savings and surplus funds of the other three sectors to fund their borrowing requirements. Public corporations (nationalised industries) receive payments for the sale of their goods and services to other sectors. The public sector spending contributes to the income of the other three sectors.

The overseas sector — there is a counterflow of funds between the overseas exporters, importers, investors and their counterparts in the UK.

According to *Financial Statistics, February 1990*, on 31 December 1988, of the total *financial* assets (£921 billion) of the UK personal sector, life assurance and pension funds accounted for £384 billion, building society accounts £149 billion, UK ordinary shares £126 billion, bank accounts £96 billion, National Savings £37 billion, British Government securities £30 billion. On the same date, of the total *real* assets (£1129 billion) of the UK private sector, UK residential property accounted for £964 billion. These figures clearly illustrate the predominant influence of residential property, life assurance, and pension funds in the wealth of the UK personal sector.

Personal-sector savings that are not required for housebuilding are lent to the government or companies through the Stock Exchange. But this lending is indirect via intermediaries such as insurance companies, pension funds, banks, building societies, and unit and investment trusts. In recent years, the personal sector has been increasing its total investments but at the same time reducing its direct investment in the stock market. The following are the main reasons why many in the personal sector prefer to hold a claim against a financial institution rather than a direct claim against the government or a company.

- Indirect investments have generally proved to be not only most tax-efficient, but also achievers of higher returns.
- Institutional investors can provide a widely diversified portfolio, therefore less exposed to risk, for a relatively small outlay and at comparatively low cost.
- Institutional investors provide professional management, which endeavours to provide the highest return for the level of risk the investor is willing to undertake.

To reverse the process of increasing institutional ownership of equities and to encourage direct ownership of equities by the personal sector, Personal Equity Plan (PEP) was introduced by the government in 1986. Further inducements to direct personal share ownership are employee share-ownership schemes and employee share-option schemes. Largely as a result of government's privatisation issues, the number of share-owning adults in the UK rose from under three million in 1979 to around 11 million in 1990: but this was 'share-widening' rather than 'share-deepening', i.e. the number of personal shareholders rose, but their percentage share of the total market fell.

∎ Monetary policy

For a fuller explanation of monetary policy, see Chapter 7.

Monetary policy is a set of measures by which the UK authorities attempt to regulate the total spending in the economy by controlling the money supply and influencing the availability and cost of credit. Monetary policy instruments generally take up to 18 months to produce the full effect. Monetarists believe that a long-term strategy, with monetary policy as base, is the most effective way of steering the economy.

There are two broad approaches in implementing the monetary policy.

1. *Restrictions* – the Bank of England, on behalf of the government, instructs the banks, because the deposits of the banking sector are such a vital component of money, to adhere to particular requirements. For example: liquidity ratios, cash ratios, special deposits, higher purchase controls. In recent years, due to the monetarist stance of the Conservative Governments, restrictions, especially quantitative directives, have become unpopular. The UK authorities now prefer to steer the economy through transactions.
2. *Transactions* – the government acts as an extremely powerful buyer and seller in the market, for example: Bank of England's open market operations (to influence short-term interest rates) and transactions in the foreign exchange market (to hold the exchange value of the pound at a desired level).

In the past few years, the only instrument of monetary policy used by the government to steer the economy and to control inflation, has been the interest rates. Some economists argue that this sustained 'one club' approach to control inflation has much to do with the economy going into the recession. In the last couple of years the government's main objective has been to control the public sector borrowing requirement (PSBR): the excess of government spending over government revenue from all sources. The PSBR is both a fiscal and a monetary concept, because there is an accounting relationship between the PSBR and M4, the broad money: the fiscal budget establishes the amount of the deficit, the monetary measures aim to fund the deficit, without increasing the M4, unduly.

The size of the PSBR and the sources from which it is funded – M4 private sector, overseas sector, banks and building societies, Bank of England – have a major effect on the money supply: the sale of government securities to the first two sources will leave the money supply, by and large, unchanged; borrowing from the last two will increase the money supply, due to the credit creation by the banks and building societies.

Monetary policy and building societies

Monetary policy regulates the economy through control of the money supply. If the economy is going through a period of high and rising inflation, due to too much money chasing too few goods, then the authorities may decide to pursue a *deflationary* monetary policy in order to reduce the money supply, via high interest rates and imposition of credit restraints. On the other hand, if the economy is suffering from recession due to rapidly falling demand, then the monetary policy stance may become *reflationary* in order to increase the total spending by increasing the money supply, via lower interest rates and relaxation of credit controls.

A high interest rate policy will tend to encourage savings, which will increase the deposits of building societies, as well as the demand for their various savings products. If the high interest rates persist for a long period, then some of the building society mortgagees will find repayments difficult and might even default, causing repossessions and arrears. Apart from 'distress' borrowing, which is interest-inelastic, the demand for personal and unsecured loans will decline. With falling demand for loans the building societies will find the servicing of their depositors/shareholders very costly. With too much liquidity on their balance sheets, they will have to compete with other financial institutions, like the banks, which would have, more or less, the same predicaments: to find profitable investment outlets at home and abroad. Overseas investments will require the purchase of costly hedging arrangements, to protect their profit margins against translation risks. With a rise in interest rates, their earlier fixed-interest lending and investments will suffer capital loss. If a sustained high interest rate policy happens to coincide with a reduction, or abolition, of the mortgage interest relief, the effects on the building societies will be disastrous, because approximately 80 per cent of their assets are made up of lending activities, of which the major portion is house mortgage for private owner-occupation.

A reflationary monetary policy will, by and large, produce the same effects for the building societies, but in *reverse*.

To the extent the building societies finance the PSBR, their ability to create credit increases, which increases their profitability. However, the highly popular privatisation issues during the past decade, to reduce the PSBR, and the increased importance given to national savings products in the financing of the PSBR has raised the cost to the societies of attracting retail funds, which has reduced their profits.

Monetary policy and insurance companies

Insurance companies sell policies to the policyholders on payment of regular premiums which provide them protection against events that may happen, e.g. fire, theft, accident, or provision for the next-of-kin against events that must happen, e.g. death, or which provide a monetary return, e.g. investment products, such as managed bonds, with-profit endowment bonds, guaranteed income bonds. Practically in all cases, early withdrawal from these investment products can involve capital loss.

In turn, the insurance companies invest the premium monies they receive in portfolio of assets designed to provide long-term capital growth. The portfolio will combine the need for safety, with investments such as cash deposits and gilts, and the need for return, with perhaps longer-term and riskier assets, such as equities and properties, included in the portfolio. In the UK the investment element in insurance products is far more important than in many other countries, partly because of the greater freedom and opportunities to life assurance companies in placing their funds and partly because of the tax advantages given to saving via life assurance. Non-life or general insurance differs quite markedly from life assurance. The contracts taken on by a general insurance company are essentially short-term, usually one year. Accordingly the assets are held in a liquid form.

The most important factor adversely affecting the business of life insurance companies was the removal of tax relief on premiums in 1984. This diminished the attractiveness to the personal sector savings of life insurance policies, and the life companies were forced to look for other ways of maintaining business and growth. The life companies in the UK are heavily involved in the personal savings market because life insurance is used by the public as a form of long-term saving. Therefore short-term interest rates may not affect the life business: the uncertainty element loses its potency over long-periods, which is why the yield curves, in the long-term, flatten out. Empirical research has shown that correlations between higher interest rates and surrender values of insurance policies are positive, i.e. higher interest rates usually provide higher surrender values in the *long run*. The effect of interest rates on surrender values in the short-term is weak relative to the effect on surrender values of other factors, such as the financial distress of the policy holder. As substantial lenders of mortgage finance, a high interest policy especially during a depressed housing market will adversely affect their profitability.

Single European Market and insurance companies

The SEM has started a surge in acquisitions, mergers and alliances which is changing the shape of the insurance industry across the continent as national insurance markets are penetrated by outside companies. National companies which were content within their own national markets are beginning to accept that they need to expand abroad, if only to defend their present position.

The deregulation of investment means that the insurance companies have to expand and compete successfully for savings with banks and other financial institutions. However the irregular pattern of deregulation in the EC states will lead to a greater increase in the supply of insurance than its demand: competition is bound to intensify, but winners and losers may be slow to emerge. In Britain small mutual companies, short of capital and distribution, should be among the first casualties in any concentration of the industry. But boom in mortgage endowment policies in 1988 and in personal pensions in 1989 made the small mutuals less vulnerable than appeared likely in the aftermath of the Financial Services Act.

Demographics and economic trends both favour insurance. As Europeans live longer, a higher proportion is looking for insurance. They are also richer, so there are more houses and cars of higher value to be insured. In the UK, for instance, the number of households with central heating increased from 37 per cent in 1972 to 75 per cent in 1992. An overall increase in demand for insurance may ease the problem for the insurance companies, in the *short-term*.

In the longer-term, smaller companies are bound to be squeezed, and inevitably they will look for larger partners. But the larger companies are finding the cost of buying an insurance company very high. In the UK several larger companies, unsure of getting value for money, are concentrating on the organic growth within their existing widespread network. The forces for change acting on the European insurance industry are making the situation very fluid; and this makes it difficult to devise an effective strategy based on acquisitions, mergers or alliances.

The key development in the life assurance industry is that the neat, historic distinction between manufacturer (the life companies) and distributor is breaking down. In due time it is likely that the market will be dominated by groups that can control distribution, capital and expertise in manufacturing life assurance. In the UK, the insurance companies are under pressure from two directions: the relationship between the insurance industry and other financial services is changing, and, at the same time, banks and building societies are becoming key distributors of insurance products. In the new balance of power between insurance companies, banks and building societies, the insurers may be in a weak position because their expertise can be replicated in the way that distribution outlets cannot be replicated. As a result there has been a rush to form links as the number of independent intermediaries has diminished. But in the post-Financial Services Act relationship between banks, insurance companies and building societies, the most potent challenge comes from the purpose-built structures combining the strengths of banks and insurance companies. For example, the salesmen of Lloyds Abbey Life, with access to over six million Lloyds Bank customers, find selling life policies four times as productive as selling to the general public.

For the non-life business in the 1990s, the competition will be more intense, and in the UK as in the rest of Europe, the capacity of the market and intensified competition must mean prolonged pressure on premiums. Direct sales via the telephone and mail are also likely to reduce margins and the market share of traditional suppliers.

In summary, the insurance industry is entering a decade of fundamental and irreversible change, due largely to establishment of the SEM. National companies are looking to expand by acquisition, merger and alliance. Insurers are looking for new methods of distribution through banks and building societies. Distribution through banks and building societies is a new enough development for its limitations to be unclear.

∎ Recent examination questions

The following questions were asked in the recent Economics examination question paper in the Associateship examinations of the CBSI. The syllabuses of the CBSI's 'Economics' and the CIB's 'The Monetary and Financial System' have been merged, and the new title for the examination from May 1994, will be The Monetary and Financial System. The outline answers to these questions, and the 'Tutor's answer', form a part of this chapter, and you are therefore strongly advised to pay great attention to the study of these questions and answers.

Question 1

How relevant is the theory of supply and demand to the UK housing market?

Question 2

'Regional policy seeks to increase employment and growth in the economy and to remove regional disparities between prosperous and less prosperous areas'.

How has regional policy been implemented in the UK and how successful has it been?

Question 3

(a) What are the principal problems affecting the collection and the use of house price statistics?
(b) Explain why there are so many different house price series published?

Question 4

Explain how you would attempt to forecast the UK personal savings ratio, over a twelve month period.

Question 5

'Prior to the 1980s the market mechanism did not work within the mortgage finance market, but during the 1980s the invisible hand was untied'. Comment on this statement.

Question 6

Discuss some of the general implications which the implementation of the Single European Act 1992 may have for the operation of capital markets?

∎ Outline answers

Answer 1

(i) Main housing demand determinants:
- price of houses
- cost of mortgage
- price of alternatives
- incomes
- tastes and preferences
- demographic trends
- availability of finance.

(ii) Main housing supply determinants:
- new housing
- household dissolution
- government policy
- house-building technology.

(iii) Intervention in the housing market:
government policies − housing construction/sale
                        − rents
                        − fiscal policies.

(iv) The extent to which the market is
- 'free' (interaction of supply and demand)
- 'regulated' (impact of government policies).

Answer 2

(i) Main objectives of regional policy:
- taking work to the workers
- taking workers to the work.

(ii) Operation of regional policy:
- at UK level
- at EC level.

(iii) Regional policy instruments:
- encouraging geographical mobility, e.g. enterprise zones
- encouraging occupational mobility, e.g. YTS
- EC funding, e.g. Regional Development fund.

(iv) Extent of regional policy success:
- give specific examples of success
- has prevented areas of economic disadvantage from worsening
- has not, as yet, removed regional disparities.

Answer 3

(i) Refer to different sampling methods:
- random and stratified samples
- sample size
- data sources.

(ii) Identify problems specific to housing:
- definition of housing categories

- counting rooms/measuring areas/size of plot
- mortgaged/unmortgaged houses
- mortgage offers/completions
- starts/completions
- asking price/actual price
- inclusion of fixtures/fittings/soft furnishings
- seasonal variations
- new/old stock/vacant possession.

Answer 4

(i) define savings and savings ratio;
(ii) distinguish between savings and money;
(iii) show diversity of stores of wealth;
(iv) show impact of changing property values upon saving/spending;
(v) show separate, but interactive, influences of inflation and high interest rates:
- impact of inflation on asset values
- impact of interest rates on asset values
- distinguish between real and nominal interest rates;
(vi) show relevance of new technology in financial services:
- diminished requirement of idle balances;
- wider access to credit.

Answer 5

(i) Explain: – 'market system' – principles of supply and demand
      – show relevance of market system to mortgage finance market both before and during 1980s, with mortgage interest rate as the 'price'.
(ii) Explain the events in the mortgage market before and during 1980s:
Before 1980s:
- market dominated by few suppliers (building societies) acting in unison (interest rate cartel) to control price;
- new entrants/competition on finance supply side (banks) not interested in housing supply;
- result: price fixing and supply (mortgage finance) rationing.

During 1980s:
- break up of interest rate cartel (main reasons: wholesale funding and competition);
- entry of new suppliers (e.g. insurance companies);
- end of mortgage rationing;
- market became demand-led, not supply-led.

Answer 6

The implications of the Single European Act 1992:
- abolition of exchange controls
- ability of EC financial institutions to operate anywhere in member states
- general advantages arising from free trade
- lesser degree of regulation of UK financial sector institutions

- greater scope for innovation and change overseas
- relevance of a wider market for specialisation
- impact of increased competition on innovation
- imposition of community-wide capital adequacy rules
- relevance of diverse domestic regulations
- relevance of diverse domestic taxation policies
- relevance of greater economic harmonisation within the EMS
- relevance of domestic monetary policy
- implications for international interest rate differentials.

■ A tutor's answer

First try to answer the following question from the knowledge you have acquired from this and previous chapters in the book, before looking at the tutor's answer.

Question

Compare and contrast the functions of the Bank of England with those of the Building Societies Commission.

Answer plan

- *Compare*: list the functions of the two institutions − factual knowledge;
- *Contrast*: show how the functions differ and are similar − analytical skill.

Specimen answer

BANK OF ENGLAND FUNCTIONS:
(a) As *banker to the government*, it:
- holds the government's main accounts, and receives and makes payments on behalf of the government departments;
- ensures that the short-term (Treasury Bills) and longer-term (gilt-edged bonds) finance is always available to the government;
- pays interest to government stockholders and reduces the total cost of government borrowing by purchasing government securities with surplus government funds;
- issues bank notes;
- implements the official monetary policy.
(b) As *banker to the banks*, it:
- holds their operational deposits and facilitates the settlement of clearing transactions between them;
- sells them Bank of England notes;
- holds their mandatory 0.35 per cent non-interest-bearing, non-operational cash ratio deposits;
- holds the accounts of overseas central banks.
(c) As *lender of last resort* to the banking system, it:
- ensures the banking system as a whole is not short of liquidity on a daily basis;
- makes good any shortages of liquidity, primarily by the purchase of eligible bills from discount houses;
- mounts lifeboat operation to save a bank in serious difficulties.

(d) As *regulator* of the banking system, it:
- gives authorisation for deposit-taking by banks;
- ensures that banks maintain capital adequacy, as per the Basle Accord;
- agrees with each bank its liquidity adequacy, and ensures banks maintain their agreed liquidity ratios;
- supervises risk by monitoring large risk exposures of banks, including foreign currency exposures;
- protects depositors' funds against bank failures.

BUILDING SOCIETY COMMISSION FUNCTIONS:
- It authorises building societies to take deposits, provided they meet the liquidity and capital adequacy criteria.
- It supervises building society industry, by:
  - making new regulations through Prudential Notes, concerning liquidity, capital adequacy, protection of depositors/shareholders funds, advertising and raising of wholesale market funds;
  - monitors closely their activities by requiring them to submit detailed returns regularly.
- It advises the government on matters affecting building society industry.

Comparison
Bank of England is:
- governed by Banking Acts;
- is a regulator;
- is lender of last resort; and
- operates as a financial institution.
Building Society Commission:
- was established by the Building Societies Act, and is governed by it;
- is a regulator only.
Both supervise financial institutions/markets, but the Bank of England, unlike the Building Societies Commission, is the government's bank and therefore has a public sector role.

∎ A step further

The daily and weekly quality newspapers regularly publish articles on the housing market, building societies and regional policy: for example, *The Times* published on 2, 24, 28 and 30 March 1993 useful articles. With the merger of the CBSI and the CIB, it is probable that the CBSI *Journal* and the CBI *Banking World* will also merge; the merged publication would be your best source of updating information. *The Economist*, *The Financial Times*, the quarterly *BEQB* should also be looked at for developments in this area of the syllabus. The CBSI publication, *ECONOMICS*, by Robert J. Souster, is recommended.

Index